Spirituality, Organization and Neoliberalism

Spirituality, Organization and Neoliberalism

Understanding Lived Experiences

Edited by

Emma Bell

Professor of Organisation Studies, The Open University Business School, The Open University, UK

Sorin Gog

Lecturer in Sociology and Anthropology, Faculty of Sociology and Social Work, Babeş-Bolyai University, Romania

Anca Simionca

Lecturer and Vice-Dean, Faculty of Sociology and Social Work, Babeş-Bolyai University, Romania

Scott Taylor

Reader in Leadership and Organization Studies, Birmingham Business School, University of Birmingham, UK

 Edward Elgar
PUBLISHING

Cheltenham, UK • Northampton, MA, USA

Published by
Edward Elgar Publishing Limited
The Lypiatts
15 Lansdown Road
Cheltenham
Glos GL50 2JA
UK

Edward Elgar Publishing, Inc.
William Pratt House
9 Dewey Court
Northampton
Massachusetts 01060
USA

A catalogue record for this book
is available from the British Library

Library of Congress Control Number: 2020938015

This book is available electronically in the **Elgar**online
Business subject collection
DOI 10.4337/9781788973304

ISBN 978 1 78897 329 8 (cased)
ISBN 978 1 78897 330 4 (eBook)

Printed and bound by CPI Group (UK) Ltd, Croydon, CR0 4YY

Contents

Contributors

Ibrahim Abraham is the Hans Mol Research Fellow in Religion and the Social Sciences at the Australian National University, Canberra. He is the author of *Evangelical Youth Culture: Alternative Music and Extreme Sports Subcultures* (2017) and the editor of *Christian Punk: Identity and Performance* (2020).

Emma Bell is Professor of Organisation Studies at The Open University, UK. Her work is informed by a commitment to understanding how people create meaning through their work and how those meanings are contested. Previous projects focused on the importance of religious and spiritual beliefs in shaping organizational cultures and leadership, popular cultural representations of management and organization and understanding embodiment, materiality and learning in organizations. A commitment to qualitative inquiry runs throughout. She has authored and edited six books and published articles in journals including *Academy of Management Learning and Education*, *Human Relations*, *Organization*, *Management Learning* and *British Journal of Management*.

Liza Cortois is a post-doctoral researcher in the Faculty of Business & Economics, Hasselt University, Belgium. She obtained her PhD (2019) with a dissertation entitled: *Becoming an Individual: A Cultural-Sociological Study of Socialization in Individualistic Scripts*. This project was funded by the Research Foundation – Flanders and dealt with socialization in the diverse narratives of individualist culture in three case studies: spirituality, civic integration and management courses. Here, she combined a theoretically informed approach with qualitative methodology. With regard to the field of spirituality, she is particularly specialized in currently popular mindfulness spirituality and how it relates to the so-called 'spiritual turn in the west' and 'business spirituality'.

Sorin Gog is Lecturer at the Sociology Department of the Faculty of Sociology and Social Work, Babeş-Bolyai University Cluj-Napoca, Romania, teaching courses on contemporary sociological theories, sociology of religion and paradigms of secularization. He has been a research fellow at University of Fribourg, Switzerland, Max Planck Institute for Social Anthropology, Germany, Institut für Wissenschaft der Menschen, Austria, New Europe

College, Romania, CEU-IAS, Hungary and Helsinki Collegium for Advanced Studies, Finland. His current research project focuses on the field of personal and spiritual development programmes and the way they are related to the current economic and political transformations of labour markets in Central and Eastern Europe.

Anna-Riikka Kauppinen is Research Associate at the Max Planck Cambridge Centre for Ethics, Economy and Social Change. Her doctoral project explored young people's efforts to make a career as 'professionals' in Ghana's capital, Accra. Her new project investigates the close social networks between West African-owned private enterprises and Charismatic Pentecostal churches in Accra and Lagos.

James Dennis LoRusso is Postdoctoral Research Associate at the Center for the Study of Religion, Princeton University. His central research concerns are the intersections of religion, work, capitalism and popular culture. James has contributed to understandings of workplace chaplaincy, the construction of selfhood at work and marketplaces of belief in the United States.

Darlene Miller is Senior Lecturer at the Wits School of Governance, University of Witswatersrand, South Africa. Her research is multidisciplinary, often focusing on food production and retailing in the context of regional political economies. Darlene is committed to decolonization, in her research, educational practice and institutional work, always seeking a balance between idealism and pragmatism.

Kseniya Navazhylava's research explores the future of work with a particular emphasis on technology, identity and occupational dynamics within a workplace. Before completing her PhD at HEC Paris, Kseniya accumulated 11 years of professional experience as a journalist in the largest national newspaper in Belarus. Currently she serves as Assistant Professor at the Ecole de Management Leonard de Vinci, Paris.

Amanda Peticca-Harris is an Associate Professor of Management at Grenoble Ecole de Management in Grenoble. Her research explores how people experience work with a particular emphasis on the body, identity, emotional labour and power relations within contemporary sites of work. Amanda has published in *Organization, Human Relations, Organizational Research Methods* and the *Journal of Business Ethics*. She currently serves as Associate Editor for *Qualitative Research in Organizations and Management*.

Genevieve Shanahan studied philosophy (2008–14) at University College Cork (BA) and University College London (MPhil Stud). She is currently working on her PhD in the field of organization studies at the Grenoble Ecole de Management, where her dissertation concerns the ways in which technology enables and impedes radical democracy in work and alternative organizations. She is interested in critical perspectives on technology and post-capitalist futures, with active research projects on cooperatives, social enterprises, platform work and unconditional basic income.

Anca Simionca is Lecturer in the Sociology Department of Babeş-Bolyai University in Cluj-Napoca, Romania. Her main research interests revolve around the transformations of work, the relationship between social and organizational settings and individual biographies. Her PhD from the Central European University, Budapest (2012) is titled 'Critical Engagements with and within Capitalism: Romania's Middle Managers after Socialism'. Together with Sorin Gog, she has recently researched the link between work and personal and spiritual development practices in Romania.

Scott Taylor is Reader in Leadership and Organization Studies, Birmingham Business School, University of Birmingham. His research on contemporary spiritualities and work includes analyses of 'spiritual management development', homeopathy, work/life balance in New Age capitalism and the promise of enchantment. This work has been published in journals such as *Human Relations*, *Sociology* and *Organization*, and in a number of edited collection chapters.

Katja Valaskivi is a media and communication scholar, currently Associate Professor for Religion and the Digital World at the University of Helsinki. She is the previous director of the Tampere Research Centre for Journalism, Media and Communication at Tampere University where she still holds an affiliation. She has also worked as the director for the Finnish Institute in Japan, Tokyo, as the head for communication and media relations at Tampere University of Technology, Finland and as a journalist. Her research interests include ideologies and belief systems, promotional culture, hybrid media events and mixed methods for the study of the digital world.

Tom Vine studied for his first two degrees at Warwick Business School before moving to Essex Business School, Colchester for his doctorate. He is presently Associate Professor of Business and Management at Suffolk Business School, Ipswich where he leads the MBA (apprenticeships) and PhD programmes. He lays claim to an identity as an ethnographer and organization theorist with specific interests in agency, belief, complexity and paradox. When he is not grappling with Nietzsche, Tom enjoys charity shop crawls, restoring old boats and racing radio-controlled cars.

Ariel Yankellevich is a PhD candidate in the Department of Sociology and Anthropology at Ben-Gurion University of the Negev. He holds a BA (Sociology and Psychology) and an MA (Sociology) from the Hebrew

University of Jerusalem. His dissertation research project explores the construction of new forms of neoliberal subjectivity among Israel's veteran middle class. His previous research examined the logics and practice of resilience-building interventions for potential victims of war and terrorism in Israel. His research interests include the sociology of therapeutic cultures, medical and psychological anthropology and neoliberal subjectivity.

Spiritualities and neoliberalism: changes and continuities

Sorin Gog, Anca Simionca, Emma Bell and Scott Taylor

Since the 1960s, sociologists of religion have been increasingly focused on the study of belief practised outside institutional religious settings. This mainly centres on what Lynch (2007) terms 'the new spirituality' – progressive practices and values informed by conceptual, material and social resources associated with established belief systems but detached from their institutional roots. The cultural expansion of such movements, in Europe and North America in particular, throughout the 1970s appeared to presage a dramatic transformation in religious practice. However, by the 1990s, it became clear that there was little evidence of large-scale change, either in the cultural importance of established religions or the number of religious practitioners engaging with established theological traditions. Consequently, engagement with the new spirituality has remained a minority interest compared to established religions. Attention has therefore turned to new spirituality as a socio-cultural presence, through spiritualized practices becoming embedded beyond the contexts of their original development, often in secularized forms (e.g. yoga). These subjectivity-related discourses have become integral to production and consumption processes in contemporary capitalism (Heelas, 2008).

As sociological debate on religion, spirituality and subjectivity unfolded, another research community was similarly engrossed with the radical material reshaping of everyday working lives through increasingly dominant neoliberal political regimes. Sociologists of work presented evidence of structural change affecting labour in and on the subcontracted fringes of organizations, as deregulation, privatization and promotion of enterprise informed political policy initiatives that reduced job security and extended the reach of market-based economic rationalities. However, the intersection of the new spirituality with new forms of work and economic life has not yet been the focus of sustained dialogue. Consequently, understandings of how contemporary cultures of progressive belief and the neoliberal governance of work intersect remains empirically limited and theoretically neglected.

The contributions to this book provide a starting point for this dialogue by offering detailed, theorized accounts of how people negotiate the complexities of belief in the new spirituality and relate this to their working lives. Above all, they show that the varieties of 'progressive belief' (Lynch, 2007) that underpin the new spirituality affect and are affected by the extension of neoliberal markets and value. Each of the contributions to this book shows, in different ways, that we can observe how 'the soul of the citizen-subject' (Brown, 2003) lives and works within neoliberal governmentality, whatever the cultural or political conditions, in complex, contested ways.

Taken together, these analyses suggest a much more complex dynamic. Lack of cross-disciplinary dialogue may be one reason why contemporary spiritualities have been positioned as having an inherent affinity between the subject that such movements try to create, and the functioning of enterprising selves under neoliberal capitalism. This approach, present in much of the research we review in this introduction, positions the disciplining mechanisms of neoliberal subjectification, and the practices surrounding spiritual development movements, as inherently interrelated. This in turn suggests that we can explain the popularity of subjectivities based on new spirituality as a response to the social change that neoliberalism promotes. However, in this introduction, based on our reading of key contributions to understanding the interplay of spirituality and neoliberalism and analyses in this book, we argue that this somewhat simplistic account of affinity between the new spirituality and neoliberal market relations provides an insufficiently nuanced and detailed understanding of the relationship between these two aspects of social life. Analyses of new spiritualities and enterprising subjectivities often assume *a priori* that spiritual practices are a response to subjective demands that the individual behave calculatively, and this further supports the functioning of neoliberal economic systems by reinforcing productive individualism.

Our selective review is structured around four key issues: the search for a new spirit of capitalism, neoliberal subjectivities, neoliberal transformations and resilient religiosities. Throughout, we use summaries of the book chapters to show how it is possible to combine understanding of the complex ways in which situated individuals interpret, engage with and respond to neoliberalism, without assuming ideological control, manipulation, obliviousness or false consciousness. This creates a more productive space in which to consider the empowering and liberating dimensions of subjectivities founded on the new spirituality, while simultaneously recognizing their exploitative potential.

LOOKING FOR A NEW SPIRIT OF CAPITALISM

The starting point of the contributions to this book is the relationship between individualistic neoliberal capitalism and the often self-centred, proactive subjectivities promoted by personal and spiritual development programmes collectively considered 'alternative spiritualities'.[1] New spiritual perspectives often focus on physical and mental health, education, personal development and work, in addition to the practice of spiritual belief independent of other life spheres. The chapters in this volume present a variety of insights from around the world to analyse how the economic and social transformations enabled by global, usually neoliberal, capitalism and the new spirituality are negotiated within communities, through socialization of selves and subjectivities. Attention is given to the spiritualities which have proliferated around the organization of work and leisure time and the creative legitimations this has produced. This raises the question of whether a new spirit of capitalism is being constructed, and if so, what this means for neoliberalism and the new spirituality.

Boltanski and Chiapello (2005a, 2005b) provide a landmark discussion of this dynamic in their account of how the contemporary interplay of belief, subjectivity, economy and work can be indicative of a 'new spirit of capitalism'. Their argument starts from the assumption that capitalism is an absurd and amoral system because of its incessant need to increase the rate of accumulation. This absurdity and amorality is exemplified in the necessary active and positive involvement of people who share little of the profit that is being made.[2] From this, they argue that capitalism needs an ideology capable of eliciting participation – a 'spirit of capitalism'. The success of this spirit stems from its capacity to equate participation in the system with promises of reward, excitement and security.

However, for Boltanski and Chiapello, the spirit of capitalism not only motivates people to engage in the current socio-economic system; it also constrains the accumulation process by exposing it to the possibility of critique. They suggest that people are capable and fundamentally inclined to constantly compare their realities with the promises inscribed in the ideology. The accumulation of situations that are evaluated as unfair in relation to these promises can contribute to the slow demise of an ideological era. Thus they 'credit people with genuine critical capacities and [believe that] critique has an impact on the world. We start out from the principle that people are able by themselves to measure the discrepancy between discourse and what they experience, to the point where capitalism must, in a way, offer – in practice – reasons for accepting its discourse' (Boltanski & Chiapello, 2005a: 4). This starting point in analysing the transformations that have taken place in the 'spirit of capitalism' is very different from a classic sociology of domination and offers important insights for the analytical framework developed in this book.

The cycle of critique is central to Boltanski and Chiapello's argument. Like its predecessors, the current spirit of capitalism is the result of capitalism's ability to incorporate critique and indigenize it. The artistic and social critiques that were so prominent in the Western social movements of the 1960s end up as building blocks for a new order of justice that capitalism is tested against. Boltanski and Chiapello judge the artistic critique, which we interpret as closely related to new spiritualities in its focus on disenchantment and inauthenticity, very clearly. They argue (e.g. 2005b: 178) that many supporters of this form of critique gradually entered the power elite that by the 1980s was entirely comfortable with capitalism. Notwithstanding, their analysis encourages us to take ordinary actors and their embodied critiques seriously. The fact that at a macro-historical level people's actions can be seen as fulfilling a bigger pattern in which exploitation is only deepened through new and more sophisticated means does not constrain researchers to treat social actors as mere passive containers of self-defeating ideology. People are not simply endowed with false consciousness. The task of the researchers (following a more pragmatic sociology of everyday life) is to take seriously the operations that people make, the ways they test reality for fairness and how they attempt to live moral lives. The fact that various elements of critique can be indigenized by capitalism does not remove or negate people's genuine capacities to make sense of the world critically. The chapters gathered in this volume take this epistemological recommendation seriously and explore the ways different types of social actors and communities make sense of recent capitalist transformations and articulate critiques or further legitimations in response to it.

Neoliberalism has been a focal topic of research in the past decade in all social sciences and has acted as both an epistemological framework and a historical background for understanding various economic and cultural processes, religious/spiritual ones included. Nevertheless, existing literature engages in a limited way with the issue of subject formation in a neoliberal age. Our reading of this field has brought three key questions to mind. First, what is distinctive about the selves that have learned to adapt to these political and economic transformations? Second, what does it mean to analyse how the new social order of neoliberalism becomes embedded in the subject? And third, how are neoliberal subjectivities formed, and challenged, by the rise of new spiritualities?

NEOLIBERAL SUBJECTIVITIES

A promising attempt to analyse the neoliberal subject was put forward recently by David Chandler and Julian Reid in their book titled *The Neoliberal Subject: Resilience, Adaptation and Vulnerability* (2016). Conceived as a dialogue between two scholars working on international relations and political science, the book presents two complementary perspectives on how subjectivity is imagined and socialized through governing bodies and procedures implemented by current neoliberal regimes. The authors depart from the classic understanding of neoliberalism as an economic system in which markets regulate all aspects of societal life by disabling state intervention, and point out that these types of economic hegemonies cannot be sustained and reproduced in the absence of cultural and political legitimations. Political economies are therefore not imposed from top to bottom; they need to be actively sustained by permeable cultural narratives. An important aspect of how these legitimations enable socio-economic governing processes is identified in the institutionalization of new moral orders, thereby embedding distinct types of subjectivities in societal life. How neoliberalism constitutes these subjectivities and the distinct regimes of identity mechanisms that neoliberalism generates, in comparison with classical liberalism, becomes the focal point of this investigation.

At the centre of their analysis lies the postulation of a rupture between the classic liberal forms of governance and the emerging neoliberal ones. Neoliberalism is seen here not as a continuation or radicalization of the political project of liberalism, but as discontinuity which produces a new mode of societal governance in an increasingly interconnected and volatile global economy (Chandler & Reid, 2016: 13–14). Chandler argues that this has a significant impact on the modes of subjectification and on the ways in which humanity and communities are reshaped:

> the discourses of neoliberalism and the concomitant focus on the agency and empowerment of vulnerable subjects is less a project of government regulation and control (whether in the cause of capitalist accumulation or liberal governmentalism) than a rejection of the liberal conception of government as standing above society. The neoliberal subject is thus a subject at home in a world in which externally orientated projects of transformation are no longer imaginable. A subject for who work on the self is understood to be liberating and emancipatory; who welcomes governance discourses of empowerment and capacity-building in the knowledge that we are all producers of our world and all share responsibility for its reproduction. In this world, with no outside, there is nothing beyond the technical or administrative management of the status quo through societal 'steering'. Politics, as a contestation over societal goals, could have no meaning in such a world. (Chandler & Reid, 2016: 15–16)

According to Chandler and Reid, resilience constitutes the main feature that neoliberalism attempts to instil in communities and subjects. By resilience they understand the capacity of individuals to bounce back in contexts of crisis and engage proactively with the turbulences and dislocations of the current world. A resilient subject or community is one that welcomes change and uncertainty and seeks to creatively adjust to the adverse or hostile conditions they encounter. This capacity of the subject is predicated upon a new regime of self-transformation in which personal development, introspection and psychological reprograming of one's interiority become important cultivated values (Chandler & Reid, 2016: 14).

This argument is important here because it moves beyond conventional post-Foucauldian 'governmentality of the self' narratives, and creates space for a more comprehensive understanding of subject formation. By capturing the creative cultural dimensions through which governing structures seek to empower the self, by encouraging a well-capacitated agency accessible to all individuals and rearranging this through societal relations, Chandler and Reid contribute to understanding how existing forms of neoliberalism structure self-identity processes.

A second important, relatively neglected, book supports this argument. In *Saving the Modern Soul: Therapy, Emotions, and the Culture of Self-Help* (2008), Eva Illouz offers a rare cultural analysis of the therapeutic discourses and practices in contemporary realities to which Chandler and Reid refer. Illouz attempts to start from the points of connection that situated individuals find in therapeutic cultures due to their relevance in addressing daily preoccupations and challenges. Illouz distances herself from the 'epistemology of suspicion' which she considers characteristic of analysis in this area. Her claim is that analyses that focus on the narcissistic effects of therapeutic discourses, or the disembeddedness from institutions and social relations that they promote, are in themselves normative in that they start from a clear idea of how social relations should be. In contrast:

> The point of cultural analysis is not to measure cultural practices against what they ought to be or ought to have been but rather to understand how they have come to be what they are and why, in being what they are, they 'accomplish things' for people. Thus, despite its brilliance, a Foucauldian approach will not do because Foucault used sweeping concepts – 'surveillance,' 'biopower,' 'governmentality' – that have some fatal flaws: they do not take the critical capacities of actors seriously; they do not ask why actors are often deeply engaged by and engrossed with meanings; and they do not differentiate between social spheres. (Illouz, 2008: 4)

A central concept that Illouz develops is 'emotional style', namely,

> the ways a culture becomes 'preoccupied' with certain emotions and devises specific 'techniques' – linguistic, scientific, ritual – to apprehend them. An emotional style is established when a new 'interpersonal imagination' is formulated, that is, a new way of thinking about the relationship of self to others, imagining its potentialities and implementing them in practice. (Illouz, 2008: 14)

The assertion made here is that the therapeutic discourse has established itself as an emotional style in contemporary culture; analysing the mechanisms through which it ended up resonating with social spheres as different as work, family and psychology should be the main aim of researchers. In this analysis, therapeutic discourses are instrumental to achieve 'coherent selves, procure intimacy, provide a feeling of competence in the realm of work, and facilitate social relations in general' (Illouz, 2008: 20).

The most relevant part of this analysis for us here concerns the interaction between the therapeutic discourse and the world of work. Illouz shows how psychology as a profession and discipline has, since the 1930s, played a crucial role in developing a new understanding of the relationship between individuals and their work environment, altering the main parameters of how individuals negotiate the relationship with their work environment. The increased importance of emotion for managers and employers in understanding productivity and efficiency maximization are directly linked to the ways in which psychologists have reframed the understanding of the working subject. The working subjects who have internalized the therapeutic emotional style have come to equate self-interest and efficiency with an entire repertoire of emotional work done on themselves and on their emotions. On the one hand, the emotional capabilities and traits of employees and managers become central to the economic prosperity of organizations. On the other hand, it becomes crucial for individuals to be able to do the emotional work on themselves that allows them to become part of the current organizational understanding of prosperity.

Chandler and Reid (2016) and Illouz (2008) inspire us to make space for more nuanced understandings of neoliberal subjectivities. The chapter by James Dennis LoRusso (Chapter 1, this volume) illustrates this in a compelling manner. His research on United States' business and managerial practices focuses on the ways in which workplace spirituality is transformed into a governmentalizing technology of producing resilient subjects. This contributes to the formation of a self which is deeply embedded in a capitalist mode of managing employees and work relations.

LoRusso criticizes David Harvey's approach to neoliberalism for its reliance on an understanding that draws on political economy. LoRusso's argument positions this order as being rooted in a hegemonic system through which free markets regulate all aspects of life. Following Peck and Bourdieu he stresses the need to understand neoliberalism as an ideological discursive formation capable of inscribing in the human subject the coherency and social consistency that existing forms of capitalism lack. In this respect, workplace spirituality is seen as a managerial cultural formation through which neoliberalism is inscribed in a supernatural ontological order. This reifies it, giving an aura of incontestability. Its social power in socializing subjects is instrumental in legitimizing current contradictions of capitalism and generating a wider consensus among employees for how capitalist accumulation works.

LoRusso asserts that spiritualities do not inevitably lead to exploitation of workers. Instead they can be significant in promoting a meaningful work environment. But the way they are employed as part of managerial interventions in order to enhance productivity by reshaping working selves tends to suggest otherwise. In some parts of the United States in particular, managers use spiritualities as a tool to advance business plans and augment human resource capabilities. It is this that LoRusso calls 'radical subject formation'. Spiritual practices and beliefs generate not only a specific form of authenticity, but also a neoliberal vocabulary which enables an understanding of everyday capitalism and a mode of self-organizing through personal life restructuring. By emphasizing the value of adaptability, creative intuition and holistic presence, the subject learns through spirituality how to think of themselves as an 'entrepreneurial project'. Similarly to Chandler and Reid (2016), LoRusso sees a major shift regarding the socialization of the self from liberalism to neoliberalism. Whereas management of the liberal order promoted a subject within a frame of bounded rationality and secular autonomy, the neoliberal order emphasizes the need for a spiritualized and holistic subject capable of overcoming vulnerability through their flexibility and adaptability to the increasingly volatile global economy.

Illustrating another aspect of spiritualities in the workplace, Ariel Yankellevich (Chapter 2, this volume) focuses on the growing number of veteran middle- and upper-middle-class Israelis who have embraced coaching and other similar self-improvement practices as a second (or third) career in later life. In recent years, a growing number of women and (some) men born in the 1950s and early 1960s have turned to coaching and similar forms of 'personal development work'. Unlike most other social categories whose precarious economic position does not allow them much choice in adopting or rejecting the contemporary ideology of self-improvement, flexibility and self-reliance, the subjects of Yankellevich's research had a clear alternative of falling back on existing social and economic prosperity. Yankellevich argues that the language of coaching allows members of this generation to negotiate their complex position as a waning but still powerful elite in search of new sources of legitimation. He offers several paradigmatic life stories in detail and shows the richness of meanings that the dilemmas and choices of his subjects entail. The middle-aged well-off Israelis use a language of 'daring to embrace change', 'openness to risk' and 'service to other' in their attempts to describe their professional decisions in meaningful ways. After having their economic, political and cultural hegemonic position threatened by the economic, political and cultural changes Israeli society has gone through, these individuals find in the language and practice of coaching a way of further proving their worth and importance as 'service elite', albeit in new circumstances.

Unlike most research commentating on the neoliberal turn in subjectivity forming, we find here that supra-individual aspects like collective national goals are central to this category of people's reasons for embracing coaching and similar practices. While their economic wellbeing was little threatened by the national-level embracing of a neoliberal economic ethos, we find here the fear that if they do not adapt to the new rules of the game they will be left behind to become 'rotten, stink and grow mold', as one of the respondents graphically formulates it. It is in this context that we situate new spiritualties as playing a role in socializing neoliberal subjectivities.

Liza Cortois' contribution (Chapter 3, this volume) approaches the issue of neoliberal subjectivity from a different perspective, as an expression of an intersection between paid work (as an employee this time), physical activity and meaning formation. This analysis builds on literature related to outdoor management development, the 1980s corporate training innovation that subjected mostly managers to team- and character-building exercises in remote locations and had little or no existential or metaphysical content. The context of Cortois' empirical work, in contrast, is built around spiritual foundations through the incorporation of mindfulness into management development in the natural environment. Cortois' analysis observes a significant, spiritual shift in how the self, or the managerial subjectivity, is treated in these events. There is much less emphasis on physical performance; trainers are less likely to be ex-military, less focused on conquering natural 'barriers' and less taken up with achieving physical exhaustion as a means of self-discovery. Instead, they are encouraged to become more authentic, more mindful and more focused, for example on controlled breathing.

This is important, as Cortois emphasizes, because it demonstrates a common method of articulating the 'new spirit of capitalism' that places high value on expressive individualism and authenticity. However, there is a further twist here, when these demands come into contact with functional organizational logics. Once again, the aspirations that employees are encouraged to develop clash with the values embedded in the dominant neoliberal economic system that the employing organization reproduces.

NEOLIBERAL TRANSFORMATIONS AND CHANGING SPIRITS OF CAPITALISM

Bringing the themes of 'neoliberal transformations' and 'changing spirits of capitalism' together is the purpose of this section. Researching the new spirituality as part of a wider global neoliberal transformation has been an important direction over the past two decades in the field of religious studies. New Age spiritualities have been a crucial area of study in sociology and anthropology of religion since at least the 1970s, but the main focus was on whether the proliferation of such spiritualities could provide insights into whether secularization had occurred in Western societies. The primary epistemological commitment centred on registering the transition from institutional forms of religions to diffuse and 'invisible' ones, and as such the corpus of research produced in this period aimed at challenging and debating various secularization theories. It is only in the past decade that analysis of spiritualities have been substantially linked with neoliberal transformations and how they inform the new 'spirit' of capitalism.

An early text that makes this connection is Jeremy Carrette and Richard King's *Selling Spirituality: The Silent Takeover of Religion* (2005). Their provocative narrative argument is designed to stimulate thought on a taken-for-granted issue, which at that time had received limited attention. The first page poses the question: 'Is something more complex and suspicious at work [than the revision of religious belief into a more contemporary form] in the glorification of the spiritual?' (2005: 1). Carrette and King locate expressions of contemporary spiritualities, such as holistic medicine, yoga and counselling, as central to many lives in Western societies in the late twentieth century. Most important, they argue, are not the beliefs or practices, but how they intersect with capitalism, its neoliberal forms in particular. Spiritualities, they suggest, enable the spread of neoliberal capitalist ideology into lives via individual actions and behaviours, but also, crucially, through accommodating or even actively promoting consumerism and corporate capitalism.

Carrette and King are unsparing in their critical analysis. They direct their commentary towards practitioners and academics. Their argument is specifically designed to engage with political debate, by assessing how economy and ethics interact. Spiritual practitioners, those selling and those buying, are accused of stripping, for example, yoga's underpinning belief systems of transformative or critical potential. Academic researchers are also held up as lacking ways of understanding, through neglect of 'cultural critique' (2005: 6). For us here, this analysis raises two concerns. First, on what do Carrette and King base their critique of individual motives and motivations? And second, what is the conceptual foundation of the 'cultural critique' that they present?

Carrette and King propose a typology of spirituality capitalism, based on how far the belief systems accommodate neoliberal ideology. This thoughtful and subtle typology ranges from revolutionary anti-capitalist (such as the deep ecology movement) through reformist spiritualities (such as the Quaker movement) and individualist consumerist spiritualities (usually described as 'prosperity religion'), to the central target of the book, capitalist spiritualities. This latter group 'mainfest[s] an uncritical assimilation of business values into their rationale' (2005: 20), and can be eclectically spiritual (e.g. Deepak Chopra) or very conventionally religious (e.g. Opus Dei).

What then is the evidence for this 'dynamic cultural continuum' (2005: 22) of spiritual-capitalist intersection? Their account of what contemporary spiritualities mean to practitioners is developed through quasi-Foucauldian readings of pop psychology manifestos and management consultancy adaptations of the Human Potential Movement's ideas. The scholarship, however, remains exceptional; the argument draws on cultural studies, theology and ecclesiology to define spirituality, for example, in contrast to the many vague or empiricist definitions of that term provided in other academic research in the field. This may be a weakness, oddly; an earlier book by Carrette (2000) demonstrates a deep familiarity with Foucault's ideas, in a detailed re-evaluation of religion as an immanent political experience with the potential to govern human life, woven into the fabric of the secular.

The cultural studies methodology on which *Selling Spirituality* mainly relies involves a highly partial empirical representation of contemporary spiritualities' intersection with the everyday economic lives of practitioners. While this is not intrinsically problematic – all social science leads to abstraction in the pursuit of theory – it can create unstable judgements such as: 'Despite the frequent appeals to a "holistic" approach [in Hatha Yoga], the popular reception of yoga in the West has largely fallen into a Cartesian trap of emphasising either the mind or the body' (Carrette & King, 2005: 118). Such authoritative assessments of a widely practised contemporary spiritual form are troubling. This overlays an empirical judgement as to how Eastern spirituality is experienced in the West, based on a secular early modern Western philosophical framework. This judgement is given more detail in the assessment that 'the metaphysical, institutional and societal dimensions of ancient yoga traditions are largely lost in the translation and popularisation of yoga in the West' (2005: 119). Again, this is something that is, at best, open to challenge and nuance.

What do these two observations, on theory and data in relation to the important argument presented by Carrette and King, mean in the context of the current edited volume? Carrette and King provide a landmark in understanding the intersection of spiritualities, and by extension all metaphysical belief systems, with everyday economic lives. However, their argument does not allow for the subtlety demanded by close empirical observation of how and why people engage with contemporary spiritualities. Hence the book is characterized by sweeping statements that position individual social actors as simple ideological carriers, rather than thoughtful, reflexive agents. This is unconvincing as a way of making sense of spiritualized practice, as the chapters in this volume highlight. That there is ideology is not in doubt; that some who promote spiritualities enthusiastically embrace neoliberalism is equally clear. However, it is unhelpful to represent contemporary spiritualities in all forms as materialistic and consumerist, as Carrette and King tend to.

More recently, Adam Possamai in his book, *The I-zation of Society, Religion, and Neoliberal Post-Secularism* (2018), approaches the issue of neoliberalism and spirituality using a Weberian framework. This enables analysis of the impact of digitalization and recent economic developments on contemporary religious practices. The book is a strongly theorized review of how spirituality can be researched, and puts forth methodological suggestions and political recommendations (such as the taxation of neoliberal religions).

Drawing on wide-ranging social theory, Possamai employs an epistemology of social research that understands neoliberalism as a process of commodification, consumerism and competition at all levels of society. This generates hyper-rationalization of everyday life and increasing social inequalities and economic imbalances. Possamai adopts a definition of neoliberalism that speaks to the marketization of everyday life and widespread deregulation of economies (including implementation of competition regulations within state structures). Neoliberalism is understood this way as a radical mode of dominance by capitalist economy which succeeds in encapsulating all spheres of life.

This classic (and limited) way of defining neoliberalism determines his understanding of the transformation of religion. Possamai analyses the relationship between neoliberalism and religion by looking at two different instances of religious consumerism: hyper-consumerist religions which enable believers' extensive and creative choices over the religious content of their everyday practices, and 'hypo-consumerist religion' in which the range of choices is limited by one 'brand' of religion. Both these religiosities are the by-product of religious adaptation to contemporary consumerist society, generating a religious field that is strongly entrenched in processes that enable the commodification of religious experiences.

Hyper-consumerist religions proceed from the assumption that each individual should have the right to create, select and consume the types of religious services desired. This is, for Possamai, a socio-economic position particularly well adapted to New Age spiritualities, which encourage practitioners to draw on many religious traditions and techniques in order to create their own spiritualized world-views. This amounts not just to a genuine religious post-modernism but also to an extensive commodification of religion. The capacity to choose and assemble a particular religious universe is mediated by a growing rise of religious entrepreneurialism and multiplication of business networks of global distribution of New Age spiritualities.

Possamai connects this with what he interprets as the ever increasing requirement of late capitalism for enhanced productivity. Hyper-consumerist religions are not only about commodification of religious practices as goods and services to be sold; they are also about enabling the formation of a subjectivity that is attuned to the demanding cycles of capitalist production. This is why, Possamai observes, businesses in the United States are thought to spend between 3 and 4 billion dollars per annum on professional workforce formation that experiments with New Age techniques and motivational workshops. Similar patterns of spending on consumerist religions can be observed in other Western European countries, according to Possamai.

This area is explored in great detail by Kimberly Lau (2000), in her book-length discourse analysis of North American 'New Age capitalism'.

Lau's focus is on the production of commodified spirituality. She analyses the beginnings of the spectacular global expansion of opportunities to consume alternative health and wellness offerings. As Lau argues, the opportunity to 'practice Chinese meditation while listening to Andean relaxation music and burning Indian incense ... on a yoga retreat in the Caribbean, enjoy aroma-therapy massages, enjoy a strictly macrobiotic diet based on Japanese foods' (2000: 13) encourages a highly individualized sense of empowerment and responsibility.

The commodification of spirituality, however, is problematic. First, it is dependent on an ability to consume, and therefore is limited to those who are (at least partially) 'winning' the capitalist game. Second, it is based on an *impression* of difference and alternative action; again, this impression is fragile, especially in its political promise that the consumer is changing them-selves and the world. Lau concludes that commodification and consumption integrate what might be metaphysically, politically and economically sub-versive practices into disenchanted capitalism. She notes the implications of privatizing progressive political action in this way, transforming its potential into consumption, for public health and society.

The chapters in this edited book revisit and build on Lau's argument. Two chapters, by Amanda Peticca-Harris, Kseniya Navazhylava and Genevieve Shanahan, and by Tom Vine, specifically explore the commodification of spiritual beliefs and value systems. Yoga offers a prominent representa-tion of contemporary spiritualities and their intersection with neoliberalism. Peticca-Harris and colleagues (Chapter 4, this volume) examine the embodied and economic precarity that characterizes yoga teaching. Teachers often work on a 'zero hours' commitment as self-employed contractors, and are paid only for the classes that they are physically present to teach. Their physical presence is thus reliant on their own health and wellbeing. They also explore the gendered nature of this work. Sociologists such as Paul Heelas and Linda Woodhead (2005) established the gendered nature of the 'holistic milieu' that includes yoga (along with many other New Age-influenced spiritual professions) where producers (teachers) and consumers (students) are mainly women. Peticca-Harris and colleagues suggest an elective affinity between this kind of spiritual work in neoliberal economies such as Canada, and post-feminist discourses promising financial liberation alongside a certain version of gender equality. This chapter is also important methodologically. A life history method that focuses on meanings attributed by the actors in context provides what Peticca-Harris et al. call a 'portal' into the lives of others. This methodological choice respects the experiences of the person and the meanings they read into their working lives, while at the same time analys-ing the often invisible structural conditions of that life.

A small number of spiritually oriented communities have acquired a global reputation. One such is the focus of Tom Vine's account (Chapter 5, this volume) of living and working at the Findhorn Foundation, which he describes as a New Age commune. Vine's chapter is based on ethnographic fieldwork which enables understanding of established custom and everyday practice within the community. He suggests the work required of visitors to Findhorn forms part of a process of resacralization that the community pursues more broadly. This is important in part because of the cultural reach of Findhorn – which has provided a cultural and structural model for many communities around the world, partly by welcoming visitors such as Vine. The Findhorn community works with branches of the United Nations, focused on sustainable living. Work at Findhorn is framed by the process of 'attunement', which he suggests resembles the socialization that employees typically experience in the first weeks working for a large corporate multinational. This is, as Vine suggests, a semi-mystical process that ostensibly conflates individual spiritual purpose with community exigencies. Vine's insights expose tensions within the community related to freedom/discipline and efficiency/meaning. A further contradiction Vine explores concerns the community's approach to work. Task-allocation processes, the tools, even the work itself, are rarely oriented towards maximizing outputs or efficiency. At the same time, Vine found relatively little metaphysical content in the work he did – it was difficult to invest much self or find deep meaning in harvesting beans and tidying scaffolding poles. Consequently, neither efficiency nor sacralization seem to be achieved.

To summarize, in Peticca-Harris et al. and Vine's chapters, commodification is manifest in and through the labouring body, either as a means of accomplishing an independent enterprising self, albeit somewhat temporarily in a physical sense. Both thereby speak to Lau's (2000) concern about the limited potential for progressive political action. These spiritual practices thus appear disconnected from the kind of public politics that provokes change beyond the individual and their immediate local community.

Finally, in considering how neoliberal transformations and new spirits of capitalism intersect, Darlene Miller (Chapter 6, this volume) focuses on urban food gardening in South Africa in the context of vast neoliberal transformations and urban unemployment affecting young people from Cape Town. The main argument of this chapter is that food gardening can act as a spiritual form of connection with the earth and mediate a process of self-knowledge among the rebellious youth that has been marginalized and dispossessed by economic reforms which have rendered them a surplus population. Food gardening constitutes an important mode in which indigeneity is articulated and performed. Food politics has been a vital component of colonialism and the repression of local traditions. Ikhaya, a specific form of indigenous food politics, addresses this past and assumes the rich traditional heritage in generating an alternative mode of food production. This is relevant in the context of a predominance of unhealthy large agriculture food production and consumerist networks of food distribution through supermarket chains. The ethnography of this chapter analyses gardening as a site of transformative knowledge production and new modes of personhood that are developed in relation with this. In doing this the gardeners become 'enchanted' and actualize a critical perspective on secular rationalist epistemology and capitalist practices of food production and consumption.

NEOLIBERALISM AND RESILIENT RELIGIOSITIES

This brings us to our final theme. New spiritualities have been repeatedly coupled with global neoliberal transformations, but more established religiosities have also proved remarkably resilient. Special attention in the field of religious studies has been devoted to Evangelical movements (Comaroff & Comaroff, 2001; Hackworth & Stein, 2012; Martikainen & Gauthier 2013), and the role they play in the global spread of capitalist imaginaries through religious narratives of personal prosperity. Possamai (2018) suggests these types of religiosities are an instance of 'hypo-consumerist religion'. In comparison with the hyper-consumerist religions described in the previous section they generate a different pattern of consumerism, encapsulated in a particular, gated, religious tradition. This does not encourage bricolage and liberal individual choice, but predetermines the 'right' type of religious consumerism believers are allowed to engage in. This monopolization of consumerism is embedded nevertheless in organized neoliberalism. Evangelical movements tend to create alternative cultures which aim to protect believers from secular cultures, and generate distinctive modes of religious consumption through Christian movies, books, music and concerts, TV stations, leisure activities, even dating networks. Possamai stresses that this hypo-consumerist pattern is encountered not only among Christian groups, but also among Buddhist groups that want to adapt their religious way to the Western world (Possamai, 2018).

Hypo-consumerist religions also emphasize increased productivity and personal development among believers, neglecting the fact that this is embedded in strong community life and social networks. Looking towards Africa and Latin America, Possamai notices social mobility-generated patterns of middle-class consumption and strong professional ethics. An extreme example of this is the global diffusion of the Gospel of Prosperity which openly equates success, wealth and abundance as signs of God's blessing for those saved. Evangelical mega-churches are seen here as laboratories of a new religious world-view in which religious consumerism is becoming the new norm (Possamai, 2018).

Possamai points out that within neoliberalism, the religious field is structurally transformed and religion changes its function. Contemporary religion, rather than having a Durkheimian collective function of mediating society, tends to be more individualistic and adapted to market competition, productivity and new labour requirements. This is suggestive as to why religion does not consolidate a sense of belonging to wider social structures, but rather enables various forms of enhancement of one's life in order to facilitate the development of adaptive capacities to neoliberalism. From his argument we can notice at least three distinct modes in which religion is appropriated in the neoliberal age: a) to empower and amplify the self in order to facilitate the inner growth and enhancement required by capitalist enterprises, both in aspects of stimulating consumerist subjectivities and in the need to develop employees' productive capabilities; b) the healing of self through meditative practices and alternative therapies, that address both the need for meaning in life and stress reduction; and c) personal entertainment, associated especially with the rise of mega-churches and the religious shows and distractions they often involve (Possamai, 2018: 75–76).

Possamai elaborates little on the ways in which neoliberal transformation of the religious field has generated new modes of authenticity, ethical reasoning or cultural ontologies that make neoliberalism meaningful in religious terms. These neoliberalized religions are not just religious ideas and practices captured by capitalism. As Boltanksi and Chiapello (2005a) emphasize, their internal development can sometimes generate critiques of capitalist arrangements. Similarly, Charles Taylor (2007) cautions against the view that new emerging spiritualities are shallow and superficial ways of authenticating the self, instead seeing them as creative modes of understanding genuine human flourishing which have their genealogy in centuries-long developments of religious practices. In this respect, two chapters in this book, by Kauppinen and Abraham, illustrate the complexity of modes through which belief systems address recent capitalist transformations.

Anna-Riikka Kauppinen (Chapter 7, this volume) focuses on the boom in markets for personal development emerging in Ghana's capital, Accra. In recent years, this industry has been characterized by Charismatic Christian discourses focused on the making of the competitive citizen subject, which claim that deeper Christian faith results in economic prosperity and national economic development. Adopting a long-term historical perspective on personal development in Ghana where 'character building' closely dovetails with nation building, Kauppinen explores this industry through the lens of young Charismatic Pentecostal media practitioners who produce spiritually motivated programmes. Situated in a context where the popularity of Charismatic Pentecostal Christianity has risen hand in hand with post-1990s currents of neoliberal economic transformations, they frame personal development as a spiritual regime that enacts productive citizenship in Christian terms. Somewhat at odds with critical scholarship on personal development as a medium of neoliberal governmentality that shifts responsibility for social change from the collective to the individual, the young entrepreneurs in question view Christian faith as a revolutionary force in advancing Ghana's collective economic position. In dialogue with recent debates on the depoliticizing effects associated with the globalization of therapeutic industries of personal development, Kauppinen draws attention to a multiplicity of historical macro regimes, post-colonial African nation building in particular, that make personal development a distinctive global scene at the interface of 'the world' and God's Kingdom.

Ibrahim Abraham (Chapter 8, this volume) also brings a substantial contribution to understanding the way religion and neoliberalism are made meaningful to religious subjects, in his focus on the moral articulation of after-work leisure among the Evangelical youth groups from South Africa. The chapter analyses recent developments within the 'serious leisure' perspective, and the role religious narratives play in generating an understanding of one's attitudes towards life in the context of youth unemployment and neoliberal emphasis on competition and productivity. Abraham carefully traces a genealogy of the neoliberal understanding of work and leisure within bourgeois culture, and discusses aspects of how this culture was engaged both by liberal economists and Christian theologians. Developments within the Protestant moral order eventually came to emphasize the importance of productive leisure activities and sought to entrepreneurialize free time, as was historically the case with attitudes toward work.

Abraham's research focuses on religious youth culture in South Africa, an important segment of population which is affected by discrepant social inequalities and extreme poverty. Sports programmes (in this case surfing) and serious leisure are employed among the disenfranchised youth (more than 50 per cent being without work) to cultivate competitive skills and commitment in order to increase the chances of succeeding in life. Evangelical youth sports trainers emphasize the need to develop a strong sense of proactive self-determination while engaging in sports activity. Leisure is in this case not about relaxation and disconnection from exhausting activities, but about cultivating, in the very process of recreation, the capabilities of an 'auto-telic self'; a self that is proficient in focused activity and emotional reflexivity. An important concept associated with the cultivation of this type of interiority is that of flexible resilience and the capacity to bounce back from defeats and temporary obstacles.

Surfing is this way not only a sport; it becomes the source for an important experience needed in acquiring the necessary survival life skills. The risks associated with this sport and the struggle to navigate the waves become a proxy for developing a sense of self that enables the management of risk, and encourages active engagement with difficult and demanding situations. Crucially, this goes hand in hand with a religious moral pedagogy that emphasizes the need for personal salvation embedded in moral resilience, and in the capability of religious subjects to lead an ethically driven life. Abraham shows how in the case of the Christian Surfers Organization the recommendation to replace casual leisure with serious leisure comes along with an awareness that this is not an end in itself. The reduction of religion to either just moralism or simple professional success is to be avoided. Abraham places this ethnographic analysis in the context of the neoliberal erosion of leisure society and its quest for authenticity as an essentially after-work recreational activity. As a result of increasing joblessness, leisure becomes problematic because of the impact of deindustrialization and global technologies.

CONCLUSION AND FUTURE DEVELOPMENTS

We began this introduction by emphasizing the importance of detailed empirical analyses that shed light on how new spiritualities and neoliberal economy interact with one other. In making this argument, we noted the range of terms available to us to designate changes that have occurred in the religious sphere, in Europe and North America in particular, since the 1960s. The contributions to this book show clearly that the new spirituality is underpinned by what Lynch (2007: 41) calls the 'cultural tool-kit' of conceptual, social and material resources that practitioners draw on to make sense of the intersections between belief and economy. We conclude here with a brief discussion of potential future developments in this field.

We deliberately did not define 'neoliberalism' at the start of this introduction, preferring instead to discuss the contested concept of spiritualities. This is in contrast to much of the literature on spirituality and economy that we have reviewed in this introduction (Boltanski & Chiapello, 2005a; Carrette & King, 2005; Chandler & Reid, 2016; Illouz, 2008; Lau, 2000; Possamai, 2018) which begins by conceptually defining neoliberalism as a political project, using this to frame the cultural, religio-spiritual changes under discussion. This literature follows a familiar trajectory in tracing political-economic changes in the late twentieth century, summarized as: neoliberalism began as an economic theory, which became 'a political discourse about the nature of rule and a set of practices that facilitate the governing of individuals' (Rottenberg, 2018: 57), and has come to dominate global economic structures and everyday working lives. Sociologists have long observed the implications of neoliberalism's emphasis on individualism, enterprise and instrumental rationality for the construction of contemporary subjectivities, including by looking to Foucauldian perspectives on governmentality and selfhood (c.f. Rose, 1990). From this perspective, the political project of neoliberalism is summarized as an attempt to reduce state responsibility for actions and choices, through creating and promoting a sense of subjective and economic freedom and personal choice (Brown, 2003). A key area for further research involves generating insight into the complexities of everyday experiences of neoliberalism, to complement the accounts of its ideological implications.

The last chapter in this book takes a direct approach to this issue and considers the way a specific feature of contemporary capitalism – innovationism – and the social values associated with this – competitiveness, creativity and success – has become a new form of secular spirituality and an implicit religion. Katja Valaskivi (Chapter 9, this volume) provides a critical interrogation of the mythological narratives that fuel contemporary global capitalism and its obsession with innovation and growth. What are the 'sacred values' and the implicit belief system at the core of the institutions, practices and actors that are engaged in decision making that shapes contemporary capitalism? Valaskivi shows how norms and values promoted by many states around the world to encourage innovation, especially technological innovation, are open to analysis as a faith that promises to resolve fundamental human challenges, including human mortality. The entrepreneurial spirit of today's global capitalism is increasingly connected with the idea of constant innovation that is not just a means through which economic growth is achieved but a particular ideological and utopic imagination that addresses the way self and society have to be reimagined in order to adapt to a competitive social environment. Working with a range of empirical materials, including observations about higher education – a key institutional location for the spread of beliefs about innovationism – combined with detailed qualitative interviews, Valaskivi's analysis brings original insight to what could too easily be dismissed as another managerial fashion. Four levels of action are identified, each with its own particular dynamics: individual, organizational, national and global. This chapter speaks to our understanding of the discourse of innovation and to sociological understandings of what constitutes a belief system. She concludes by suggesting that innovationism, while clearly not a religion in the conventional sense, manifests the aspects of an implicit religion. Innovationism is thus understood as an emerging religion of technology, with all of the ideological markers, both immanent and transcendent, that a faith requires. In this respect the chapter provides further insight into the spiritual and mythological imagination of current capitalism.

To summarize, it is clear that there have been significant global political shifts in the period defined by the new spirituality, including fundamental changes in the accepted role of the state in many parts of the world. In bringing together this edited collection we have sought to avoid a reductionist approach to understanding religion and spirituality in neoliberal societies. The chapters in this book instead show how neoliberal societies produce resilient subjectivities that are adapted to the current global capitalist economy. Consequently, the 'new spirit of capitalism' is understood not as a form of false consciousness that reifies the relations of production, but as a complex cultural formation through which capitalist transformations are made meaningful. The chapters emphasize the way in which spirituality and religions enable social actors and communities to be reflexive in relation to capitalism, and generate new social practices and modes of being. The way these spiritualities produce resistance to, or legitimations of, capitalism is always mediated in a complex way and engages the emotions, sensibilities and reflexivity of social actors. In this respect, the contributors to this volume provide comprehensive accounts of how the social spaces that connect contemporary spiritualities with the global transformations of capitalism are materially and culturally produced.

NOTES

1. The sociology of contemporary spiritualities is a difficult definitional area. As noted above, we prefer the term 'the new spirituality', used by Lynch (2007). Heelas and Woodhead (2005) write of the 'holistic milieu', Campbell (1987) prefers the 'New Age' (1987), Carrette and King (2005) simply 'spirituality' (although always in inverted commas). We prefer Lynch's term because it is developed through consideration of theological and cultural changes that have resulted in a distinctive ideology.
2. Boltanski and Chiapello's strong sweeping argument has of course proven highly controversial, empirically and conceptually. Some of the strongest critique centres on their definition of 'benevolent' participation in the capitalist activities. The definition of capitalism provided almost completely ignores the global features of the system and, through this omission, ignores the immense number of people whose labour is essential to the basic functioning of the system, and whose involvement is not gained through subtle justifications that the (representatives of the) system need to constantly upgrade, but through sheer force. The fact that much of the Third World's population involvement in the global capitalist enterprise would be better described in terms of slavery or forced labour completely escapes the model built by Boltanski and Chiapello. Finally, even in the French case, the accounts are far more relevant for the middle classes and for the secure working class than for the growing number of what has recently been called the precariat, or those working in the gig economy. Nonetheless, we believe there is something to be rescued from this line of critique.

REFERENCES

Boltanski, L. & Chiapello, E. (2005a) *The New Spirit of Capitalism*. London: Verso.
Boltanski, L. & Chiapello, E. (2005b) 'The new spirit of capitalism', *International Journal of Politics, Culture and Society*, 18: 161–88.
Brown, W. (2003) 'Neo-liberalism and the end of democracy', *Theory and Event*, 7(1). Accessed 31 October 2019, https://muse.jhu.edu/article/48659

Campbell, C. (1987) *The Romantic Ethic and the Spirit of Modern Consumerism.* Oxford: Blackwell.

Carrette, J. (2000) *Foucault and Religion.* London: Routledge.

Carrette, J. & King, R. (2005) *Selling Spirituality: The silent takeover of religion.* London: Routledge.

Chandler, D. & Reid, J. (2016) *The Neoliberal Subject: Resilience, adaptability, and vulnerability.* London: Rowman and Littlefield.

Comaroff, J. & Comaroff, J. (2001) 'On personhood: An anthropological perspective from Africa', *Journal for the Study of Race, Nation and Culture*, 7(2): 267–83.

Hackworth, J. & Stein, K. (2012) 'The collision of faith and economic development in Toronto's inner suburban industrial districts', *Urban Affairs Review*, 48(1): 37–63.

Heelas, P. (2008) *Spiritualities of Life.* Oxford: Blackwell.

Heelas, P. & Woodhead, L. (2005) *The Spiritual Revolution: Why religion is giving way to spirituality.* Oxford: Blackwell.

Illouz, E. (2008) *Saving the Modern Soul: Therapy, emotions, and the culture of self-help.* Berkeley: University of California Press.

Lau, K. (2000) *New Age Capitalism: Making money east of Eden.* Philadelphia: University of Pennsylvania Press.

Lynch, G. (2007) *The New Spirituality: An introduction to progressive belief in the twenty-first century.* London: IB Tauris.

Martikainen, T. & Gauthier, F. (eds) (2013) *Religion in the Neoliberal Age: Political economy and modes of governance.* Farnham: Ashgate.

Possamai, A. (2018) *The I-zation of Society, Religion, and Neoliberal Secularism.* London: Palgrave Macmillan.

Rose, N. (1990) *Governing the Soul: The shaping of the private self.* London: Routledge.

Rottenberg, C. (2018) *The Rise of Neoliberal Feminism.* New York: Oxford University Press.

Taylor, C. (2007) *A Secular Age.* Cambridge, MA: Belknap Press.

1. Towards radical subjects: workplace spirituality as neoliberal governance in American business

James Dennis LoRusso

There is only one social responsibility of business—to use its resources and engage in activities designed to increase its profits so long as it stays within the rules of the game, which is to say, engages in open and free competition without deception or fraud. (Milton Friedman, *New York Times Magazine*, September 1970)

In these words written nearly 50 years ago, Milton Friedman, the Nobel Laureate economist and father of the Chicago School of economics, expressed the prevailing view of American business at mid-century: that business exists solely for the pursuit of profits. Anything else is superfluous. Surely, the notion that companies should devote any of their energies towards other ends would have seemed foreign, perhaps even nonsensical. The truism, often attributed to long-time chief executive officer (CEO) of General Motors Alfred P. Sloan, that 'the business of business is business,' certainly still rang true. Yet today, the culture of business couldn't appear more different. Companies, at least on their public face, more often present themselves as responsible stewards of society, boasting aspiration mission statements, entire divisions devoted to 'corporate social responsibility,' and core values committed to respecting the dignity of their employees. Every year since 1998, *Fortune* magazine publishes its coveted list of the 'Best Companies to Work For,' measured not by their profit margins but how they ensure a fulfilling and rewarding *experience* for their workforces.

The expectation that work should be 'more than a paycheck' but also intrinsically rewards seems almost unexceptional to working people today. The workplace of the twenty-first century aims to be a space to which individuals can bring their 'whole selves.' Business schools and corporate training programs instill ideas about management and 'leadership' as a form of service to others, specifically for their clientele and their staff. Indeed, for a growing number of firms, business leaders, and even mid-level managers, this quest has taken on 'spiritual' significance. Companies offer extracurricular courses that claim to draw on spiritual disciplines in order to promote employee well-being. Google, for example, introduced a two-day workshop called 'Search Inside Yourself,' that instructs employees in meditation techniques that will presumably help them avoid burnout and achieve better 'work–life balance' (Lebowitz 2016).

Scholars in the business world and the humanities have dubbed this latter trend to introduce various spiritual perspectives into their organizations, 'workplace spirituality.' Religion scholar Lake Lambert III understands workplace spirituality as 'important religious movement shaping and being shaped by American business culture' (Lambert III 2009, p. 18). Others offer a more critical assessment of this development. Sociologist Douglas Hicks (2003) worries that these efforts risk becoming 'religions *of* the workplace,' corporate cultures that use spiritual perspectives to elicit increased productivity and profit margins.

The vast majority of research into workplace spirituality overwhelmingly stems from scholars in the business world, where professional interests in understanding effective management strategies blur the line between disinterested scholarship and overt advocacy. In fact, American scholars of management, beginning in the mid-1990s, were among the first to articulate and identify this trend in the business world, and in fact, it was they who first coined the term 'workplace spirituality.'[1] Too often, however, the study of workplace spirituality has tilted towards outright advocacy, envisioning the trend as a positive development for business and working people alike, while ignoring its broader implications for society.

The purpose of this chapter is to begin to highlight the power dynamics of this trend, to provide some measure of historical context, and to ponder the way in which workplace spirituality exacerbates existing forms of socioeconomic imbalances. Eschewing conventional qualitative and quantitative methods that dominate the field of management, this chapter privileges critical approaches offered by social theorists, indicative of the work of cultural historians, discourse analysis, and practice theories. The basic claim of this chapter is that workplace spirituality, contrary to the claims of most management scholars, represents a distinctly neoliberal form of managerial control. Rather than a radical departure from conventional management thought and practice, it is an extension of existing strategies that reproduce the very conditions from which they purport to liberate and improve the lives of working people. Workplace spirituality not only functions as an effective tool for management, it represents what Michel Foucault calls a 'technology of the self,' engendering new forms of subjectivity suited to the conditions of twenty-first-century work. In short, when spirituality becomes part of the fabric of a workplace culture, individuals adopt interpretive strategies and enact practices that render them, perhaps unwittingly, participants in their own subordination to the interests of management and to a broader neoliberal status quo. After establishing the conceptual relationships between neoliberalism, workplace spirituality, and subjectivity, the chapter will examine how these elements intersect with two domains of American business. First, I explore how workplace spirituality reinforces neoliberalization in management education. Second, the chapter draws on ethnographic fieldwork conducted at a coffee shop chain located in the western United States that has explicitly adopted 'spiritual' discourses as a central component of organizational culture. Each of these cases illustrates how spiritual regimens operate to recast individuals as neoliberal subjects suited to their particular location, whether frontline workers or business professionals, within the class structure of American society. In this way, we can begin to see how spiritual discourses participate in much broader cultural processes that uphold neoliberal capitalism.

WORKPLACE SPIRITUALITY AS NEOLIBERAL SUBJECT FORMATION

Conceptualizing Neoliberalism

Neoliberalism is a concept that defies simple explanation. Perhaps more prevalent in European than North American public discourse, it has been defined variously and inconsistently, and therefore I can only hope to offer some precision in how I will conceptualize this term herein. David Harvey, whose grasp of this elusive concept surpasses most, suggests that neoliberalism is a theory of political economy, grounded in the belief that human wellbeing is best secured by promoting free trade, free markets, and a strong defense of private property rights. He characterizes it as hegemonic, as the 'common sense' of today (Harvey 2005, pp. 2–3).

I agree with Harvey's assessment that what he labels neoliberalism is *the* normalized way of understanding the world, especially in the capitalist West, yet his depiction remains inadequate. Because Harvey presents neoliberalism as a ruling ideology, his conceptualization obscures the myriad contested and dynamic social processes that often fall under its banner. The wide array of factors that converge in the concept cannot be reduced to Harvey's portrait of neoliberalism as a set of coherent, interconnected, and largely stable set of principles that give rise to a consistent assortment of formal policies. Rather, as Jamie Peck argues, we must attend to the inherently unstable quality of *neoliberalization*, which 'does not follow the pristine path of rolling market liberalization and competitive convergence; it is one of repeated, prosaic, and often botched efforts to *fix* markets, to build quasi-markets, and to repair market failures' (Peck 2010, p. xiii). Peck does characterize neoliberalism as a discursive formation, but he frames it primarily as a practical discourse strategically mobilized to uphold the ideological purity of capitalist markets, rather than an ideology in and of itself. Whereas Harvey asserts neoliberalism as a political project to restore class power (2005, p. 16), Peck takes us further. It is not only fueled by a resistance to the welfare state or working-class power, but by the failure of really-existing-capitalism to live up to the utopian promises of its most fervent adherents.

Marnie Holborow likewise recognizes this slippage between 'what neoliberalism says and what it does' (2015, p. 9). While proponents of free markets decry government interference with supply and demand, they actively utilize the state to create, sustain, and shape markets in order to defend the interests of capital. The chasm between, on one hand, capitalist ideologies, and the policies its advocates support, on the other hand, defines neoliberalism. Ideologies justify the practice, and in turn, the practices legitimize the ideology, all of which renders the social contradictions inevitable.

The sense that somehow the conditions produced by capitalism are inevitable and a reflection of the natural order is crucial to understanding neoliberalism as a dynamic cultural phenomenon. Rather than a set of standard *orthodoxies*, as Harvey suggests, neoliberalism resides beneath the mantle of overt discourse, what Pierre Bourdieu refers to as *doxa*, a set of subjective principles that, in the quotidian world, lie beyond even the possibility of critique because they are experienced as self-evident, irreducible, objective conditions of the natural world (Bourdieu [1972] 1977, p. 164). It is literally a crucial element of the discursive air we breathe, woven into the collective cultural fabric in which individuals in capitalist societies become 'human.' Thus, it is here, at the level of human subject formation that I hope to illuminate the way that neoliberalism nonetheless persists and even thrives through attempts to overcome its most pernicious effects. Conceptualizing neoliberalism in this manner draws it out of hiding, transforming it from a *doxa* beyond recognition to a set of historically situated *orthodoxies* capable of critique. We will be able to see that human beings are not naturally or inevitably entrepreneurial. They are made that way through neoliberal disciplinary regimes.

If a critique of neoliberalism attempts to denaturalize what is typically taken for granted, to rehistoricize that which is commonly framed as sui generis, and to repoliticize that which otherwise has persisted as descriptive empirically rather than prescriptive ideologically, then I propose that neoliberal spiritualities, including workplace spirituality, operate at an inverse trajectory. They further mystify the logic and institutions of capitalism as more than natural, indeed, *supernatural*, as not merely ahistorical but a keystone of some cosmic order. Neoliberal forms of spirituality are not merely the way the world is but the perfected, if unattainable, telos of human existence. I want to suggest that workplace spirituality, as articulated by its champions, performs this precise ideological work.

Workplace Spirituality as Neoliberal Project

On its face, workplace spirituality is, as advocates suggest, a way of fulfilling an employer's obligation to care for both the material and immaterial needs of its employees. They see it as a part of a long-term effort to improve the quality of work, a remedy for traditional patterns of management practice, which tended to treat workers as simply one more factor of production. Not only should companies provide for the livelihood of their employees, they should actively promote their overall wellbeing, which includes spiritual health. Organizations have pursued this end in numerous ways. Some firms, like Google, Nike, and Salesforce, have embraced this practice, carving out physical spaces where individuals may 'recharge' through relaxation, meditation, or engage in daily prayers (Garvey 2018). Others allow their employees to form affinity groups, or 'employee resource groups,' that bring together staff, typically under the watchful eye of human resource departments who share a particular religious identity.[2] Faith-based and interfaith employee groups treat workplace spirituality as an extension of diversity and inclusion with religion as an important marker or identity in need of formal recognition and respect from the employer. Still others, like Tyson Foods, provide corporate chaplains, trained professionals ready and willing to serve as counsel for individuals of any faith background.[3] Some businesses directly articulate their organizational culture or corporate mission in explicitly spiritual or religious terms.

Researchers from the study of management and other disciplines consider each of these examples as comprising a broader trend within American business in recent decades to attend to the spiritual needs of working people. David Miller, the director of the Faith and Work initiative, argues that the 'Faith at Work movement' represents a response to various social, economic, and cultural factors that came to a head during the late 1980s and early 1990s. Miller (2007) claims that religious institutions (namely the Church) have failed to equip their members to adequately deal with the anxieties brought about by the effects of globalization, corporate downsizing, and the diminishing prospect of lifelong employment. Consequently, laypeople have formed their own voluntary associations that draw on religious resources for sustenance. Management scholar Judi Neal, a long-time advocate for workplace spirituality, also attributes the rising business interest in spirituality to broad global socioeconomic trends. Yet, while Miller decries the absence of a robust theology of work on the part of churches, Neal (2006) explains rising corporate interest in spirituality as the result of a tectonic 'spiritual awakening' originating in the counterculture of the 1960s and early 1970s. While other scholars offer various explanations, they generally concede that workplace spirituality represents a movement to reform the culture of business in ways that empower working people to be their 'whole selves' on the job.[4]

From the perspective of scholars like Miller and Neal, spirituality in the workplace or the Faith at Work movement function as a religious response to changes normally associated with neoliberal capitalism: globalization, deregulation, etc. For them, workplace spirituality represents a radical, perhaps even revolutionary, departure from conventional managerial norms that too often dehumanize and subordinate the lived experiences and interests of working people to the needs of the firm. Despite such claims, however, it remains a deeply neoliberal project. The emergence of workplace spirituality in American business thought during the late twentieth century coincides with the triumph of neoliberal political culture, embodied first in the election of Ronald Reagan to the United States presidency and later in Bill Clinton's embrace of 'free trade' and reform of the welfare state. Yet, this rise is more than mere coincidence. Rather, interest in spirituality at work can only be adequately explained as an extension of existing trends in management thought that contributed to this shift towards a neoliberal orientation. Indeed, workplace spirituality advances the neoliberal project, as outlined by its critics. As we shall see, it naturalizes the capitalist logic, indeed *super*-naturalizes it by reconfiguring it as a truly utopian project. The market is not merely a reflection of human nature; it is the echo of a divine order, and the telos of all human striving is to perfect the mundane expression of this celestial form.

Radical Subject Formation

Workplace spirituality is not merely neoliberal, it is a form of neoliberal governance in two ways. First, it is, and always has been, a managerial tool, a set of tactics and habituated practices intended to reduce sources of friction in production. Yet, workplace spirituality also engenders modes of self-governance; it serves as a technology of the self, a practical regimen aimed at inculcating within workers more than a set of habits, but a way of experiencing reality, a way of knowing and being in the world that places subjective experience above and beyond all else. In short, it produces the quintessential capitalist subject, a radically individualistic subject for whom reality is itself merely the results of individual choices about how it is to be experienced.

Foremost, regardless of claimed aspirations to empower individuals and allow them to be authentic at work, workplace spirituality is, and has been since its inception, a business management strategy, a particular way of framing management decisions in order to facilitate production. Champions of workplace spirituality frequently resist these claims by distinguishing between those who, on one hand, use spirituality as a way to increase profits and themselves who envision spirituality as an intrinsic good. Yet, in the same breath, they will often make the case that tending to the spiritual needs remains 'good for business.' Such concerns betray an awareness among advocates that workplace spirituality possesses a latent potential for exploitation. As easily as they express these concerns, they nonetheless resist seeing this potential in their own models.

Of course, treating spirituality as a means rather than an end doesn't necessarily imply exploitation. Workplaces can conceivably promote respectful culture for employees and therefore breed high levels of job satisfaction without taking undue advantage of their labor. However, in practice, workplace spirituality, like any other management strategy, is often mobilized in ways that undermine the interests of subordinates and bolsters managerial authority.

Workplace spirituality not only constitutes managerial strategy, but also a mode of subject formation. It quite literally holds the potential to reshape the individual. Managers use workplace spirituality as a way to approximate organizational interests *as* those of the employee, but it also takes hold at a much more fundamental level of social relations, reshaping not only individual perceptions about their interests but the basic epistemic mode of which the self is perpetually reproduced, reality is perceived, and consequently the horizon of possible action in the world. Individuals therefore acquire an ontological map and way of knowing compatible—perhaps identifiable—with a neoliberal social order. In short, they are (re)cast as neoliberal subjects.

Judi Neal acknowledges this relationship between subjectivity and workplace spirituality in her concept of the *Edgewalker*. She declares 'that a new kind of human being is emerging on the planet and that this has major implications for business, governments, religion, education, and all of our social institutions' (Neal 2006, p. xv). According to Neal, these 'edgewalkers,' who walk between this world and the spiritual realm, are autochthonous beings of exceptional abilities destined to lead humanity into a new paradigm. She characterizes them as the twenty-first-century iteration of the medicine men of 'ancient cultures' (p. 2). Edgewalkers represent 'the corporate shamans who walk into the invisible world and bring back wisdom and guidance for their organizations' (p. 10).

I agree with Neal's assessment that a new kind of individual is emerging, not as the charismatic herald of a new age but a rather ordinary type of subject suited to this new (i.e. neoliberal) age. The enactment of workplace spirituality—its practices and beliefs—is one way in which this subjectivity is sustained. In this way, it performs a pedagogical function, akin to Foucault's notion of a *technology of the self*. These technologies 'permit individuals to effect by their own means or with the help of other a certain number of operations on their own bodies and souls, thoughts, conduct, and way of being, so as to transform themselves in order to attain a certain state of happiness, purity, wisdom, perfection, or immortality' (Foucault 1988, p. 18). As Foucault states, these technologies of the self operate in tandem and in relation to other

'matrices of practical reason,' including technologies of *production, power,*
etc., the confluence of which enforces a particular set of social dynamics and
structures. Unlike its role as a resource for strategic management of individuals
by organizations, this dimension of workplace spirituality is not imposed by
authority but taken up by employees themselves, in a nominally voluntary and
often tacit manner. The application and habituation of this practical regimen
results in a neoliberal subject suited to the local requirements demanded by
sites of production (i.e. in workplaces) and for the maintenance of global
capitalist social structures. If the previous section demonstrated workplace
spirituality as a form of managerial governance, this section focuses on how it
operates as a neoliberal governmentality, cultivated within subject.

I refer to this novel form of subjectivity as neoliberal precisely because it
is constituted by what Doreen Massey labels 'vocabularies of the economy,'
a *neoliberal* lexicon employed not only to 'talk about the economy in particular' but as a way of organizing life more generally (2013, p. 10). Massey characterizes the framework as an interpretive filter through which individuals 'are
primarily consumers, whose essential duty (and source of power and pleasure)
is to make choices' (p. 10). Certainly, the 'human-as-consumer' plays a crucial
role in perpetuating neoliberal ideology, but more elementary is Massey's
observation that these neoliberal vocabularies operate on and reinforce the
assumption that 'individual interests are the only reality that matters; that those
interests are purely monetary; and that so-called values are only a means of
pursuing selfish ends by other means' (p. 10).

These vocabularies accomplish more than establishing selves as consumers,
for they also cast individuals in their role as producers according to neoliberal
logic. Whereas the modern *liberal* subject is perceived as a stable, autonomous, and rational actor in the political economy, the *neoliberal* subject is
flexible, holistic, and intuitive. Rather than active, she remains *reactive* to ever
shifting market forces.[5] As Carla Freeman suggests, 'the self as an entrepreneurial "project" under constant renovation is a key signpost of neoliberalism
and its perpetual quest for flexibility in the changing global marketplace'
(Freeman 2014, p. 1). Similarly, the work of Dardot and Laval asserts that
neoliberal subjects become 'enterprises'—agents competing in a social order
organized around market principles—as the basic model for the self (Dardot
and Laval [2009] 2017, p. 259). Moreover, Ulrich Brockling's scholarship specifically links the popularization of entrepreneurial modes of the self with late
twentieth-century 'management literature' (Brockling 2016, p. 101). Taking
this further, I want to suggest that the language of spirituality, as illustrated in
workplace spirituality, has proven especially central to the fabrication of this
new, flexible form of subjectivity. Indeed, even Brockling cannot help but
employ concepts to describe this entrepreneurial self. 'Faith in the creative
potential of the individual,' he declares, 'is the secular religion of the entrepre-

neurial self' (p. 101). In the remainder of this chapter, I will explore in a more concrete manner how workplace spirituality facilitates the formation of radical subjects suited to our neoliberal moment.

PARSING THE CASE: NEOLIBERAL SPIRITUALITY IN AMERICAN BUSINESS EDUCATION

The neoliberal character of contemporary workplace spirituality appears most visibly with the emergence of the 'management, spirituality, and religion' (MSR) subfield in the Academy of Management, the largest professional society of scholars engaged in management research. Formed in the first years of the new millennium, MSR was the brainchild of a small band of academics who believed that conventional approaches to the study of management needed reform. Research, they asserted, relied too heavily on empirical, and in particular, quantitative methods, often overlooking the kind of 'person-centered' realities facing day-to-day managers. They founded MSR as a program unit within the academy as a way to promote generative research into the contributions that religious and spiritual perspectives might make to the existing body of knowledge. Over the years, MSR has situated itself as a kind of central hub, a clearing house for the latest perspectives on spirituality in the workplace.

Over the years, scholars pursuing research on workplace spirituality have formulated various founding mythologies to justify their shared identity. Typically, these mythic narratives explain workplace spirituality as an emergent movement within business aimed at transforming the nature of work specifically and society generally. The group often characterizes the movement as restorative, perhaps even redemptive. For them, the incorporation of spirituality into the workplace is not an innovation but rather a return to a more natural order, a rejection of the modern rationalization of society in favor of an imagined pre-modern arrangement when work and social relations were imbued with sacred meaning and purpose. Indeed, in the process of crafting this broader mythology, a handful of historical figures have emerged as 'founding fathers' of the movement whose scholarship provides the conceptual basis for much of the MSR research conducted to this day.

One such figure often touted as a pioneer of workplace spirituality is Willis Harman (1918–97), an electrical engineer who turned away from his profession to embrace futures research at the Stanford Research Institute during the second half of the twentieth century. Judi Neal, former director of the Tyson Center for Faith and Spirituality in the Workplace and co-founder of the MSR group, credits Harman as one of the earliest proponents of bringing spirituality into the workplace, but I want to suggest that a closer examination of his intellectual legacy demonstrates how workplace spirituality represents a comprehensive vision for the creation of a neoliberal social order and the formation of radical subjects.

While advocates of workplace spirituality see Harman's views as transformative, his thoughts mirror those of Drucker and the new generation of management philosophers. Industrial society, he maintains, suffers from an overly rationalized and fractured worldview that separates work, home, and worship, thereby denigrating the individual. Modernity, while it has produced unparalleled prosperity, has impoverished the individual by turning workers into factors of production deprived of, first, meaning, and eventually as a result of technological advances, jobs (Harman 1974, p. 9). Given this situation, Harman fervently believed that a radical shift in consciousness was required, one that would fundamentally reconfigure the role of work. In the future, he opined, only a fraction of the labor force would be engaged in actual work to meet the material needs of society, but nonetheless work would still serve as the source of self-worth. Under such conditions, '*employment is primarily the activity of self-development*, and secondarily the production of goods and services' (Harman 1974, p. 9).

This new era of self-improvement would be defined by a reintegration of inspired forms of knowledge into the workplace. 'There are today,' he claimed, 'multifold signs of a respiritualization of Western society, with emphasis on self-realization, transcendent meaning, and inner growth leading to wisdom and compassion' (Harman 1988, p. 121). What he repeatedly refers to as the 'Perennial Wisdom' of the world's religious traditions will gain new epistemic authority, infusing each and every experience with profound meaning and purpose.

Harman tied this self-improvement ethic of work to a particular kind of social order, which in retrospect undeniably endorses neoliberal worldviews. It would be the business world, not nation-states, that would lead this shift in consciousness. 'The modern business corporation,' he wrote in 1988, 'is probably the most adaptive institution humankind has ever devised' (Harman 1988, p. 131). It would be the biggest private-sector actors—corporations—who should 'assume responsibility for the whole of society' (p. 131). In pursuing his program to reintegrate society, Harman would become an integral part of the burgeoning efforts to (re)introduce spirituality into American business. He spent the last decade of his life as director and co-founder of the World Business Academy, a liberal think-tank dedicated to facilitating this 'trans-industrial age.' However, it is important to note that, as a futures researcher, Harman was not merely *prescribing* radical social reform, he saw his project foremost as *descriptive*, identifying trends already taking place. Discerning this sleight of hand remains crucial to understanding the neoliberal ideological work that Harman's philosophy performs. For him, business has already eclipsed the nation-state and social relations already only make sense in terms of the capitalist markets. The perfectibility of humankind will *inevitably* take shape only insofar as we acknowledge this paradigmatic fact.

Harman crafted a neoliberal mythology that he passed to his intellectual progeny like Judi Neal and others in the MSR universe. When Neal boldly declared at a conference in 2011 that 'business is the way we can transform consciousness precisely because it is so powerful today,' she is not merely restating platitudes often voiced by champions of the marketplace but, rather, affirming a key ideological aspiration of workplace spirituality: to remake the world in terms that can only be understood as neoliberal. This expressed goal of 'transforming consciousness' indicates that workplace spirituality targets more than societal reform; it has its sights aimed squarely on the formation of subjects themselves, and here Harman's intellectual project offers key insights into the mode of subjectivity it seeks to produce.

Harman begins from the assumption that the industrial society of the twentieth century, characterized by its 'direct measures' for dealing with the problems of poverty and inequality, has reached an impasse and is giving way to a new *transindustrial* paradigm.[6] If the industrial era is characterized by attention to 'physical frontiers of geography and technology, in the transindustrial society concern would shift to the inner frontiers of mind and spirit,' he asserts (Harman 1979, p. 1). Accordingly, he suggests that his radical epistemological turn inward will reconfigure individual and society alike. 'It would assume the existence of a *spiritual order*, discoverable and explorable, and in some sense testable, against which human value choices could be assessed; emerging from this spirituality would be a creative work ethic, placing a high value on aware participation in both individual and social evolution' (pp. 2–3).

In linking this paradigmatic shift in human consciousness to an ethos of work, Harman is essentially offering a primer for the neoliberal subject. Drawing on the work of Aldous Huxley, he suggests that the principles of the 'perennial philosophy' will guide humanity in the coming age. Turning towards spiritual resources nurtures a 'higher awareness' that 'all knowledge and power is ultimately accessible to the mind looking within itself, and that all limitations are ultimately self-chosen' (Harman 1979, p. 105). Harman, again, links this new perspective to a novel attitude of work, that it will produce 'the desire to participate consciously, to labor and serve, in the evolutionary process, the fulfillment of mankind' (p. 105). Thus, the trajectory of this perceived shift, its ultimate end, is the production of a new type of worker whose impetus to work stems not from material needs but from a *desire* for the holistic spiritual advancement of society, a neoliberal society shorn of the trappings of the welfare state. He continues, 'But the reverse side of this attitude is *acceptance*, the choosing of what is, since at some deep level the self already chooses this' (p. 105). At this point, Harman appears to contradict himself in this final caveat. On one hand, the transindustrial subject must realize that 'all limitations are self-chosen,' but on the other, she must accept 'what is.' Yet, in reconciling this seeming incongruity, Harman offers a glimpse of what I refer to as the *radical subjectivity* engendered through the enactment of workplace spirituality.

In order to resolve this dichotomy, Harman suggests that the transindustrial human operates according to a particular ontology, or theory of reality: *perception creates reality*. In *Global Mind Change* (1998), he takes seriously the largely unsubstantiated claims of thinkers like Fritjof Capra, who suggested in his widely popular New Age book *The Tao of Physics* (1975), that quantum physics affirmed Taoist and Buddhist assertions that 'mind seemed to have some effect in the physical world' (Harman 1988, p. 13). The industrial age was marked by what Harman refers to as 'Materialistic Monism' where it is understood that 'matter gives rise to the mind,' whereas the transindustrial age is giving rise to 'Transcendental Monism in which the mind gives rise to matter' (Harman 1988, p. 35). The transindustrial age will presumably bring about an awareness that 'by deliberately changing the internal image of reality, people can change the world' (p. 157).

Harman proposes a *radical subject* sharply distinct from the modern *liberal subject*. The latter—the liberal conception of the subject—persists in a cartesian world in opposition to the objective world. The liberal self experiences reality *out there* through its particular subjective lens, and effects reality through its external activities. For the *radical subject*, however, the objective conditions collapse into subjective perception itself, rendering *perception* as the measure of what counts as the real. 'Mind or consciousness is primary and matter-energy arises in some sense out of mind,' he explains, and 'ultimately the reality behind the phenomenal world is contacted not through the physical senses, but through deep intuition' (Harman 1988, p. 34). The subject therefore becomes radical in the sense that its conquest of the object is complete, rendering the objective world *out there* as little more than a reverberating echo of one's conscious or unconscious choices made from *within*. The implication, then, is twofold. The radical subject is, at once, empowered to shape their perception of experience and compelled to accept these experiences not as the result of objective conditions but as the product of their own making.

Of course, as a futures researcher, Harman understands his project as *predictive* of trends already occurring, as one possible social order in the process of becoming. Indeed, in the context of his broader prediction for society, this radical subject appears just. As the industrial paradigm wanes, so does its unnatural predilection for unceasing economic growth, environmental destruction, and global competition for resources. Likewise, Harman treats the relatively equitable distribution of wealth and power between labor and capital that emerged after the Second World War as immutable. Under such hypothetical conditions, it is conceivable that individuals, having achieved relative material and economic security, could come to experience work as 'primarily for self-development,' as he suggests (Harman 1988, p. 146).

Yet, while his predictions for a transindustrial era have not come to fruition, his *prescriptions* for the integration of spirituality and work have been taken up, refined, and put into practice, not, as we shall briefly explore, as part of a larger shift towards a more just and equitable social order, but to uphold the very structures that sustain the very suffering Harman sought to defeat. Also, it is important to note that while not all proponents and practitioners of workplace spirituality have been directly influenced by Harman's work, his philosophy illustrates a general pattern for how workplace spirituality operates as a technology of the self. The engendering of *radical subjectivities* through workplace spirituality reshapes employees into willing participants in a neo-liberal social order that, ironically, only diminishes their ability to *choose their own reality*.

Harman's ideas echo part of the wider discursive world of workplace spirituality among the MSR community and in business schools. Consider, for instance, how one MSR leader mobilizes these discourses within the frame-work of a business class to engender radical forms of subjectivity, equipping business elites with tools to navigate life under neoliberal conditions. The course, titled 'Spirituality for Business Leadership' and facilitated by the late Andre Delbecq, professor of management at Santa Clara University and long-time proponent of integrating spiritual perspectives into business educa-tion, introduces enrollees (MBA students and executives) to a diverse regimen of readings from 'the spirituality tradition.' As described by Delbecq (2000), the course culminated in a two-day retreat at Villa Holy Names, a retirement complex for Catholic nuns in the foothills of Santa Cruz in northern California. Delbecq describes the retreat as an opportunity to rehearse the teachings to which the students and executives had been exposed during the course.

The course itself clearly frames spiritual practice as a recipe for coping with and flourishing under the pressures of the marketplace. Delbecq, for example, depicts daily meditation as a way of 'listening to the inner voice in the midst of turbulent business environments' (Delbecq 2000, p. 119) and suggests that contemplation can mitigate the 'hectic space of a business leader's life' (p. 122). Yet the course also leverages spirituality as a pathway to reflect on broader socioeconomic concerns. It addresses Christian, Buddhist, and Taoist teachings on wealth and poverty and considers the obligations of the privileged for helping 'the destitute' (p. 121). However, Delbecq interrogates these issues with students through an overtly neoliberal lens by marking CEOs as 'wealth creators' and limiting discussion to solutions that uphold the principles of eco-nomic liberalism. Eschewing state-led efforts altogether, the course reduces social justice to the deeds of individual market-based actors. Focusing on 'almsgiving, justice giving, charity giving, philanthropy, stewardship' domesticates social justice for neoliberal capitalism by occluding the possibility of structural reform. Moreover, Delbecq redescribes 'poverty as a spiritual path,' which, like Harman, renders an objective socioeconomic position as a matter of perspective.

The retreat at the end of the course transmutes these ideas into embodied practice. Each morning begins with a 'mindful walk' followed by personal reflection on spiritual readings. At the end of the first day, Delbecq sends the attendees out to witness 'a place of suffering' that they 'most feared' (p. 122). Participants chose various sites—a center for disabled children, a homeless shelter, a hospice—for their field activities, but ultimately these experiences are only valued for their relevance to professional life with the intent of cultivating a malleable self capable of weathering the demands of the neoliberal workplace. Consider Delbecq's account of the debriefing on suffering following the field experiences:

> Examples of suffering might include the selflessness required by the intensity of the leadership role with its demand on time, emotional energy, and absence of privacy; the inexorable criticism and backbiting directed toward leaders; the loneliness of the office and demands of confidentiality; the anxieties when addressing the new strategic challenges; the special burdens of bearing bad news in firings and layoffs; the humbling uncertainties when stepping down from high prestige roles; and so on. (p. 125)

Attendees therefore finish the retreat with admittedly powerful first-hand experiences of acute human suffering, but they acquire a perspective that erases the stark and substantial objective differences in suffering. Homelessness, acute physical disability, and terminal illness stand alongside 'the loneliness of the office,' the 'special burdens' of laying off employees, or the 'humbling uncertainties' of 'stepping down from high prestige roles.' The exercise casts suffering as a subjective experience to which everyone, even business elites, is subject, and ultimately finds resolution in the habituation of the proper mindset vis-à-vis spiritual practice. In the end, the 'Spirituality for Business Leadership' course accomplishes more than preparing business elites for the tumultuous and unpredictable marketplace; it exonerates the existing social structures from which they directly benefit.

PARSING THE CASE: RADICAL SUBJECTS IN AN AMERICAN WORKPLACE

While Delbecq and Harman certainly remain revered figures among business scholars of workplace spirituality, it is important not to overstate their broader significance. Indeed, the MSR community persists at the margins of management scholarship, evidenced by its ongoing failure to gain full recognition as a 'division' in the Academy of Management, instead settling for the less prestigious label of 'interest group' since its inception in 2000. Courses like Delbecq's that teach spiritual perspectives on business remain scant and frequently are framed as experimental in nature, rarely if ever comprising part of the standard curriculum. The literature on workplace spirituality stands at the boundaries of the scholarly canon and, moreover, largely disconnected from the actual executives and managers practicing their craft in the American marketplace. It would therefore be grossly improper to claim that workplace spirituality, as an academic discourse, impacts the culture of American business in any substantial way. However, in the context of American business, there exists a growing, if still marginal, segment of organizations, business owners, and entrepreneurs who are putting these very ideas into practice and positioning spirituality as the hub of their workplace cultures, even if they remain wholly unaware of their counterparts in the management academy. As I have argued elsewhere, the genesis of interest in spirituality in the workplace can be observed from multiple vantage points—at the intellectual as well as the practical levels—and as emerging out of numerous cultural forces, including New Age religious perspectives, shifting popular attitudes and expectations about work, and seismic socioeconomic changes like globalization and post-industrial modes, particularly in the West.[7] My point is that, while seemingly unrelated, scholarly interest in workplace spirituality and the integration of spirituality into business cultures are products of the same discursive environment and are therefore allies in the broader proliferation of neoliberal subjects.

The MSR community and courses like Delbecq's equip elite actors (in business and the academy) with subjectivities capable of thriving under a neoliberal order, whereas businesses that enact workplace spirituality promote distinct modes of radical subjectivity more suited to more vulnerable constituents (e.g. middle managers, working-class Americans). In the case that follows, we take a closer look at how one particular business mobilizes discourses on spirituality as part of its workplace culture in ways that reproduce neoliberal orthodoxies, reshape subjects, and, ultimately, protect or advance organizational interests.

Founded by Matthew and Terces Engelhart, Café Gratitude is a West Coast coffee chain that subscribes to a novel business philosophy known as 'Sacred Commerce.' The Engelharts have shaped the entirety of their business model around the conviction that business can be a 'path to spiritual awakening' (Engelhart and Engelhart 2008). They understand this exclusive brand of spirituality as a way of life and encourage their employees to enact its principles both inside and outside the workplace. Sacred Commerce, as practiced, represents an all-encompassing set of values and convictions that regulate all aspects of the enterprise, from large-scale strategic planning to day-to-day decision making and even the way employees interact with each other and with customers.

The Engelharts have even developed an array of employee training workshops that serve to instill the virtues of their business philosophy. As part of my research, I was permitted to participate in one such workshop called *The Abounding River* in the Spring of 2012. While employees are 'encouraged' to attend the workshop, they are not compelled and, for a not unsubstantial fee (at least for someone like myself surviving on a graduate stipend), members of the general public are welcome to attend.

Over the course of the two-day course, *Abounding River* helps individuals discover that 'abundance' is a state of mind, 'a quality of spirit, of the divine, a flavor' or human experience. Through a combination of lecture, discussion, and activities, the workshop challenges participants to reassess and transform their relationship to money in order to experience true fulfillment. As the *Abounding River Logbook* (given to participants) states, 'being abundance' requires 'living in the assurance of being supplied as a mindful practice to connect to Spirit in everything' (Engelhart and Engelhart 2007, p. 22).

The Engelharts present the workshop as a practical regimen for spiritual transformation, but it also accomplishes significant ideological, specifically neoliberal, work. The lessons, anecdotes, and activities each reinforce capitalist logic as the irreducible fabric of human society; fabric that American norms, according to the Engelharts, pervert. Money, for example, is characterized as the ultimate 'sacrament,' 'a body fluid that holds us all together,' and 'an expression of Spirit and Abundance flowing through us, connecting us all' (Engelhart and Engelhart 2007, p. 62). The more one spends, the more one impacts the lives of others. One's spending is another's paycheck, and the more we spend, the more we promote wellbeing and the social good. Consequently, institutions that hinder this sacred flow, namely regulatory apparatuses, are disrupting the spiritual and material lifeblood of humanity. 'When we hoard money,' Matthew told the class, 'we stifle life itself … Keep the cycle of giving and receiving going—keep things in the flow.'

According to the Engelharts' two-dimensional map of reality, society is comprised of the sum total of market actors, and these actors are equal and ultimately responsible for their choices. Like more traditional defenses of free markets, the Engelharts understand suffering as a character flaw, rather than the result of unjust socioeconomic regimes. However, even when real forms of economic injustice appear undeniable, they suggest these are but illusions to be eliminated through the cultivation of the proper attitude. To justify this claim, they recounted to workshop participants the story of a homeless woman they had met. After repeated refusals of their help, the woman had explained to the Engelharts that living on the streets had been more of a blessing than a curse. 'She had lost weight at last, had more time to read, and had a great community of friends who share and look out for one another,' recalled Terces (Engelhart and Engelhart 2007, p. 60). Surprised by the optimism of the woman, the Engelharts had learned an important lesson, they declared: 'homelessness is just another way of life. It's not worse. It just looks different from my perspective. This woman was healthier than she'd ever been in her entire life,' she concluded.

In addition to crafting a neoliberal worldview, the case of Café Gratitude illuminates how spirituality in the workplace can become exploitative. The Engelharts remain ambivalent about the role of spirituality in Sacred Commerce. At times, they deny spirituality as a management strategy but as the end of their business itself. Their philosophy, Sacred Commerce, envisages business as 'a sacred container for the transformation of the participants, expressed as prosperity and abundance' (Engelhart and Engelhart 2008, p. 7) Rather than spirituality as a tool for improving the workplace, it is the workplace, run according to the principles of Sacred Commerce, that 'is going to birth a new community and a new human being' (p. 7).

Yet, my research into the culture of Café Gratitude reveals how Sacred Commerce operates in practice as a form of managerial power. In their book *Sacred Commerce: Business as a Path to Spiritual Awakening* (2008), the Engelharts write 'when we get attached to members of our staff or begin to treat members of our management team as if they were irreplaceable, it becomes easy to accommodate the wants and desires of a single personality at the expense of the entire business' (p. 10). Here, they make a dramatic course correction from their claim that Sacred Commerce is strictly a way for business to transform individuals and society. The interests of the business remain central, and concern for employee wellbeing should not undermine them. The Engelharts and their managers frequently mobilize their spiritual philosophy to justify this position, as illustrated in the following anecdote in their book:

> One of our managers wanted to go to Hawaii but rather than come to our meeting and request time off, she bought a ticket and then presented it as 'I already have my ticket so I need to get time off.' We supported her in seeing that she not only diminished her experience of being supported and celebrated by her management team, but she diminished their experience of being people who would of course want her life to be great and would alter their schedules to make her trip happen. She created a prerequisite and then made her request because she did not trust us to grant it without it. (Engelhart and Engelhart 2008, p. 71)

In this excerpt, it is unclear and unlikely that the employee violated any company policy when she chose to purchase a ticket before asking for time off. After all, she could decide how to proceed if she were unable to secure the time off from work for the trip. Nonetheless, the Engelharts condemn her actions on the grounds that even presuming to make the purchase without their prior approval transgressed the principles of Sacred Commerce. They present her actions as a spiritual malady, as a result her experience and those of others is 'diminished.'

Sacred Commerce is similarly used to justify lower pay for employees by redescribing such criticisms as misguided perceptions. Individuals are simply 'creating being so justified in feeling underpaid and overworked right now' (Engelhart and Engelhart 2008, p. 96). To suggest that wages are low, working hours too long, or workload too demanding is to make a subjective claim. Sacred Commerce reformulates the *objective conditions* of employment into *subjective* (and therefore malleable) perspectives, a move we will more closely examine later in this chapter.

The extent to which these anecdotes reflect the culture of Sacred Commerce as practiced in Café Gratitude proved elusive in my research. The company strictly regulated the manner of my access to interview subjects. Their chief administrator (presumably at the behest of the owners) dictated which locations I could contact for recruitment. Moreover, the general managers instructed me to sit in their cafés, and they would send those employees willing to speak with me. Curiously, or perhaps not so curiously, all of the individuals that agreed to an interview were either shift managers (hourly) or assistant managers (salary). In short, not a single non-managerial employee shared their views with me, which raises more questions. Are managers simply more flexible to leave their duties and speak with me? Or does this suggest a more profound distrust of front-line employees by management, or a voluntary hesitation on the part of these individuals to express their views out of fear of retribution? Or, do these workers simply not care because they lack any investment beyond their daily shifts?

Unfortunately, these questions must inadequately be addressed, but, at times, my conversations with managers did reveal some clues. For instance, when I asked one manager about their training experience, they repeatedly stressed that required training was minimal and mostly on the job, but the workshops like *Abounding River* were 'always recommended, never required but recommended. The same,' she said, 'with the Landmark Forum.' The Landmark Forum is a company that offers a comprehensive array of self-improvement programming. It is a direct heir of the earlier Erhard Seminars Training, a widely popular seminar during the 1970s that was subject to criticism for its somewhat aggressive methods. One journalist describes the Landmark Forum as 'a trusted ally of companies—big and small—looking to increase the "personal productivity of their employees"' (Curbed 2014). Café Gratitude, the manager explained, 'pays a fifty percent scholarship to attend the Forum' as supplemental training for employees who have the desire to attend. They neglected to mention, however, that Café Gratitude was in the midst of dealing with numerous complaints over their training policies related to the Forum.

A few years earlier, the company came under public scrutiny when a former manager claimed that she was improperly demoted and subsequently fired for refusing to attend the supposedly voluntary Landmark seminar (Levin 2009). Eventually a number of employees came forward to disclose similar experiences, resulting in formal litigation. In fact six months after the completion of my brief fieldwork, Terces Engelhart announced in a social media post that Café Gratitude would be closing all of its northern California locations in the wake of the scandal (Engelhart 2011). Although I could not substantiate the details of the litigation, one local media source reported that 'the lawsuits in question stem from former Gratitude employees who left the restaurant with a bad taste in their mouths, so to speak. *East Bay Express*, a weekly newspaper based in Oakland, California, published a 2009 article that claimed, among other things, employees were fired for not attending Landmark Forum classes' (SFIST 2011).

Given the tempest into which I had waded, the manager's emphasis on the voluntary nature of the workshops comes as no surprise, but her further remarks on the matter prove equally illustrative of coercion in the practice of Sacred Commerce. Referring to the Café Gratitude workshops like *Abounding River*, she opined, 'It's kind of like why would you not go. It's free to you and you're here. So most people end up going to at least one or two of the workshops. And they're amazing.' After celebrating the classes, the manager makes one last telling observation. 'People who really take on the curriculum, and do the workbook, and go to the workshops, they are the ones who get so much out of working here. And people who stay on the periphery, they might have a more peripheral experience.' Although she saw the 'peripheral experience' of those who failed to embrace, learn from, and grow in extracurricular spiritual regimen, be it Landmark Forum or the various internal workshops, I couldn't help but wonder if this inverted the lived experience for many employees. Did the skills acquired in the workshops better prepare them for success in the company? Or was participation simply a gateway to advancement? It seems quite likely that these workshops serve as a veritable 'glass ceiling,' keeping the less compliant on the 'periphery' and therefore less of a threat to interests of the status quo.

In the end, one thing seems certain. Café Gratitude's owners, when disgruntled former employees threatened their material interests, chose to sell off their assets and cast their workers back into the labor market. Although I have no way of knowing if the Engelharts had any other viable option open to them, their rapid decision to close—something that just six months earlier seemed unthinkable to me during my fieldwork—appears at odds with their espoused commitment to the spiritual wellbeing of their workforce. Sacred Commerce purports to use business as a vehicle to transform others, but the telos of this transformation appears to be one of subservience to those who own the means of production, best captured in their own words: 'Like any initiate, the Sacred Commerce manager's life is a continuous act of surrender. The merchant priest lives in the paradox between emptiness, knowing nothing, and being a warrior of daring action. Their impossible promise to a transformed world is so extremely challenging and highly inspiring that their personal wants and habitual shadows have less sway over them' (Engelhart and Engelhart 2008, p. 50). Thus, Sacred Commerce constitutes a managerial strategy for enforcing organizational interests, but it potentially operates at a much deeper level, at the level of individual subjectivity, reminiscent of Delbecq's course on spirituality in business. Yet, if Delbecq's course inculcates a radical subjectivity through which business elites may prosper, the Sacred Commerce program at Café Gratitude represents one way that workplace spirituality inscribes similar modes of being for members of the working class but for very different ends. In this case, radical subjectivity serves as a psychic survival strategy for the powerless in society, who adopt a neoliberal vocabulary inside and outside of the workplace.

Each day when employees arrive and before leaving work at Café Gratitude, they practice a ritual known as 'Clearing.' In their *Sacred Commerce*, owners Matthew and Terces Engelhart state that 'Clearing is the foundation of Sacred Commerce' (2008, p. 25). The practice enlists a supervisor to 'clear' a subordinate as they begin and end their workdays (the Engelharts leave 'unclear' who 'clears' the ranking manager on duty). 'Clearing,' they explain, 'is a basic technique for distinguishing how the past is impacting the present and then presenting an opportunity to create something new and shift one's attention to something more empowering' (p. 25). The entire session may last just a few minutes or longer, depending on the needs of the one being cleared, and pursues two lines of inquiry asked in succession. First, the Clearer asks, 'what are you present to?' or some variation, to which their interlocutor responds. The second question aims to 'shift one's attention to something new; to be present now, to love one's life' (Engelhart and Engelhart 2008, p. 30). Once satisfied, the Clearer closes the exchange with an expression of gratitude for the person being cleared.

Superficially, the Clearing appears as nothing more than a way of getting focused for work and beginning one's shift with a show of respect. However, as a routinized practice, it holds the potential to reshape the way individuals perceive work and life. As part of my fieldwork at Café Gratitude, one of the general managers was eager to invite me to be cleared, giving me a unique opportunity to glimpse, in an embodied sense, the transformative potency carried across its performance.

Sitting on the patio together, having just finished lunch, the manager asked me, 'are you committed to being cleared today?'

I agreed, and she closed her eyes for a moment of silence. Upon reopening her eyes, the manager stared intensely into mine, our gaze remaining fixated on each other for the duration of the Clearing.

> **Manager:** First question: what's something you are afraid of being judged for?

In an effort to be authentic and not merely act 'as if' I were an employee, I confided in her my anxieties and feelings of insecurity related to completing the dissertation and attaining a PhD.

> **Me:** Being the product of state universities, I worry about whether I can live up to the high standards expected at an elite private school; I worry that my training and preparation have been inadequate, that I am just not smart enough to compete.

Already, I could feel my initial discomfort ease as I shared some of my most intimate fears with her.

> **Manager:** So what I heard you say is you're fearful about whether you are good enough to be in graduate school. When you're present at that, when you're putting your attention on your fear of being judged, what are the emotions you're feeling when you're thinking about that?

> **Me:** Anxiety, apprehension, that I don't want to do it, that I want to run from it.

Again, after repeating back my response verbatim, she says,

> **Manager:** What do you think is underneath the anxiety? What are some of the emotions you might see?

I say, 'fear,' and she responds with gusto, 'Got it! Thanks for sharing that.'

> **Manager:** Just take a few minutes and be there with that. *That is a creation, right?* When I'm *putting my attention on* being afraid of being judged for not being smart enough, I … See that!?

Here, the manager has begun the process of reframing my negative fears as products of my own creation, as perceptions that I have chosen to *put my attention on*. Predictably, I start to feel a sense of detachment from these emotions; these fears, I think to myself, are not perceptions of the *out there*, but projections of my private insecurities onto the objective, neutral world. At this point she pivots to the second line of inquiry.

> **Manager:** Now when you're ready, tell me what do your friends or people you know, what do they love about you?

Me: That I am sincere, honest ... and that I am a good listener.

After announcing these affirmations about myself, my mood noticeably brightened. The Clearing had taken me through a process of exposing, detaching from, and rewriting deep-seated anxieties. As if I did not feel empowered already, she smiles and concludes, 'I want to acknowledge you for that. I want to acknowledge you for being committed to making a difference in the world, for impacting the quality of life on this planet through your work, and I also want to acknowledge you for being an amazing friend and for really caring about the people in your life.' The message couldn't be clearer. Simply by practicing a shift in how I perceived myself and the world, I was changing, even improving it. Moreover, as she explains, the clearing is not merely a conversational practice, 'it's actually an alchemical experience where the person getting cleared is getting to see. Where we put our attention is our experience. That's the basis of all of this ... Your experience has changed, *not because we fixed the circumstances, but because you shifted your attention*, which is like a magic trick of life.' Here, the picture of the *radical subject* manifests plainly; the source of suffering lies within subjective perception, not in the objective conditions.

Of course, I am not an employee of Café Gratitude and therefore my experiences can only approximate rather than recreate the quotidian experience of the Clearing among staff. The power dynamics between employer and employee have been replaced by a social interaction between myself, a novice field researcher, and my subject, a manager likely motivated to present their employer in an exemplary fashion. Surely, it is conceivable that some front-line workers merely tolerate the daily clearings as a part of the emotional and psychological labor demanded of their job.

Still, it is equally plausible that in subtle ways, the daily practice of learning to 'put one's attention' on the right perspectives becomes a basic way of organizing one's personhood. Consider, for instance, how one hourly shift manager with whom I spoke described the way Café Gratitude transformed her life. The employee, who self-identifies as of mixed 'white' and 'Native American' heritage, stated that she came to Café Gratitude at a pivotal time in her life. Upon returning from a trip to Peru after graduating from culinary school, she began 'thinking about how I don't want a job just to make money. What is more important to me,' she continued, 'is finding a place where I feel good. I can say what I feel, and I feel support from the managers. That's *what I really started to put my attention on*.' Finding Café Gratitude, she characterizes as her 'first *spiritual manifestation* of where I saw myself in the workplace.' The culture of Sacred Commerce, she explains, 'showed me how to look into myself and see what was the root problem.' As these remarks demonstrate, not only has this individual adopted the practice of shifting her focus inward to locate the source of suffering, she is actively redescribing her past prior to Café Gratitude through the language of Sacred Commerce (i.e. 'putting my attention on'). This suggests that these practices become central to both her ongoing identity work and her attempts to identify with the organization, each now inextricable from the other. This disposition obscures the objective social position that she occupies in the organization, subsuming her immediate interests to those of the employer and therefore establishing an opportunity for exploitation.

Nonetheless, despite the potential for abuse, the employees with whom I interacted appeared quite content in their jobs and convinced that these spiritual practices have positively transformed their lives. Consequently, to suggest that Sacred Commerce specifically, and workplace spirituality generally, only represents a form of managerial governance would misrepresent and devalue the sentiments of its practitioners. As a form of governmentality, as a technology of the self, however, it equally serves as a way for those subordinated to the structures of neoliberal capitalism to make sense of their worlds, and perhaps draw some measure of dignity from a social order fundamentally inflected to serve a global elite.

CONCLUSION

From a bird's eye view, workplace spirituality remains quite inconsequential to American business. As stated previously, the MSR group remains a marginal presence in the Academy of Management, having failed to attain full division status. And companies like Café Gratitude, which overtly associate their values and culture with spirituality, constitute an almost imperceptible niche within the juggernaut of the American economy. However, their relative insignificance obscures a more profound affinity with the trajectory of American corporate culture, providing insight into the way neoliberal ideologies inhabit our most personal dispositions. It is apparent in quite unexceptional business practices of corporate America. Mission and vision statements declare with moral authority the higher purpose of their goals, and it would be a rare find to discover any employer, whether in business, education, or even government, today that did not aspire to meaningful work and care for their employees.

At the individual level, these discourses penetrate, possess, and produce the expectations and dispositions of persons. And like radical subjects, we experience this turn towards a more humane workplace as human progress, even as the empirical reality suggests that our objective position in society has diminished. Working hours are longer, real wages are flat, and economic security is increasingly a fleeting hope for a dwindling American middle class. In writing this chapter, my most ardent hope has been to illustrate how workplace spirituality can be understood as a synecdoche for American corporate culture.

If only because the integration of spirituality and work strikes the rest of us as exotic and starkly other, it sharpens our ability to perceive the often concealed and soft power relations that shape human labor under neoliberal capitalism. In its apparent abnormality, workplace spirituality reveals itself to be utterly conventional. After all, is there a substantial difference between practices labeled 'spiritual' and those dubbed 'mindful'? Is the rhetoric inscribed around 'core values,' 'guiding principles,' or 'mission statements' significantly distinct from 'spiritual wisdom' when either are deployed in the pursuit of profit? Can a project to use the marketplace as a medium to 'transform human consciousness' be anything but a neoliberal pursuit?

NOTES

1. The *Journal of Management Inquiry*, for example, dedicated an entire special issue in 2003 to research on workplace spirituality.
2. Faith-based employee resource groups mimic other employee affinity groups that first emerged in the mid-1970s as a way for employees from vulnerable underrepresented groups (i.e. African American, women, and LGBTQ+) to share their unique experiences and advocate on behalf of their particular interests in the context of their workplace. To date, I have not located any extant scholarly research into faith-based or interfaith employee networks specifically, although my preliminary findings suggest that these groups typically began to emerge during the late 1990s, coinciding with the rise of interest in spirituality in management thought.
3. For more specific information on corporate chaplaincy, see Miller et al. (2016).
4. Even more critical assessments, such as Hicks (2003) and Lambert III (2009), argue that spirituality in the workplace is driven by largely altruistic motives to render the workplace more humane.
5. The concept of the modern liberal self as an autonomous, inwardly stable, self-reliant rational agent has been articulated by a number of scholars in a wide-ranging number of disciplines. See Taylor (1989) for a thorough treatment tracing the intellectual history of the modern self, or Erik Erikson's numerous works in developmental psychology on the life cycle.
6. Harman (1979, pp. 21–2) condemns 'price and wage controls,' 'urban renewal programs,' 'welfare regulations,' 'minimum wage laws,' and 'programs dedicated to the reduction of inequalities of opportunity between the races' as ultimately counterproductive and indicative of the scientific materialism undergirding the industrial paradigm.
7. For a thorough treatment of how interest in workplace spirituality reflects deep cultural and structural shifts around economic production, see LoRusso (2017).

REFERENCES

Bourdieu, P. (1972), *Outline of a Theory of Practice*, trans. R. Nice (1977), New York: Cambridge University Press.
Brockling, U. (2016), *The Entrepreneurial Self: Fabricating a New Type of Subject*, London: Sage.

Curbed (2014), 'Café Gratitude and the Cult of Commerce,' *Curbed: Los Angeles*, October 23.

Dardot, P. and C. Laval (2009), *The Neoliberal Way of the World: On Neoliberal Society*, trans. G. Elliot (2017), London: Verso.

Delbecq, A. (2000), 'Spirituality for Business Leadership: Reporting on a Pilot Course for MBAs and CEOs,' *Journal of Management Inquiry*, **9** (2), 117–28.

Engelhart, M. and T. Engelhart (2007), *The Abounding River Personal Logbook: An Unfamiliar View of Being Abundance*, Berkeley, CA: North Atlantic Books.

Engelhart, M. and T. Engelhart (2008), *Sacred Commerce: Business as a Path to Spiritual Awakening*, Berkeley, CA: North Atlantic Books.

Engelhart, T. (2011), 'To Our Café Gratitude Community,' *Café Gratitude Facebook Page*, November 29, accessed December 22, 2018 at www.facebook.com/permalink .php?story_fbid=10150995099355074&id=528890073

Foucault, M. (1988), 'Technologies of the Self,' in L.H. Martin, H. Gutman, and P.H. Hutton (eds), *Technologies of the Self: A Seminar with Michel Foucault*, Cambridge, MA: University of Massachusetts Press, pp. 16–49.

Freeman, C. (2014), *Entrepreneurial Selves: Neoliberal Respectability and the Making of the Caribbean Middle Class*, Durham, NC: Duke University Press.

Garvey, M. (2018), 'Meditation Rooms Are the Hottest New Work Perk,' *MarketWatch*, October 26.

Harman, W. (1974), 'Humanistic Capitalism: An Alternative,' *Journal of Humanistic Psychology*, **14** (1), 5–32.

Harman, W. (1979), *An Incomplete Guide to the Future*, New York: W.W. Norton.

Harman, W. (1988), *Global Mind Change: The New Age Revolution in the Way We Think*, New York: Warner Books.

Harvey, D. (2005), *A Brief History of Neoliberalism*, New York: Oxford University Press.

Hicks, D. (2003), *Religion in the Workplace: Pluralism, Spirituality, Leadership*, New York: Cambridge University Press.

Holborow, M. (2015), *Language and Neoliberalism*, New York: Routledge Press.

Lambert III, L. (2009), *Spirituality Inc.: Religion in the American Workplace*, New York: New York University Press.

Lebowitz, S. (2016), 'I just spent a day in a mindfulness program developed at Google and left with 5 key lessons,' *Business Insider*, November 5.

Levin, S. (2009), 'I am annoyed and disappointed,' *East Bay Express*, August 5.

LoRusso, J. (2017), *Spirituality, Corporate Culture, and American Business: The Neoliberal Ethic and the Spirit of Global Capital*, New York: Bloomsbury Academic.

Massey, D. (2013), 'Vocabularies of the Economy,' *Soundings: A Journal of Politics and Culture*, **54**, 9–22.

Miller, D. (2007), *God at Work: The History and Promise of the Faith at Work Movement*, New York: Oxford University Press.

Miller, D., F. Ngunjiri, and J. LoRusso (2016), 'HR Perceptions of Corporate Chaplains: Enhancing Positive Organizational Culture,' *Journal of Management, Spirituality, and Religion*, December, 196–215.

Neal, J. (2006), *Edgewalkers: People and Organizations that Take Risks, Build Bridges, and Break New Ground*, Westport, CT: Praeger.

Peck, J. (2010), *Constructions of Neoliberal Reason*, New York: Oxford University Press.

SFIST (2011), 'Café Gratitude Announces NorCal Closures,' *SFIST*, November 29.

Taylor, C. (1989), *Sources of the Self: The Making of Modern Identity*, Cambridge: Cambridge University Press.

2. Running to stay in the same place? Personal development work and the production of neoliberal subjectivity among Israel's "last republican generation"[1]

Ariel Yankellevich

In recent years, a growing number of veteran middle- and upper middle-class Israelis, men and (mostly) women born in the 1950s and early 1960s, have turned to coaching and similar forms of "personal development work" (Swan, 2010) as a second career. Daphna,[2] a former high school principal in her late 50s, is one of them. Like many middle-class women in her generation, she married young, became a teacher[3] and later on a school principal. During the 1990s, after more than two decades in the education system, she turned to the incipient field of management consulting. Following her phenomenal success in her new profession, in recent years she has added coaching to her set of skills and today she mostly works as a freelance coach and mentor in organizations. When I asked about her career changes, she came up with the following story:

> I strongly believe in Alice in Wonderland. Do you know the story? She met a fairy and the fairy told her at a certain point to run and Alice ran and the fairy told her to run faster, and faster and Alice accelerated and she got tired. So after a while the fairy told Alice "Ok, now we can rest" and then Alice looked around and said "but we are in the same place. In my world when you run so fast you get to another place." So the fairy told her: "In our world, in order to stay in the same place you have to run very hard." So I tell you that the world changes and you have to change yourself; I preach about it, both in organizations and in my work with managers. And I change all the time myself … It takes courage. I always took economic responsibility and I left very lucrative workplaces because I started to get bored and I felt that I am stuck in the same place … My former colleagues tell me "you had luck" because I moved to another job and they stayed. Now they are starting to retire from teaching. I wasn't lucky, I had courage. It isn't luck. They were also great. They could have been a thousand times better than me, but they didn't dare. So I dare.

Daphna's story exposes the paradoxical nature of the encounter of her generational unit, which I term here "the last republican generation,"[4] with emerging neoliberal therapeutic discourses such as coaching. This encounter takes place at an historical juncture where this veteran, mostly Ashkenazi (Jews of European origin) social elite has lost much of its hegemonic status in Israeli society (Kimmerling, 2005), which was based on a republican model of citizenship that stressed and rewarded contribution to the collective (Shafir & Peled, 2002). This model started to crumble with the demise of the Labor Zionist collectivistic ethos and the turn to neoliberalism in recent decades, thus forcing this group to adapt to a changing cultural and socio-economic reality.

In the first part of the above quote, Daphna recounts a tale from Alice in Wonderland in which in order to keep pace with a constantly changing world, you have to be always running. In this world, continuous personal change is not an option, but an absolute necessity if you do not want to be left behind and wither. In this sense, the tale describes rather accurately what personal and economic life look like in the new global post-Fordist economy,[5] an economy which Israel has eagerly embraced since the mid-1980s. In order to survive in this hyper-competitive economy, companies and workers must continuously strive to improve themselves and adapt to changing circumstances mostly outside of their direct control (Boltanski & Chiapello, 2005; Rosa, Dörre, & Lessenich, 2017; Sennett, 2006).

But in the second part of the quote, where Daphna speaks about her own experience of change, a somewhat different picture emerges. In this picture, change is the result of boredom and a sense of being stuck, not of job insecurity or workplace restructuring. In contrast to the Alice of the story, Daphna did not have to run fast in order to stay in the same place. Like most of her former colleagues, she could have stayed in the education system for all of her working life and retired with decent pension benefits. Economic arrangements dating back to the welfare state that Israel built in the first decades of its existence (and has been dismantling since the turn to neoliberalism in the 1980s), such as tenure, subsidized mortgages, salaries tied to seniority and non-contributory pensions, are still in place for most members of her generation. Her career changes, by contrast, entailed taking economic risks and facing uncertainties that she could have easily avoided by staying in the school system for the rest of her working life. But as we learn from her account, this choice also had its price.

Seen in this context, stories like Daphna's trajectory of continuous change (both as a personal experience and as a professional belief and tool) raise questions about the social and cultural conditions of adoption of new neoliberal therapeutic discourses of self-improvement and entrepreneurialism. What makes middle aged, well-to-do Israelis such as Daphna so receptive to these new discourses? How does this new ideology of continuous change, adaptability and self-growth intersect with a generational experience marked by security, predictability and collective commitments? Having been spared from the economic precarization brought on by neoliberalism and post-Fordism in Israel, what is the meaning of "staying in the same place" for this generational unit?

In order to answer these questions, I draw on 46 in-depth interviews with members of the last republican generation who chose coaching and related self-improvement practices as a second (or third) career in later life. The interviews were conducted in 2016–17 in different locations in central and southern Israel and lasted two hours on average.[6] Research participants were initially recruited from personal websites, an email sent to affiliates of the Israeli Coaching Bureau[7] and personal acquaintances. I then used a snowball sampling technique, asking interviewees to provide the names of other potential participants. Roughly two thirds of participants were women, which seems to reflect their predominance in the profession.[8] Virtually all participants had academic degrees and many of them turned to coaching after long and successful careers in the public or quasi-public sector.

In what follows, I will focus on three representative narratives of self-transformation and career change in order to expose how members of the last republican generation employ the new therapeutic language of coaching as a cultural resource for repositioning and reorienting themselves vis-à-vis the new Israeli neoliberal order. Each narrative illustrates in a condensed and context-sensitive manner a key theme or pattern of self-change that came up in many other interviews. Through a detailed analysis of these stories, I will show how the language of coaching allows members of this generation to negotiate their complex position as a waning but still powerful elite in search of new sources of legitimation. By daring to embrace change, risk and uncertainty, they prove to themselves and the rest of society that they are still worth their privileged social and economic status. In this process, they redefine their role as a "service elite" (Shafir & Peled, 2002) committed to the fulfillment of collective and national goals, while adhering to the neoliberal logics of self-appreciation and self-value accrual (Feher, 2009; Skeggs, 2011).

NEW THERAPEUTIC TECHNOLOGIES AND THE NEOLIBERAL SUBJECT: MINDING YOUR OWN BUSINESS AS A SURVIVAL STRATEGY

The ascendance of new therapeutic discourses and practices such as life coaching, positive psychology, happiness studies and self-help has often been linked to the rise of neoliberalism. As various studies from across the globe have shown, post-Fordist working conditions, labor market insecurity and the precarization of life under global capitalism provide a fertile soil for the development of new therapeutic technologies that cater to the struggling middle class (Freeman, 2007; George, 2013; Illouz, 2008; Mäkinen, 2014; Matza, 2012, 2014; Mazzarino, 2013; McGee, 2005; Nehring, Kerrigan, Hendriks & Alvarado, 2016; Salmenniemi, 2016; Salmenniemi & Vorona, 2014).[9] These new therapeutic technologies aim at the production of autonomous, self-responsible, "enterprising selves" attuned to the challenges of work and life under neoliberalism (Du Gay, 1996; Rose, 1996). Blending psychological and economic discourses (Illouz, 2008), technologies like coaching conceptualize the self as a business or commodity, continually striving to enhance its "human capital" through the cultivation and optimization of its personal skills and abilities. They foster qualities such as flexibility, adaptability and openness to change, which are seen as essential in order to succeed and survive in the post-Fordist workplace (Binkley, 2011b; Brown, 2003; Mäkinen, 2016; Swan, 2010; Urciuoli, 2008; Vallas & Hill, 2018). At the same time, they regard qualities as dependence, docility and collective commitments as problematic (Binkley, 2011a) and promote an instrumental approach to social relations based on the principles of market exchange (Mäkinen, 2014; Pagis, 2016a).

Hence, these new therapeutic technologies seem to provide "a neoliberal recipe for atomised, individual survival in the rat race of the early 21st century" (McGee, 2005: 163). This is especially the case in societies that have experienced rapid economic and social change, such as those in the post-socialist world, where a rising therapeutic culture has served to index "disorientation in the face of the jarring conditions of labor market imposition and neoliberal reform" (Matza 2014: 51). This culture, comprised of a wide variety of psychological services, workshops and self-help texts, provides "new idioms for aligning market demands and self-development," thus helping to "affix subjectivity to expectations of successful or unsuccessful self-transformation in competitive conditions" (51–2). For example, in a study of self-help reading in post-Soviet Russia, Salmenniemi found that by engaging with therapeutic technologies, research participants "sought to understand 'how the world works' and how to succeed, or at least survive, in the new capitalist system" (2016: 9). In the context of the increasing insecurity and instability of everyday life in Russia, self-help seemed to offer "tools to master the new capitalist rules of the game" (11) and "to make sense of and come to terms with the new neoliberal value system" (8; see also Salmenniemi & Vorona, 2014).

A few recent studies of the incipient coaching field in Israel have made a similar connection between the growing popularity of this new therapeutic technology[10] and the rise of neoliberal individualism. In these accounts, coaching is described as a tool for the production of a vernacular version of neoliberal selfhood (Kaneh□Shalit, 2017) and for negotiating the challenges of individualization and self-creation in a context of increasing labor market insecurity (Pagis, 2016a, 2016b). For example, Pagis argues that it is no coincidence that the first coaching institutes in Israel were opened in the same year of the high-tech bubble crash. In her view, "the lack of stability in the job market created a space that on the one hand pushed people to study coaching and on the other hand attracted their future clients" (2016b: 37). Therefore, these studies join previous work that views coaching and related therapeutic technologies as a way to cope with the "precariousness of individuality and the fear of failure" (Mäkinen, 2014) characteristic of neoliberal capitalism.

My aim in this chapter is to complicate this view of the relationship between therapeutic culture and the production of neoliberal subjectivity by focusing on the adoption of coaching by a generational unit that for the most part has remained protected from the perils of neoliberal precarity and "insecurity culture" (Pugh, 2016). As we will see, the development of self-responsible, entrepreneurial selves by members of this group obeys to a distinct set of preoccupations anchored in structural shifts in Israeli political economy and culture.

THE LAST REPUBLICAN GENERATION AND ISRAEL'S NEOLIBERAL TURN

The biographies of members of the last republican generation are deeply entrenched in the economic and socio-cultural changes that Israel has experienced in the last three decades. During the first decades of its existence, Israel's economy was organized according to a developmental state model in which the state was the main catalyst of economic activity (Maman & Rosenhek, 2012). The state controlled the allocation of economic resources and tightly regulated economic activity. This economic arrangement followed a state-building logic based on Zionist principles and interests, such as immigrant absorption and settlement, accelerated industrialization and the development of a segmented welfare state. It was also in line with the Zionist socialist and collectivistic ethos that was dominant in the early years of the state.

Following the 1973 war, the Israeli developmental state experienced an extended economic crisis that paved the way for neoliberal economic reforms starting in the mid-1980s. These reforms included the deregulation of the labor market, the lifting of restrictions on the movement of capital and goods, the privatization of public assets and restrictive fiscal and monetary policies (Maman & Rosenhek, 2012; Shalev, 2000). In the socio-cultural realm, the neoliberal turn brought about a profound ideological shift. From a collectivistic society that espoused job stability and social welfare policies, Israel turned into an individualistic society that fosters free enterprise, competition and workforce flexibility (Ram, 2000, 2008).

The ethno-class generational unit I term here "the last republican generation" (born in the 1950s and early 1960s) grew up and had its formative experiences in the era before the neoliberal turn in Israel. As members of the veteran Ashkenazi dominant social group, they were socialized into the Labor Zionist collectivistic and nationalistic ethos, which tied individual self-realization with the fulfillment of collective goals and loyalty to the state. This ethos was crystallized in a republican discourse of civic virtue that placed this group as a "service elite" and rewarded it accordingly (Shafir & Peled, 2002: 43). On the other hand, this was the first generation of the Ashkenazi middle class that adopted a Western, bourgeois style of life (Almog, 2001) and sought to realize its personal and professional abilities in the sphere of work. As Uri Ram (2000: 227) observes:

> the middle class which was made by the state and for the state is now turning away from the service of all to the service of the few. The middle-class successors of the older state and military elite are withdrawing from the older career-path and turning to the more attractive and rewarding trajectories offered by civil society and the burgeoning market.

In the economic realm, the last republican generation got the best of both worlds: on the one hand, it was the last generation to fully enjoy the benefits of the centralized Fordist economy and the Israeli welfare state (subsidized housing, full employment, tenure at work and more), while on the other hand, its members were the big beneficiaries of the economic prosperity (and the tax cuts) following the neoliberal turn and the integration of Israel's economy in the global market (Ram, 2008; Rosenhek & Shalev, 2014; Shalev, 2000).

While in the individual economic realm this generational unit has done pretty well, its economic, political and cultural hegemony has been threatened on a number of fronts. First, the economic changes described above stripped the Labor Zionist elite from its control over the allocation of economic resources, thus opening new economic opportunities for other social groups that were assigned a subordinate place in the developmental state model. Second, the political "turnover" that ended three decades of continuous Labor Party government in 1977 brought new political actors from marginalized social groups to the fore and curtailed the political power of the old Labor Zionist elite. Third, on the cultural plane, the hegemony of the secular Ashkenazi Zionist culture was thrown into question by the rise of a new system of competing countercultures associated with marginalized social groups, leading to an escalating cultural war and to the onset of a state of cultural plurality (Kimmerling, 2005; Shafir & Peled, 2002). All these processes have contributed to the transformation of the last republican generation into a waning economic, political and cultural elite. It is in this historical and cultural context that we should analyze the adoption of coaching by this social group.

FROM CARING FOR THE WELFARE OF WORKERS TO HELPING WORKERS HELP THEMSELVES: DOV'S STORY

I met Dov, a coach in his early 60s, at his large modern house in Kfar Bustan, a *moshav*[11] in the center of Israel. Kfar Bustan, once a symbol of the labor settlement movement, has recently become a real estate gem for the affluent, owing to its combination of privileged location and a "rural atmosphere." Like many members of the last republican generation, Dov, a social worker by training, spent most of his early career in the public sector. After graduating from college, he worked for two decades in the area of worker welfare at Isratech, one of Israel's biggest and prestigious state-owned companies. The highlight of his career came in the early 1990s, as the company, an emblem of Israel's state-sponsored military-industrial complex, was heavily downsized. During this painful process, his duty was in his own words "to take care of the downsized workers." One of his biggest achievements was the establishment of an exceptions committee for people who didn't fulfill the criteria for early retirement benefits. He recalls the negotiation with the Ministry of Finance:

> I had the mandate to save or rescue, I don't know how to call it, X people who didn't fit the criteria, to get them early retirement benefits … Because I said that there are some workers that I know will take a blow, a hard blow, since they have no chances of reentering the job market, because in most cases these are folks that were hurt in major work accidents, no employer will offer them a job.

In this excerpt, Dov explains why he insisted on setting up an exceptions committee. In his view, these workers deserved compensation from the state for their long-term contribution to the company (which in some cases entailed physical injury) and through it to Israel's security. Most of them did not plan to leave the company and were sure that they would stay there for the rest of their working lives. Therefore, Dov stresses the state's responsibility towards them, a responsibility that includes "saving" them from the vagaries of a faceless and merciless job market. This view is at odds with the coaching credo of assuming personal responsibility and avoiding dependence (Binkley, 2011b). Here Dov speaks in a different voice, reminiscent of Labor Zionism's republican citizenship discourse (Shafir & Peled, 2002). This view stresses such values as loyalty, commitment and mutual responsibility, values that, according to Dov, are rapidly disappearing from Israeli society. And indeed, during this process at Isratech, Dov understood that Israel is experiencing profound social and

economic change and that things that were taken for granted for his generation
are no longer true:

> I think that at Isratech I realized that the rules of the game are changing and what
> used to be socialist and right and equal is starting to move in the direction of …
> capitalism then was still on the plane on its way to Israel, it wasn't here yet. I began
> to realize that the rules of the game are changing and that big companies and organ-
> izations are starting to dismantle. Not only in Isratech, they started signing personal
> contracts everywhere, personal employment contracts for senior posts. This process
> started to take shape, so it was clear in my analysis of reality that in three, four, five
> years, that's what society will look like … So my view of this change in the rules
> instilled in me the idea that I'm moving forward, that I have a lot to offer.

As we learn from this quote, in contrast to his laid-off peers at Isratech, Dov
didn't see these changes as a threat, but as an opportunity. On the one hand, he
knew that owing to his seniority at the company, he could have stayed there
until retirement, thus achieving an occupational and financial security that later
generations can only dream of. On the other hand, he realized that staying at
Isratech, which in his view has become a "vegetative patient" kept alive artifi-
cially by the state, would have meant staying behind at a much deeper cultural
level. As he recalls, "I knew I was a protected wildflower and I could have
stayed at Isratech until this day. I'd have probably rotten, stink and grow mold,
but I could have stayed." Here Dov traces a parallel between the company's
twilight and the personal decay of its workers (including himself had he stayed
there).[12] Like Daphna, who also worked at a national institution that is way past
its days of glory (the public school system), Dov escaped this fate by seizing an
early retirement opportunity and turning to freelance consulting and coaching.
As he describes:

> I have some sort of economic security and therefore I adopted coaching and
> I adopted it as a way of life. Call it coach, mentor, life guide, it is someone that has
> done so many things in his life that now can bring his experience to his coaching
> practice. I really feel that I can give people value, significant value.

Dov's description of his career change reflects a significant shift in his generational unit's logics of action, even if not in its sense of purpose. In Israel's
new neoliberal regime, Dov's self-appointed task is no longer to take care of
workers' welfare and rights, but "to give people value." If in his first career
he assumed responsibility for his company's laid-off workers, now he teaches
individuals to take responsibility for themselves in the face of state retrench-
ment and economic liberalization. Adopting coaching as a way of life then
allows him to translate his cultural and social capital as a member of a national
service elite into a new field of action where he still "has a lot to offer." In
this way, he redefines his social leadership role in a context where the old

Labor Zionist collective structures have become obsolete. Moreover, much like his hometown Kfar Bustan, which in recent years has buried all traces of the workers' moshav it once was on its way to becoming an affluent suburban neighborhood, Dov's trajectory exemplifies how a generational unit bred on the values of Labor Zionism mutates into the frontrunner of local neoliberalism by identifying itself with a new fashionable therapeutic discourse.

FROM COLLECTIVE STRUCTURES TO INDIVIDUAL RESPONSIBILITY: TAMAR'S STORY

The shift from social leadership anchored in collective structures to a focus on personal responsibility and self-value accrual is also at the center of Tamar's story of occupational change. Tamar, a woman in her early 60s, is a former teacher and school principal from a city in the center of Israel. Like Dov, she turned to coaching after a long career in the public sector, which accrued her generous pension benefits and overall economic security. During our interview at a coffee place near her house, she explained that her decision to quit her job as a school principal was due to "burnout." As she recalls:

> The burnout was not related to the work itself, but to the burden of responsibility. Being a school principal is a 24/7 job, including vacations and holidays. When something happens, you are on the front. The responsibility is yours. They go on a trip, the responsibility is yours, they go to a play, the responsibility is yours. You come to school in the morning, you know how you come in but you never know how you go out. It's very exhausting, this internal unrest that goes with you all the years. I didn't get burned out from working, because I am still working now. It was the responsibility. Enough, I don't want to deal with and *take responsibility for what are actually others' actions* anymore. Because when a child pushes another child, this is not something that I'm responsible for; *I didn't educate him to do that*. But if he hurts his head, I have to pay the price. When a teacher speaks inappropriately to a child, I would have to sit in the evening and think how tomorrow in the meeting between the parents and the teacher we reach a win–win situation, when it is not my fault at all. I became tired of being in the position of having to deal with the responsibility for other people's words and deeds. I wanted to *take full responsibility for myself*, to know that what I do is what happens and I take responsibility for it. (Italics are mine)

In this excerpt, Tamar relates her feelings of occupational burnout to the burden of responsibility inherent to the role of a school principal. While this role still confers social prestige in Israel, the meanings associated with it have changed dramatically in the last decades. From its early days in the pre-state era, the education system was a central pillar of the Zionist nation-building project. For the veteran Ashkenazi elite, being an educator was deemed a sacred national mission, an occupation that conferred a sense of social purpose and collective responsibility for the future of the nation (Almog, 2000: 24–6). This started to change in the 1970s, with the incipient erosion of the Zionist master narrative and the increasing feminization of the teaching profession. For many women of Tamar's generation, becoming a teacher and advancing in the education system was more of a matter of professional fulfillment and career advancement than an activity imbued with national or social purpose. Still, the national ideological context that defines education as a national mission is nonetheless present in everyday educational discourse and practice. Therefore, when Tamar says that she does not want to take responsibility for others' actions anymore (a teacher who speaks inappropriately to a child or a child who acts violently), she seems to be relinquishing her role as a member of a service elite committed to the education of the masses.[13] By saying "this is not something that I'm responsible for; I didn't educate him to do that," she deflects the responsibility for the education of children from the school system to the violent child's parents. In this sense, her words seem to reflect the increasing privatization of Israeli society, in which individuals like Tamar only assume responsibility for themselves.

This newly adopted ideal of individual responsibility is expressed in her practice as a coach. When I ask her if being a coach does not entail taking responsibility for the client, she says:

> I don't take responsibility for anything … I help people, but the responsibility is theirs and I tell them that. During coaching sessions I tell them "listen, I am like a fitness trainer: if you want a six pack, you have to do what he tells you. He can be the best trainer, very talented, much recommended, but if you don't do what he tells you, you won't have a six pack. The same goes for coaching. I can give you tools, I can help, I can mirror your feelings, but you have to act and if you won't take responsibility and you won't act and be active, we won't get anywhere."

In her answer we see how Tamar's new self-concept resonates with the coaching emphasis on personal responsibility and autonomy. In contrast to education, in life coaching the sole responsibility for the results of the process is on the client's shoulders. The coach is only a facilitator of someone else's project of self-transformation. She does not have any stakes in this project, neither does she assume any responsibility for its outcome. In contrast to the paternalistic and hierarchical teacher–student relation in the Zionist nation-building project, the coach–client relation is a purely contractual relation between two autonomous persons with no social or affective bonds between them and with no shared purpose or view of the common good. In this sense, the coaching bond is modeled after market relations, in which each part of the transaction seeks its own personal interest (Mäkinen, 2014; Pagis, 2016a). As Ilana Gershon has noted, this framing of social relationships as market alliances in which responsibility and risk are distributed so that each partner can maintain its own autonomy as a market actor is characteristic of neoliberalism (2011: 540).

We can see this logic at play in one of Tamar's new occupational activities as a coach. A year after she quit her job as a school principal, Tamar was offered a job as a freelance coach and mentor for public-school principals and staff at EduIsrael, a private company that provides outsourcing services to the Ministry of Education. Much like in individual life coaching, her task at EduIsrael is to identify the strengths of high-performing schools and build on them in order to bring the schools to a higher level of functioning. On a personal level, Tamar describes this job as "a gift" that fell upon her:

> This is a gift because the work itself helps me a lot, gives me a lot and brings me forward as a human being, my capabilities, and also economically … I've been working in the program for three years now. I work with different schools and at the same time I also learn and I use all my skills, my natural and intuitive skills and also the skills I learned.

In contrast to her previous career, which entailed giving and working for the sake of others, Tamar frames her new coaching job as something that gives *her* value by letting her use and develop her "natural and intuitive skills." In this sense, her new self-project is based on the ability to make her dispositions a form of property or capital, which according to Skeggs (2004) is a landmark of the contemporary middle-class subject of value. Whereas her previous sense of self-worth was anchored in the republican ethos of nation building through education (combined with a Fordist ethos of professional competence and career advancement), her current self-project is that of an independent and autonomous person seeking her own self-fulfillment through the maximization of her "human capital." Still, what is noteworthy in this new, individualized self-project is that it is actualized in the framework of an updated, neoliberal version of her old educational role. In a sense, Tamar never left the public education system; she just found (or more exactly, it found her) a new, more fulfilling way to enact her social leadership role as a member of a national service elite in its midst.

GETTING RID OF LIMITING BELIEFS, FINDING A NEW ANCHOR FOR IDENTITY: GILA'S STORY

In the two previous stories, we learned how members of the last republican generation craft a neoliberal self on the ruins of the old collective structures associated with the Labor Zionist nation-building project. But as the next story shows, this is not always a seamless process. For members of this generation, becoming a neoliberal subject often entails getting rid of old beliefs and dispositions rooted in those collective structures. Gila, a woman in her late 50s, started her professional career as a teacher-soldier[14] in a primary school. After her release from the army due to pregnancy, she continued working as a teacher for many years, eventually becoming a school principal. Like many women in this study, in the course of the years she became fed up with her job at school and started looking for new occupational opportunities. She first heard of coaching in the early 2000s through her involvement in alternative medicine circles. Those were the early days of coaching in Israel, with only one or two active coaching institutes. Gila took a sabbatical and then an unpaid leave from work in order to study coaching and alternative medicine. By making use of these arrangements dating back to the old Fordist regime, she could test the waters outside the protected world of the school system without giving up her accumulated rights or incurring major financial risks.[15] By the end of her year of unpaid leave, she applied for early retirement and headed for a new start as a coach and alternative therapist.

The transition from salaried employee in a bureaucratic organization to self-employed coach was far from smooth. At first, Gila was ridden with fears and doubts about her ability to make a living as a coach. She remembers the first session at the coaching course after she quit school:

> I told the whole class and Gideon [the institute founder and director], "folks, you can start looking for a job for me because I left school" and Gideon stared at me and told me "What do you mean 'find me a job'? You are a coach, find yourself a job."

In this exchange, Gideon, the course leader, reprimands Gila for clinging to her old dependent habits instead of showing initiative like a real coach would do. Gideon's scornful remark signaled to Gila that she still had a long way to go if she wanted to become a coach. She came to realize that this process of self-transformation required letting go of well-established beliefs rooted in the Labor Zionist education she received at home, such as her aversion to businessmen and big money. She describes the moment when she discovered this "limiting belief":

> In one of the classes we were asked to write who is our client base. So I wrote everybody, except businessmen. All kinds of people: children, adults, with all kinds of needs. I don't work with businessmen. And the course title was life and business coaching ... So she [her personal coach during the course] asked me why and I said "listen, I can't work with them, it gives me a heat rash. I just can't." During that session everybody had to write on a poster what their client base is, so in order to get them off my back I wrote "small businessmen." Gideon, with his acute eye, when it was my poster's turn said: "small men or small businesses?[16] Who are you going to work with?" I told him "small business?" "I don't know, take a look at it." So I realized that I have a big issue here. I called my sister on the ride home and I asked her "Ela, which businessmen do you know?" She gave me names, the same

names I had in mind. I sent an e-mail to my brother ... "David, which businessmen do you know?" He said the same names that my sister and I had said. We didn't have any other names in mind. I called my mother, "Mom, which businessmen do you know?" She said: "myself". I told her: "Mom, you are not a businesswoman." She said: "excuse me, your father and I have a travel agency, aren't we businessmen?" I told her "but you are not liars." "Fine, that's why we don't have money in our bank account, but we are businessmen" ... So I realized that I have to work on myself, because I am going to be self-employed and a business owner, and if those are my beliefs how will I make money.

In this excerpt, Gila is confronted with her deeply held beliefs about the inherent immorality of the business world; beliefs that according to her "come from home." These embodied beliefs, which in her case are expressed by a physical aversion to businessmen, can be traced back to Zionist socialist ideology and its repudiation of careerism (Almog, 2001). They are a central component of a "generational habitus" (Eyerman & Turner, 1998) corresponding to a social, economic and ideological regime that is long gone.[17] The above scene includes two distinct moments of confrontation. In the first moment, the course leader notices Gila's escape strategy and confronts her with her odd choice of words. He refers to working with small men as a metaphor for Gila's insecurity as a coach. By choosing to work with small men, she proves she is still a small woman herself.

The second and decisive moment of confrontation occurs when Gila asks her mother which businessmen she knows. Her mother's response, "myself," comes as a total surprise for Gila, who never thought of her parents as businessmen. In her cultural imagination (and her siblings' too), the term "businessmen" refers to big business owners and tycoons, not to the petty owners of a small travel agency. Growing up under the aegis of Labor Zionist socialist ideology, her parents' status as businessmen was denied at home. It was only through the coaching course influence that she could come to recognize her parents as businessmen and to consider becoming a businesswoman herself.

The process of becoming a coach required not only getting rid of "limiting beliefs" anchored in an outdated generational habitus, but also entailed finding a new basis for her identity, in order to turn from someone who needs help to find a job to someone who can create business opportunities by herself. A few months after she finished the coaching course, Gideon asked her to lead a course with him. As she recalls:

He said "tell me how much money you want." Wow, it was a big issue for me, to come and say how much money I want. Me and money? ... Now I know the cost of the course's tuition. I come to Gideon, I tell him how much money I want for each day that I go there. I don't remember the sum I told him, but I remember that it was a big sum. His reaction was "Gila, I will have nothing left for me." "Gideon, I know how much it takes from me to come. It means that I have to give up on this and that.

This is the way for me to come. If it's ok for you, good. If not, we can say goodbye as friends." I put down the phone and I roared so loud that the whole block heard me. And the roar was for the fact that I dared to ask for such a sum. My roar came from here [she points to her heart]. It was not about whether he will or will not accept. I didn't care about that anymore. It was the fact that I said aloud, "this is what I'm worth." He said "come" and we led a whole coaching course together.

In this quote Gila comes full circle. If at the beginning of the story she was rep-rimanded by Gideon for asking others to find her a job, now she proves to him her self-worth by demanding a high salary to work at his own firm. But more importantly, by asking a big sum of money from Gideon, she proves her own value as a person to herself. As her former experience as a teacher and school principal can no longer offer a basis for a desirable identity in neoliberal Israel, Gila adopts money as an alternative measure of self-worth. By commodifying herself and becoming a businesswoman (a pejorative identity in the Labor Zionist ideology she grew up with), she asserts herself as a neoliberal "subject of value" (Skeggs, 2004, 2011).

DISCUSSION

In this chapter, I set out to explore the increasing attraction of Israel's last republican generation to new neoliberal therapeutic discourses. In order to understand this connection, I focused on three representative narratives of self-transformation by members of this generational unit who chose coaching and similar forms of personal development work as a second career in later life. These narratives, I suggest, complicate existing accounts of the construction of neoliberal, entrepreneurial subjects by unraveling the relationship between new therapeutic technologies and insecurity culture. I found that in the case of the last republican generation, the adoption of the ethos of coaching in later life does not come as a way "to stave off the burdens of flexibility" (Freeman, 2007: 261) in the new post-Fordist economy. On the contrary, flexibility and related entrepreneurial qualities such as risk taking and openness to change are readily embraced by members of this generational unit as a cultural script for repositioning themselves and coming to terms with the decline of Labor Zionism as an all-encompassing master narrative that gave meaning and value to their life trajectories. As we saw earlier, the consequences of these economic and ideological shifts for the last republican generation have been mixed: on the one hand, most of its members have become "protected wildflowers" in an otherwise ruthless and precarious labor market, but on the other hand they have come to fear that if they do not adapt to the new rules of the game they will be left behind to "rot, stink and grow mold" in Dov's apt metaphor. In this sense, the turn to coaching seems to fulfill "a need to find new symbolic signposts to which to attach oneself and in relation to which to refashion oneself as an ethical subject" (Salmenniemi, 2016: 6).

Moreover, as the three stories presented in this chapter show, this refashioning of the self is not just a strategic or adaptive move, but it also entails a deeper kind of moral or even ideological transformation. At the heart of this transformation is the need to morally justify their commitment to capitalism and to make it attractive. If, as Boltanski and Chiapello argue, "integration into the capitalist process is singularly lacking in justifications" (2005: 7) due to the absurd and amoral nature of the system, personal-development culture, and coaching in particular, infuses members of the last republican generation with strong arguments and shared representations that make capital accumulation and profit making for its own sake not just acceptable, but also desirable. In this sense, their new commitment and joyful engagement with capitalism is not just practical or strategic (in the Bordieuan sense implied in Skeggs' notion of the neoliberal subject of value), but also deeply ideological.

Still, this refashioning of the self through the adoption of coaching's version of the "new spirit of capitalism" (Boltanski, 2005) does not necessarily entail the abandonment of collective commitments nor a withdrawal to the private sphere. In recent years, a growing body of literature dealing with the construction of neoliberal subjectivity has consistently argued that the generalization of the enterprise from within the social body (Foucault, 2008: 241–2) atomizes our understanding of social relations and erodes conceptions of the public domain (McNay, 2009: 64), thus leading to increasing depolitization and social disengagement. This literature, mostly inspired by the Foucauldian concept of "governmentality" (Foucault, 1991), reproduces a conceptual "seesaw model" which assumes that individual self-fulfillment and commitment to the public good counterpose one another and are essentially incompatible (Lichterman, 1995). Thus, for example, in a recent article on "the psychic life of neoliberalism," Christina Scharff (2016) finds that while "entrepreneurial subjects draw on a range of discourses in their talk ... some discourses ... are also markedly absent, such as political perspectives that highlight the need for social change. Instead," she says, "desires for change are directed away from the socio-political sphere and turned inwards." While there is much value to this critique, we still need to develop a more nuanced and less dichotomous understanding of neoliberal subjectivity if we want to fully grasp the ambiguities and paradoxes that constitute it as a lived reality. For instance, as we saw in the cases of Dov and Tamar, the adoption of coaching's neoliberal language and ideology may be used to assume and redefine social leadership roles in a context where old collective structures have lost their engaging force.

Going back to the "Alice in Wonderland" story that Daphna told at the beginning of this chapter, it seems that for the last republican generation, the metaphor of constantly running to stay in the same place has a different meaning than it does for younger Israeli generations working in the flexible post-Fordist economy. Living in a society that no longer values their republican virtue (expressed in activities like teaching or caring for the welfare of workers), they need to reinvent themselves as entrepreneurial subjects in order to avoid becoming obsolete and assert their self-value. By becoming life coaches and embodying neoliberal traits such as self-responsibility, autonomy and adaptability, they symbolically join the capitalist "race" and ratify their relevance in the new Israeli social order.

NOTES

1. The research for this chapter was supported by The Israeli Science Foundation (grant No.16/496)
2. All names of people, companies and places are fictional.
3. This career path was very common for Ashkenazi women in the first decades of the state, as the personal stories in this chapter make clear. Working as teachers left women time to fulfil the duties of wives and mothers of the nation that the Zionist project assigned them (Berkovitch, 1997).
4. I would like to thank Uri Ram for suggesting this term.
5. It is no coincidence that Zygmunt Bauman chose this same story to describe the perils of individuality in liquid modernity (see 2005: 23).
6. All interviews were conducted in Hebrew, and all translations are mine.
7. One of the two main coaching professional associations in Israel.
8. This is my own estimation, since there are no reliable statistics on the demographic composition of the coaching profession in Israel. As with most of the counselling professions, women seem to outnumber men among rank and file practitioners, while the leadership is predominantly male.
9. These neoliberal therapeutic technologies have also been described as "practices of governing the poor" (Mäkinen, 2014) and have been widely applied in "economic empowerment" and "welfare to workfare" programs (see Helman, 2013; Sa'ar 2016). I will not focus on this aspect here.
10. Since the early 2000s, coaching has enjoyed great popularity in Israel, both in the workplace and in the sphere of personal life. A myriad of institutes and higher-learning institutions offer coaching training programs and thousands of Israelis have chosen coaching as a vocation (even if they do not actually work full time as coaches), thus making Israel the country with the highest number of trained coaches per capita in the world (see Kaneh-Shalit, 2017). For a more detailed analysis of the development of the coaching field in Israel see Atad, Galily & Grant, 2013; Pagis, 2016b; Shahak, 2012.
11. A type of cooperative agricultural settlement pioneered by Labor Zionism.
12. In this sense, Dov's description of work at downsized Isratech is reminiscent of the moralizing, anti-statist tale of the clerk and the entrepreneur (see Simionca, 2012).
13. While she does not make it explicit, her renouncement of collective responsibility has also ethnic overtones. Many children in the city schools come from Mizrachi (Jews from Arab countries) families, which Ashkenazi hegemonic culture usually depicts as uneducated and uncivilized.
14. From the early days of the state, the military in Israel fulfilled a nation-building role. This role included the education of immigrants in the geographical and social

periphery of the country. Many women conscripts from the last republican generation fulfilled this duty as soldier-teachers.
15. This latter point is especially compelling, since coaches often preach about the importance and moral value of taking risks.
16. The double meaning here gets lost in the English translation. The term "businessmen" in Hebrew is composed of two words: business and men. The adjective "small" then may refer to each of these words, depending on context. The expression "small businessmen" to refer to small business owners is slightly awkward in Hebrew and this is what caught the course leader's attention.
17. For a similar point regarding the obsolescence of skills and dispositions accrued under socialism for navigating the new capitalist social order, see Salmenniemi, 2016: 9; Simionca, 2012.

REFERENCES

Almog, O. (2000). *The sabra: The creation of the new Jew*. Berkeley: University of California Press.
Almog, O. (2001). Shifting the centre from nation to individual and universe: The new "democratic faith" of Israel. *Israel Affairs*, *8*(1–2), 31–42.
Atad, O. I., Galily, Y. & Grant, A. M. (2013). Life coaching in Israel: An overview of Israel's burgeoning life-coaching industry. *International Journal of Evidence Based Coaching and Mentoring*, *11*(2), 112–23.
Bauman, Z. (2005). *Liquid life*. Cambridge: Polity Press.
Berkovitch, N. (1997). Motherhood as a national mission: The construction of womanhood in the legal discourse in Israel. *Women's Studies International Forum*, *20*(5), 605–19.
Binkley, S. (2011a). Happiness, positive psychology and the program of neoliberal governmentality. *Subjectivity*, *4*(4), 371–94.
Binkley, S. (2011b). Psychological life as enterprise: Social practice and the government of neo-liberal interiority. *History of the Human Sciences*, *24*(3), 83–102.
Boltanski, L. & Chiapello, E. (2005). *The new spirit of capitalism*. London: Verso.
Brown, M. (2003). Survival at work: Flexibility and adaptability in American corporate culture. *Cultural Studies*, *17*(5), 713–33.
Du Gay, P. (1996). *Consumption and identity at work*. London: Sage.
Eyerman, R. & Turner, B. S. (1998). Outline of a theory of generations. *European Journal of Social Theory*, *1*(1), 91–106.
Feher, M. (2009). Self-appreciation; or, the aspirations of human capital. *Public Culture*, *21*(1), 21–41.
Foucault, M. (1991). Governmentality. In G. Burchell, C. Gordon & P. Miller (Eds), *The Foucault effect: Studies in governmentality* (pp. 87–104). Chicago: University of Chicago Press.
Foucault, M. (2008). *The birth of biopolitics: Lectures at the Collège de France, 1978–1979* (G. Burchell Trans.). New York: Palgrave Macmillan.
Freeman, C. (2007). The "reputation" of neoliberalism. *American Ethnologist*, *34*(2), 252–67.
George, M. (2013). Seeking legitimacy: The professionalization of life coaching. *Sociological Inquiry*, *83*(2), 179–208.
Gershon, I. (2011). Neoliberal agency. *Current Anthropology*, *52*(4), 537–55.

Helman, S. (2013). How cashiers, cleaning workers and cashiers turned into entrepreneurs: Workfare programs and the construction of the entrepreneurial self. *Israeli Sociology, 14*(2), 312–35. (In Hebrew.)

Illouz, E. (2008). *Saving the modern soul: Therapy, emotions, and the culture of self-help*. Berkeley: University of California Press.

Kaneh☐Shalit, T. (2017). "The goal is not to cheer you up": Empathetic care in Israeli life coaching. *Ethos, 45*(1), 98–115.

Kimmerling, B. (2005). *The invention and decline of Israeliness: State, society, and the military*. Berkeley: University of California Press.

Lichterman, P. (1995). Beyond the seesaw model: Public commitment in a culture of self-fulfillment. *Sociological Theory, 13*(3), 275–300.

Mäkinen, K. (2014). The individualization of class: A case of working life coaching. *Sociological Review, 62*(4), 821–42.

Mäkinen, K. (2016). Valuable selves: Potentiality and temporality in work-related coaching. *European Journal of Cultural Studies, 19*(1), 69–84.

Maman, D. & Rosenhek, Z. (2012). The institutional dynamics of a developmental state: Change and continuity in state–economy relations in Israel. *Studies in Comparative International Development, 47*(3), 342–63.

Matza, T. (2012). "Good individualism"? Psychology, ethics, and neoliberalism in postsocialist Russia. *American Ethnologist, 39*(4), 804–18.

Matza, T. (2014). The will to what? Class, time, and re-willing in post-soviet Russia. *Social Text, 32*(3, 120), 49–67.

Mazzarino, A. (2013). Entrepreneurial women and the business of self-development in global Russia. *Signs, 38*(3), 623–45.

McGee, M. (2005). *Self-help, inc.: Makeover culture in American life*. Oxford: Oxford University Press.

McNay, L. (2009). Self as enterprise: Dilemmas of control and resistance in Foucault's the birth of biopolitics. *Theory, Culture and Society, 26*(6), 55–77.

Nehring, D., Kerrigan, D., Hendriks, E. C. & Alvarado, E. (2016). *Transnational popular psychology and the global self-help industry: The politics of contemporary social change*. London: Palgrave Macmillan.

Pagis, M. (2016a). Fashioning futures: Life coaching and the self☐made identity paradox. *Sociological Forum, 31*(4), 1083–103.

Pagis, M. (2016b). Translating positive psychology into the workplace: The case of coaching in Israel. In J. Brunner & G. Plotkin-Amrami (Eds), *Beyond the consulting room: Psychological discourse in contemporary culture* (pp. 23–48). Tel-Aviv: Resling. (In Hebrew.)

Pugh, A. J. (Ed.). (2016). *Beyond the cubicle: Job insecurity, intimacy, and the flexible self*. New York: Oxford University Press.

Ram, U. (2000). The promised land of business opportunities: Liberal post-Zionism in the glocal age. In G. Shafir & Y. Peled (Eds), *The new Israel: Peacemaking and liberalization* (pp. 217–42). Boulder: Westview Press.

Ram, U. (2008). *The globalization of Israel: McWorld in Tel Aviv, jihad in Jerusalem*. New York: Routledge.

Rosa, H., Dörre, K. & Lessenich, S. (2017). Appropriation, activation and acceleration: The escalatory logics of capitalist modernity and the crises of dynamic stabilization. *Theory, Culture and Society, 34*(1), 53–73.

Rose, N. (1996). *Inventing our selves: Psychology, power, and personhood*. Cambridge: Cambridge University Press.

Rosenhek, Z. & Shalev, M. (2014). The political economy of Israel's "social justice" protests: A class and generational analysis. *Contemporary Social Science*, *9*(1), 31–48.

Sa'ar, A. (2016). Emotional performance as work skill: Low income women in Israel learning to talk the talk. *Ethos*, *44*(2), 171–85.

Salmenniemi, S. (2016). "We can't live without beliefs": Self and society in therapeutic engagements. *Sociological Review*, doi: 0038026116677194

Salmenniemi, S. & Vorona, M. (2014). Reading self help literature in Russia: Governmentality, psychology and subjectivity. *British Journal of Sociology*, *65*(1), 43–62.

Scharff, C. (2016). The psychic life of neoliberalism: Mapping the contours of entrepreneurial subjectivity. *Theory, Culture and Society*, *33*(6), 107–22.

Sennett, R. (2006). *The culture of the new capitalism*. New Haven: Yale University Press.

Shafir, G. & Peled, Y. (2002). *Being Israeli: The dynamics of multiple citizenship*. Cambridge: Cambridge University Press.

Shahak, M. (2012). *Life coaching and the commodification of selfhood*. Unpublished MA thesis. The Hebrew University of Jerusalem.

Shalev, M. (2000). Liberalization and the transformation of the political economy. In G. Shafir & Y. Peled (Eds), *The new Israel: Peacemaking and liberalization* (pp. 129–59). Boulder: Westview Press.

Simionca, A. (2012). Neoliberal managerialism, anti-communist dogma and the critical employee in contemporary Romania. *Studia UBB Sociologia*, *57*(1), 125–49.

Skeggs, B. (2004). *Class, self, culture*. London: Routledge.

Skeggs, B. (2011). Imagining personhood differently: Person value and autonomist working class value practices. *Sociological Review*, *59*(3), 496–513.

Swan, E. (2010). *Worked up selves: Personal development workers, self-work and therapeutic cultures*. London: Palgrave Macmillan.

Urciuoli, B. (2008). Skills and selves in the new workplace. *American Ethnologist*, *35*(2), 211–28.

Vallas, S. P. & Hill, A. L. (2018). Reconfiguring worker subjectivity: Career advice literature and the "branding" of the worker's self. *Sociological Forum*, *33*(2), 287–309.

3. Expressive individualism in the new spirit of capitalism: mindfulness and outdoor management development

Liza Cortois

INTRODUCTION

> I think it is really important that people stay close to themselves, that people are authentic. If you don't know what you stand for, and I give you some good arguments, then I can blow you away. But if you are convinced: 'No, I really believe in this', then you will argue back. The company needs that resistance, to become better.

This quote from an outdoor management development (OMD) coach emphasizes the key importance of authenticity as the practice of expressing your 'real self' in the work context. The display of the authentic personality, once limited to the private sphere, has now entered the public sphere where scholars have traced its emergence and flourishing as a condition of individual and organizational growth (Costea, Crump & Amiridis, 2008; Heelas, 2003; Rose, 1989). The study on which this chapter is based focuses on mindfulness and OMD training courses in Belgium. A key assumption made by coaches and consultants who run these courses is that managers and employees need to go beyond bureaucratic enactment of their organizational roles and display authentic aspects of their personality in the professional context. As the opening quote illustrates, this is viewed as potentially enhancing organizational performance. Hence the organization is portrayed as a context of self-development.

With regard to management training focused on authenticity, two types stand out. First, the loose category of OMD relates to the expression of authentic personality via participation in outdoor activities (Bell & Taylor, 2004; Burke & Collins, 2004; Jones & Oswick, 2007). An early example of this is the scouting and military-inspired 'outward bound' training that involves team building situated in nature (Burletson & Grint, 1996) through activities such as rafting, skydiving, survival training and so on. The general idea is that outside the organizational context, people can leave behind their professional roles, and thus more genuine personalities, leadership or team spirit will develop organically. Subsequently, authentic connections and personalities rediscovered in connection to nature are brought back in the organizational context. A second category involves training that emphasizes care for the self, for instance to counter work-related stress or to prevent burn-out. Courses range from therapeutic techniques to New Age spirituality such as yoga, neuro-linguistic programming or mindfulness (e.g. Wilson, 2014). As this indicates, spirituality is no longer limited to alternative subcultures, but has found its way into mainstream culture, including business and organizations (Case & Gosling, 2010; Corner, 2009). Many people signing up for courses related to spirituality do so for work-related reasons (Aldred, 2002; Greeson, Webber, Smoski & Brantley, 2012). In many courses, people are encouraged to go beyond their organizational role and get in touch with a 'deeper self'. For sociologists of religion, this phenomenon is referred to as 'self-spirituality' (Heelas, 1996). In OMD and spiritual management development there is a strong focus on an authentic, individual self.

Many social scientists have observed and described this centrality of authenticity in organizations (Costea et al., 2008; Fleming, 2009; Fleming & Sturdy, 2011; Rose, 1989). Fleming (2009: 2), for instance, observes that 'a growing number of managerial commentators, consultants, and practitioners ... argue that authenticity is today a pivotal reference point for understanding worker motivation and productive performance'. I will locate this emphasis on authenticity using the broader sociological concept of 'expressive individualism' (Bellah, Madson, Swidler, Tipton & Sullivan, 2008; Parsons, 2007). In their interpretation of authenticity in organizations, several scholars take a critical stance. They see authenticity as a hidden form of exploitation in contrast to the overt use of power in organizational contexts. They point out that this form of control reaches deeper into the personality of the worker and makes the boundary between life and work problematic (e.g. Case & Gosling, 2010; Fleming & Sturdy, 2011). I argue, however, that this reveals only one aspect of how expressive individualism is applied in work-related contexts. Other applications also prevail in practice and illustrate a more active interpretation of this ethos by employees that stimulates them to question organizational control. More particularly, in this chapter I will distinguish, based on Merton's (1968) anomie typology, between diverse uses of expressive individualism. To do this, I will draw on in-depth interviews and participant observation of managers and employees at two management training programs in Belgium that focus on expressive individualism, one OMD and a mindfulness course. The argument will be developed as follows: first, I situate the theoretical background and central concepts such as 'the new spirit of capitalism' and 'expressive individualism'. In the following section, information is provided about the two research settings, their relation to expressive individualism and the training methods used. Finally, four potential manners of using expressive individualism in the organizational context based on Merton's typology (1968) are presented.

THE NEW SPIRIT OF CAPITALISM AND EXPRESSIVE INDIVIDUALISM

The current emphasis on authenticity exemplifies a cultural shift in organizations that enables justification of the capitalist system as a distinct historical 'spirit' (Boltanski & Chiapello, 2005). The first spirit of capitalism is characterized by utilitarian morality and can be situated at the end of the nineteenth century. Its central figure was the bourgeois entrepreneur who owned a small family business. The second spirit had its climax between 1930 and 1960 and stood for the reign of the large bureaucratic industrial firm with its central figures of organizational control the director or the manager. Rationalization and standardization were the main organizational principles, in line with Taylorist scientific management and the Fordist assembly line. Ehrenberg (1991) describes the anthropological foundation of this spirit as 'the Taylorist man-bullock and the Fordist man-chimpanzee' where man was reduced either to his strength or his repetitive manipulations of a product. While opposing paradigms also arose that took workers' motivation and human relations into account (Mayo, 1945), the institutionalized organizational mainstream was mostly characterized by utilitarianism, passive employee discipline and authoritarian control in these early spirits of capitalism (Boltanski & Chiapello, 2005: 17–19).

The contrast with organizational culture today, especially with how more aspects related to personality are incorporated into the labor process, is sharp. The turn to a 'new spirit of capitalism' was initiated during the so-called 'counter-culture' of the 1960s. This bohemian or hippie subculture posed a challenge to mainstream culture, and targeted the utilitarian, materialistic and authoritarian features of capitalism. The most important critique here is what Boltanski and Chiapello (2005) refer to as 'the artistic critique' which emphasizes 'on the one hand, the disenchantment and inauthenticity and on the other the oppression, which characterize the bourgeois world associated with the rise of capitalism' (Boltanski & Chiapello, 2005: 38). The central value in this artistic critique during the counter-culture was expressive individualism, as Parsons and Platt (1973) indicate by referring to this period as 'the expressive revolution' (see also Turner, 2005). Expressive individualism can be defined as the belief in a pre-social and authentic self that subsequently has to be expressed (Bellah et al., 2008; Cortois & Laermans, 2018; Taylor, 1991; Tipton, 1982). From a sociological point of view, authenticity is not an ontological feature of an individual, but forms a shared cultural value that developed historically and a social norm that we collectively comply with.[1]

Charles Taylor (1989, 1991), who has analyzed authenticity as a cultural ideal philosophically, explains that at a certain point in history 'we came to think of ourselves as beings with inner depths' (Taylor, 1991: 26). The counter-culture was one of these points in history that conceptualized subjectivity and morality in terms of authenticity, but it was followed by other periods where this moral perspective was gradually developed. Crucial was the Romantic period, and thinkers such as Rousseau, Herder and the romantic poets. All of them shared the conviction that morality is achieved through transparent knowledge and unbiased contact with our inner selves. A factor that might threaten this pure relation to the self is instrumentality. If one approaches oneself instrumentally, for instance as a source of production in the labor process, an authentic connection with one's inner voice may be lost. A further implication of authenticity is that each of us has a unique way of being human. In this sense, there is a close relation between the value of authenticity and creativity or originality, or as Taylor expresses it: 'each of our voices has something of its own to be said' (Taylor, 1991: 29). A thread to this unique nature of the self, Taylor (1991: 29) points out, is conformity to our social environment that pressures us to follow social conventions. This can be seen most clearly in the social roles people are expected to play that deviate from their underlying personality. The paradox here of course is that being authentic is not exempt from social conformity, but the social role in a culture of expressive individualism is precisely one of the authentic person.

In relation to the meaning and potential threats of authenticity, it is not surprising that during the expressive revolution, it was the 'capitalist system', as both potential locus of conformity and utility, that was critiqued from this perspective. The threat of conformity explains the aversion from the counter-cultural point of view to institutions, dogmas or bureaucracy that avert the attention of the deeper, authentic self. Organizations are an evident place where the self is approached from a utilitarian perspective. However, as analyzed by Boltanski and Chiapello, the expressive individualist critique of capitalism did not destroy capitalism, but in a subsequent phase became part of its ideology. This altered cultural foundation of capitalism is termed the 'new spirit of capitalism' (e.g. Boltanski & Chiapello, 2005; De Keere, 2014). Instead of standardized and controlled repetitive labor, volatile networks and new projects succeed one another, and creativity becomes a key feature of work itself, especially in the 'culture industries' (Boltanski & Chiapello, 2005; Lash & Urry, 1994). In the (stereo)typical neo-liberal vocabulary, one has to be always 'flexible' and principally 'employable' or, as Boltanski and Chiapello express it themselves: 'never to be short of a project, bereft of an idea, always to have something in mind, in the pipeline, with other people whom one meets out of a desire to do something' (2005: 110). Authenticity forms a key value in this new spirit of capitalism, exemplified in trends such as 'authentic leadership' or general advice to 'just be yourself' (Fleming, 2009; Fleming & Sturdy, 2011). Current management literature illustrates that both managers and employees are no longer expected to play an ascribed role or to be merely utility-focused, but to show their true personality in their work.[2]

Many organizational scholars are critical of this cultural shift towards expressive individualism in the workplace and view it as a new level of 'bio-power' that blurs the distinction between life and work (Fleming, 2014). While under the previous spirits of capitalism power relations were overt, now power is at a more hidden level but is arguably at least as pervasive, since it colonizes the entire personality. Fleming (2009: 5), for example, approaches

> the managerial edict to be authentic as an ideological attempt to suture the lack [of a life] through a kind of false positivity ... The corporatized 'truth of being' – encouraging superficial displays of difference, identity and lifestyle – represents the display of authenticity into an instrumental discourse. Even if it packages itself in the lexicon of freedom, the 'just be yourself' discourse follows more the grammar of appropriation than redistribution and recognition.

A similar argument is observed in literature that perceives 'business spirituality' as a commodified and instrumental means of reconciling the employee with his or her work (e.g. Bell & Taylor, 2003; Carette & King, 2004; Case & Gosling, 2010). Bell and Taylor (2003: 342) for instance observe: 'In an attempt to resolve the ambivalent relationship between self and organization in the West, it appears managers are turning to the instrumental use of technologies that appropriate spirituality in order to establish what they are encouraged to perceive as total obedience among a workforce.' These authors observe how the expressive ethos merely serves as a means of achieving utilitarian or organizational goals. Thereby, the normative critique is made that the expressive ethos functions as a hidden form of exploitation. A similarity can be observed with (neo-)Marxist analysis of religion or culture as an ideology that averts attention from what really matters, i.e. the underlying relations of production (e.g. Negri & Hardt, 2000).

In this chapter, I will argue that this critical stance discloses some of the mechanisms of a discourse focused on authenticity in relation to power, but also disregards the complexities and multiple uses of expressive individualism. This may be due to the fact that these researchers tend to study static, institutionalized forms of the discourse of this new spirit, such as management advice literature (Boltanski & Chiapello, 2005; De Keere, 2014), or focus on the perspective of managers and other powerful organization members and how they seek to benefit from the expressive individualist discourse. They less frequently consider how managers and employees appropriate this discourse reflexively and potentially challenge power relations associated with it. The central research question addressed here then becomes: How do people interpret and apply expressive individualism, as an object of socialization in management training programs that relate to the work context? To answer this, I selected two settings where employees and managers are socialized in the expressive individualist ethos and investigated how participants on these courses apply the expressive individualist ethos in their organizations.

CASE SELECTION: OUTDOOR MANAGEMENT DEVELOPMENT AND MINDFULNESS

To examine the use of expressive individualism under the new spirit of capitalism, two work-related courses were studied that embody this ethos. The first uses OMD and attributes a central role to introspection, giving and receiving feedback on one's personality and leadership qualities and developing self-knowledge (see also Bell & Taylor, 2004). The relationship to authenticity and expressive individualism is especially apparent through the emphasis on nature. The underlying idea is that the managers are taken out of their usual organizational roles and inauthentic office environments, and even out of the clothing that symbolizes their professionalism. Instead, they are dressed in sportive gear and take part in adventurous, competitive activities. A strong opposition between nature and society is posited, where nature is seen as truly authentic and devoid of social roles, influence or hierarchies. In connection to nature, one is assumed to discover one's own nature more easily. By leaving their professional roles behind, it is thought that the managers will be forced to fall back upon their 'true identity'. Deeply romantic assumptions characterize OMD, including of a more authentic self that can only arise if it is brought back in connection to nature (Taylor, 1989).[3]

This particular course consists of adventurous assignments in the woods, theoretical seminars on leadership and teamwork for junior and senior managers from multinationals in the profit sector. Besides the outdoor aspect, there are several individual and team coaching moments and a 'business challenge' where insights gained from the outdoor training are translated back into the office context.[4] The final objective is to bring the newly discovered authentic self back into the social sphere of the organization. The course can last up to a year and is comprised of a series of short-term residential outdoor modules each lasting between four and five days. Between modules there are often several months to apply the learned insights in the organizational context. The course provider has well-known multinational corporate clients in the financial, research and development, logistics and food sectors and employs a total of 15 coaches. It is located in Belgium and the outdoor modules of the trajectory I focused on were situated in the woods of the Belgian Ardennes.

The second selected course was aligned with spirituality and focused on mindfulness. It was specifically directed at enabling participants to deal with stress. Mindfulness can be defined as 'paying attention in a particular way: on purpose, in the present moment, and nonjudgmentally' (Kabat-Zinn, 1994). It makes use of Buddhist meditation and breathing practices and can be seen as a form of New Age spirituality interpreted in a broad sense (Hanegraaff, 1996). Mindfulness is thus situated as part of a broader interest in spirituality, in mainstream Western cultures where scientific legitimation is often used to argue for its functionality (Hammer, 2001). Cognitive psychology and neurological studies are often referred to and mindfulness has been modeled to an eight-week program for the prevention of stress (Mindfulness Based Stress Reduction) and to prevent relapse in depression (Mindfulness Based Cognitive Therapy) in medical contexts (Barker, 2014). Despite this rational-ized approach to spirituality, the view of the self it professes is closely related to expressive individualism and its central value of authenticity. Instead of a spiritual authority, it is the search for meaning in the deeper self that becomes central. This self should not be led by social conformity or other people's expectations, neither by an internalized 'judgmental' attitude. The purpose of meditative practice is to restore an authentic relation to the self in line with its philosophy of self-care. In the literature, this specific articulation of expressive individualism has been termed 'self-spirituality' (Heelas, 1996).

The selected mindfulness course was not delivered in, or organized by a company, but was given in a hospital and open to everybody. Nevertheless, three out of four respondents in the sample indicated that they followed the mindfulness course out of work-related motives. The main indicated motive for participants was burn-out, followed by other reasons such as balancing family and work demands, adapting to a new working environment, etc. Even in a course not explicitly organized in a work context, the links to work explicitly drawn illustrate the pervasiveness of this new spirit of capitalism. The course took place in Belgium and the particular trainer who gave it is con-sidered the founding father of mindfulness in the region. From prior interviews with other mindfulness trainers, it became apparent that he was the trainer with the most 'spiritual capital' in this area (Cortois, Aupers & Houtman, 2018).

In both cases, participant observation and in-depth interviews were con-ducted. In the mindfulness case, an entire eight-week program was observed and notes were taken. Half a year after the course, 30 interviews were undertaken with course participants between September and October 2015. Sampling was enabled by an announcement in the newsletter of this particu-lar, well-known mindfulness trainer and comprised some of his past course participants. With regard to the OMD course, participant observation was conducted during the outdoor module. I observed the activities for four days in the Belgian Ardennes. One year later, 15 interviews were collected between June and August of 2017 with senior and junior managers. The managers were from three multinational organizations that participated in the program, one in logistics, one financial organization and a research and development company. In each company, five former participants were selected for interview. Similar questions were asked in both case studies. First, interviewees were asked to elaborate on their motivations and initial expectations on the course and how they experienced the activities. They were also asked to elaborate on the important things they learned from this course about themselves and how they have applied these in the context of work.[5]

THE NEW SPIRIT FROM THE PERSPECTIVE OF MERTON'S ANOMIE THEORY

The categorization of diverse applications of expressive individualism will be systematically presented from the perspective of Merton's (1938) anomie typology also known as his 'means–ends theory' or 'strain theory'. Merton distinguishes five categories that he terms 'conformists', 'innovators', 'ritualists', 'retreatists' and 'rebellions'. This categorization originally formed a 'study of socio-cultural sources of deviate behavior', but it can also be used to describe social behavior in general. The categories form combinations of what Merton describes as 'culturally defined goals' and 'acceptable modes of achieving these goals' (Merton, 1938: 38) or simply the means to these goals. Each of the categories forms different combinations of means and ends. The *conformists* use legitimate means to achieve legitimate goals. *Innovators* on the other hand subscribe to the prescribed goals but achieve them through different or illegitimate means. *Ritualists* use the available means without being able to achieve their goals and *retreatists* withdraw both from accepted means and goals. The fifth category of the *rebellions* is similar to the former, but replaces the culturally accepted means and goals with alternative means and goals.

This categorization can be applied to the diverse interactions that were found in the case studies between expressive individualism and institutionalized goals in the organizational context. Expressive inspired courses such as mindfulness or OMD are used as 'means' to achieve utilitarian, organizational 'goals' such as getting a promotion or in general 'professional success'. It was found in the cases that the manner in which this expressive ethos is applied differs and is either used as an 'affirmation' of the organizational growth discourse (indicated in Table 3.1 with a '+') or in a 'critical' application of this discourse (indicated in Table 3.1 with a '−').[6] In the case of the category of the innovators, who, as will be shown, give a peculiar meaning to 'criticism', expressive individualism is used to criticize the specific means that are available to managers to realize their professional goals, in this case related to company culture. The combination '+/−' stands for the formulation of alternative means and goals that come to replace the generally accepted ones of professional success. In the case studies, four of the five combinations that

Table 3.1   Relation means and ends that result in four categories of Merton's (1968) anomie theory

Category Merton	(Organizational) ends	(Expressive) means
Conformists	+	+
Innovators	+	–
Ritualists	–	+
Rebellions	+/– (alternative)	+/– (alternative)

Merton describes can be identified as a manner of approaching the relation between expressive individualism and organizational goals. The fifth category of 'retreatism' was not present as completely abandoning the new spirit of capitalism or organizational goals was not found in the case studies. The four categories of Merton's anomie typology present in the case studies are summarized in Table 3.1.

The Conformist: OMD for Personal Growth

For most of the practitioners in the OMD, expressive individualist means and neo-liberal organizational goals continuously meld together, forming one inseparable discourse focused on 'personal growth': 'For me, this was an opportunity to grow' (Brooke, phase engineer, logistics company). This personal growth is understood as showing a more authentic self at work and guiding team members from a style of 'authentic leadership'. The latter involves outgrowing the controlling and authoritarian role of manager and instead being an agentic and creative leader, who transparently expresses his or her expectations (e.g. Bennis, 2009). At the same time, from an organizational and instrumental point of view, personal growth is conceptualized as an entrepreneurial view of a self that continually wants to develop its human capital (Bröckling, 2015; Du Gay, 1994). Merging both understandings as one view of the self forms the explicit goal of the coaches of the OMD. This was illustrated by the quote at the beginning of this chapter that strongly connected authentic leadership to the company benefit. The coaches in general often referred to 'the impact of authentic leaders' that is deemed greater than that of those that do not act in accordance with their personality: 'People who are authentic have a lot of impact and are often described as charismatic' (Andy, coach).

The equation between expressive and utilitarian thinking about the self is illustrated in the narratives of the former participants. They see the training as an investment in themselves, their capacities and competences that in turn has a positive influence on the company's overall effectiveness. In fact, the self is seen after the model of a company one has to invest in (e.g. Becker,

1976; Foucault, 2010; Vallas & Cummins, 2015). Consequently, a congruence results between personal and company growth. All of the managers confirmed this congruence of growth at both levels, for instance as Curt expresses it: 'It can help the efficiency of the organization to give people better understanding of their own behavior and their own mindset' (sales manager, research and development company).

Some managers went a step further in their interpretation of OMD. While personal growth is the shared vocabulary of managers used to express 'the impact' of the OMD, for some this led to hierarchical promotion in the organization. Many explicitly indicated during the interview that the training gave them the impetus to apply for a new position. Whether their promotion was directly caused by the training is of course a difficult question to answer. It is, however, also significant that most of the managers interpret their upward move like this. Ray, for instance, relates believing in himself and having the courage to climb the organizational ladder: 'By getting me out of my comfort zone, believing in myself, having higher goals for myself … the training gave me the courage that I can occupy this position. At that moment, I realized that I also really needed … a new stimulus. I realized this during the talent program, and together with what I learned there, it made me apply for my current position' (Ray, program director, logistics company). The conformist managers follow the expressive means that became mainstream under the new spirit of capitalism to achieve their goals of growth in the company. In terms of Merton's typology, they can be seen as typical conformists, subscribing to a broadly shared new spirit of capitalism. The discourse of authenticity is merely used as a subordinate means to achieve the company's goals.

The Innovator: OMD as Organizational Critique

The fusion of personal and organizational growth was not shared by all the participants to the OMD. For some managers the emphasis on self-development did not match the opportunities they were offered by their company. To the contrary, because of the management training, the former participants started questioning their company culture. The expressive individualist content of the course formed a cause for reflexivity on their organizational situation. While before they were already mildly critical of their context, the emphasis on growth and development of the training sharpened their feeling of discomfort. Curt, for example, explained that the training made him aware of his potential and how this cannot be properly developed in his organization:

> The training was especially about: what is your function in the company and how do you see yourself developing? And I just notice that I cannot develop enough in this company. And I talked a lot about that with the coach. I realize this more often,

> that I bump against a wall in this company … I'm one of the few young people in
> this company … I have more than 10 years' experience in sales … Do something
> with that! I'm really committed … but yeah, the reality … [with a discouraged tone].
> (Curt, sales manager, genetics company)

Curt uses the metaphor 'to bump against a wall' to express his feeling of facing
an obstruction to grow. The valuation of the capacities of the managers can
have a positive influence on their performance in the company, as could be
observed in the case of the conformists, but it can also cause them to question
the company conditions, like in Curt's situation.

One of Curt's colleagues, Bettany, shared his feeling. She explains that
during the training it was emphasized that she was an extrovert, which made
her more aware of the fact that her 'real' personality is not valued in her current
company: 'In this organization, they prefer it if I talk less, if I formulate less of
my ideas. Well, then I'm very far removed from my own core. So I can better
search for another organization that does appreciate this' (Bettany, marketing,
genetics company). In accordance with the centrality of authenticity, she
emphasizes that her work should be in line with 'the core' of her personality.
Since this is currently not the case and she cannot be herself at work, she
decided it was time to look for another job.

When further exploring this phenomenon of people considering quitting
their job after the program, the coaches of the OMD explained that often
participants start questioning their current professional role and whether it
matches their identity.[7] The coaches did not perceive this critical perspective to
be a misinterpretation of their training and actively encouraged it:

> *People who come to the conclusion, because of the training, that they actually don't*
> *want to be leaders or who want to quit their job, how do you deal with that?*
>
> Fantastic! That is what I call major self-knowledge! … I hope that they quit their
> job, or have a deep conversation with their manager, I sincerely hope that. (Ella,
> coach, OMD)

This response might lead one to assume that the coaches are in favor of a critical interpretation of the company culture through the emphasis on authenticity.
However, this does not imply that they are critical of the notion of the entrepreneurial self; to the contrary. The coaches align individual development,
even if the managers cannot develop this individuality in their organizational
context, with developing their human capital beyond specific organizational

boundaries, and express it in the general neo-liberal vocabulary as a 'win–win situation':

> It is of no help to our society, if someone works somewhere against his will. There are so many companies that probably relate so much better to that person's norms and values.
>
> *From the point of view of the person that is probably better, but from the perspective of the company?*
>
> That is also a win, right? You can better have someone on the right place. Maybe you have to search longer for that person that is in the right place and likes to work for your company, than for someone who merely works to earn a salary but actually constantly thinks in the back of his head: 'I don't belong here.' I think it can be a win–win situation for both. (Ella, coach, OMD)

Here it can be observed again that human capital, in terms both of human and company capital, is not opposed to authenticity, but both ideals seem to uphold each other. In the end, the recurring argument is that doing what is in line with your personality will also benefit a company in the long run. While the interlocutors criticize their company, the new spirit of capitalism in general is not questioned.[8] In the end, the philosophy of human capital and entrepreneurial subjectivity which forms the cornerstone of the training is not limited to specific company boundaries, but forms an all-round 'new spirit of capitalism'. The expressive ethos is in a minimalistic sense used to criticize, but only directed at the particular institutional setting. The company is not criticized for being neo-liberal or utility-focused, but for not allowing the managers to be themselves. This category can fall under the label of 'innovator' in Merton's terminology.[9] They subscribe to the goal of self-development in neo-liberal society, but not by means of a classic career in one company.

The Ritualist: Mindfulness as Coping Strategy

In the mindfulness case study, a clear bifurcation in interpretations and application in the organizational context was found. The two interpretations of mindfulness differ from the OMD training. In the first group, a pragmatic use of the mindfulness technique was found. These practitioners indicate that because of mindfulness meditation, they are able to continue functioning in their work context or restart their work at the usual pace after a difficult period or a burn-out. For them, meditation takes the form of a coping strategy to deal with the demands of their job. Some have the impression that due to mindfulness they are calmer, and as a result, they can focus better.

In this functional and utilitarian interpretation, the concept of 'self-control' was central. Mindfulness formed a way to control the mind, body and more

broadly the self. For example, Emma (61, lecturer, higher education) perceived
it as a way to control one's body: 'Those Buddhists, they can even control
their body temperature'. Frederic also reiterates the discourse of control and
connects it to a sense of personal autonomy: 'The feeling: "I'm in control,"
I decide. Not the stress, not the thoughts. I. I decide. I thought that was a rev-
elation, to notice how a person can calm himself down' (Frederic, 53, writer).

Self-control through meditation is, however, not used for improving one's
performance or personal growth in the work context, as was the case for the
conformists, but for the less ambitious goal of keeping up with the current
pace of their work. Work under neo-liberal conditions is endured rather than
embraced as an encompassing life goal. Leen illustrates this more ritualistic
interpretation of mindfulness. It helps her to notice her physical and mental
boundaries faster. She had to stop working for some time due to burn-out, but
mindfulness helped her to re-engage in her job, in a more responsible manner
than before. 'I think I feel faster when it becomes difficult for myself ... when
I reach my boundary, I feel a little faster: 'Be careful! Take care of yourself!'
I also think I'm less critical for myself and I learned to realize: 'I react like this,
because of that'. And I don't become frustrated because of that, but I'm mild to
myself and sort of learn to accept that' (Leen, 56, architect). Other mindfulness
practitioners cope with their work situation by including meditative breaks.
Frederic and Philip, for instance, indicated that they took several moments
each working day to take a short break and meditate. Sarah did not literally
meditate, but took a moment to sit alone and taste her cup of tea 'in a mindful
and aware manner' as she describes it.

Mindfulness is for these interlocutors not a way to criticize neo-liberal work
expectations, but rather forms a coping strategy. On the other hand, the meditation techniques are not used to grow in the organizational context either, like
for the conformists, but merely to keep up with the demands of the job. These
respondents were not interested in achieving new goals in the work context.
Seen from Merton's anomie typology, they can be approached best with the
category of 'ritualists' (Merton, 1968). These practitioners accept the expressive technique of mindfulness and the focus on self-development it involves,
but they do not aspire to success or growth in a neo-liberal context. They
engage with their work in a more reflexive way in the sense that they protect
themselves from being too involved in it. Reflexivity, however, does not lead
to radical criticism of their work conditions.

The Rebel: Mindfulness as Alternative

There was an equally pronounced group that used mindfulness to formulate
a critique of the organizational context. For them, mindfulness enabled them
to pursue different goals in life than organizational success. Examples of these

alternative paths are the reduction of working hours, an earlier pension or even a different job. Ilse, for instance, a retired engineer, says that she 'thinks mindfulness had a result, and that was that I actually quit my job earlier'. Kristel and Jane, who are mid-career, indicated that after following the mindfulness course, they both independently decided to work less in order to take better care of themselves or their families:

> It gave me the courage to take the decision to work less. Finally, I could see: 'Help! What is this?' Because of this, we [she and her husband] started thinking: the financial aspect is not the only thing that matters … and finally, we made the decision, and there is less [income] now … but our life is just as good. And our children, they are so pleased! (Kristel, 45, insurance agent)

> I am more aware of myself and my family, and yeah, my work is affected by it, in the sense that I decided to do less. I had to, the pace was not realistic anymore. (Jane, 47, researcher)

The alternative choices practitioners made after the course relate to several aspects of life. Susan, for example, joined a Buddhist community, which was for her the start of a more Buddhist-inspired lifestyle. Many people also reported a change in drinking and eating habits, such as quitting alcohol and becoming vegetarian. Luc gradually started questioning several aspects of his life, especially work:

> It meant so much for me, mindfulness and Buddhism, that I started to question being a lawyer. All the values and convictions, that I had always had of course, but that had been neglected because of work etc., they came to the surface. This didn't always make my life easy, because if you work at a bank, and you come with certain values and norms, then life becomes more difficult, there is more tension. I had a burn-out, I'm just getting out of it … Because mindfulness helped me so, I'm also following a trajectory to become a trainer myself … I still have to change a lot in my life, because I have the feeling that with every change, I'm coming closer to myself. Because of mindfulness. Absolutely. (Luc, 46, lawyer)

In line with an expressive individualist argumentation, he says that his true personality and values arose increasingly after the repeated practice of meditation. After rediscovering his repressed personality, the mismatch with his career as a lawyer at a bank became more pressing. For this category of practitioners, mindfulness becomes a means not only to cope with the organizational context, but to actively question and eventually reject it. Because of mindfulness, Luc quit his job as a lawyer and radically switched careers and is preparing to become a full-time mindfulness trainer.

The crucial aspect here is that mindfulness practitioners do not frame reducing the hours they work or the change to an alleged 'less prestigious' job as a personal failure to live up to neo-liberal standards. Instead, these changes

Table 3.2   Relation between expressive individualism and
organizational context approached from Merton's anomie
theory

Case	Category	Ends	Means	Category Merton
OMD	Personal growth	+	+	Conformists
	Question company	+	-	Innovators
Mindfulness	Self-control	-	+	Ritualists
	Alternative self-discovery	+/-	+/-	Rebellions

are perceived as conscious choices that lead to a more ethical way to live.
Mindfulness serves here not as a means to subscribe to the general neo-liberal
expectations, but instead to actively question them. The expressive individualist ethos is in this case not subordinate to organizational goals, but caused participants to formulate alternative values. This group of practitioners actively
shapes their life in accordance with these alternative ideals. In Merton's
anomie typology, this category can be seen as a 'rebellious application'.
Instead of ritualistically following up neo-liberal expectations, the expressive
ethos is used to question the conditions under which they work. This suggests
that the expressive individualist counter-cultural critique of capitalism has
not been completely absorbed by the new spirit of capitalism (Boltanski &
Chiapello, 2005), but some critical residue has been preserved in how these
practitioners use mindfulness as a critique.

From the analysis, the initial scheme can be completed in Table 3.2 with
the concrete categories that were found in our case studies, to illustrate how
Merton's scheme might be useful to approach the relation between expressive
individualism and organizational goals.

CONCLUSION

This chapter began with a discussion on the new spirit of capitalism and the
central place it attributes to expressive individualism and the related value of
personal authenticity in the organizational context. During the counter-cultural
era, expressive individualism was used to critique capitalism as an inauthentic
and merely utilitarian system. Ironically, the emphasis on authenticity became
part of that same capitalistic system (Boltanski & Chiapello, 2005). Many
social scientists take a critical stance to the centrality of expressive individualism in the organizational context and approach it as a hidden mechanism
of control (Bell & Taylor, 2003; Case & Gosling, 2010; Fleming, 2009).
Moreover, they indicate that under the banner of being authentic at work, the

distinction between life and work increasingly disappears. Thus, they conclude that the employee is not only controlled in his or her professional role, but the whole personality is placed under scrutiny. The analysis in this chapter shows that expressive individualism can, however, be used in multiple manners in the organizational context, some of them affirming this approach in terms of a 'mechanism of control', others showing a more reflexive, or even critical, use of expressive insights. To systematize these findings, the anomie typology of Merton was used. In the analysis of the case studies it was observed that expressive individualism is often used unreflexively by managers or employees in line with the organizational logic (Boltanski & Chiapello, 2005). This is most obvious for the conformist case where the managers put organizational efficiency and personal growth on a par, and do not make a clear-cut distinction between the two. The category of the ritualist shows some resemblance with the conformist in the sense that the expressive individualism of mindfulness is used to function in the organizational setting. However, the ritualists do not aspire to personal-cum-organizational growth, they merely want to cope with the organizational context, without pursuing professional success. Both the ritualists and the conformists can be seen as in line with the literature that considers expressive individualism as a 'hidden form of exploitation' (Carette & King, 2004; Islam, Holm & Karjalainen, 2017). Authenticity became part of the neo-liberal context in both of these applications and thus reconciles employees' aspirations with organizational goals. Both categories, however, show some diversity in how precisely expressive individualism is used as a mechanism of control – a question that the critical literature does not sufficiently answer. While conformists are not critical at all of how personal and organizational goals are related, and in fact perceive this whole discourse as in their advantage, ritualists are reflexive about merely achieving organizational success. Both categories show a different way of relating to the organizational discourse focused on authenticity.

The category of the innovator at first sight comes across as a critical use of the expressive discourse, since these managers doubt their organizational context. Nevertheless, it can be asked how critical this category in reality is. The critical use of expressive individualism is limited by the lack of space for self-development in their particular company. Instead, both the managers and coaches plead for professional-cum-personal growth beyond company boundaries and an all-pervasive new spirit of capitalism. This category shows us that the actor of control is not the organization as such, but the pervasive cultural discourse of expressive individualism. This makes the innovator another application of expressive individualism as a mechanism of control, but again a different variation of it. The final category of the rebellions is the only one that truly takes a reflexive stance towards the new spirit of capitalism and poses an actual challenge to it. Here, expressive individualism shows a resemblance to its original counter-cultural and critical use and functions as an encouragement to search for meaning outside the neo-liberal context. Conceiving of authentic identity beyond capitalist confines becomes an option for these practitioners. For this category, there was also more room for criticism, since the mindfulness course they followed was not arranged in their organization and they participated out of their own initiative. These courses are interesting, since they have an impact on the organizational context, and often beyond organizational interests. Here, more critical applications are likely, since there is more room for interpretation by participants. The proposed categorization on the basis of Merton's (1968) anomie theory thus forms an addition to the existing theory on the new spirit of capitalism in two ways. Firstly, the three categories of conformism, ritualism and innovation show diverse ways of how expressive individualism can be used as a mechanism of organizational control, a question that is only touched upon in very broad lines in this literature. Secondly, the category of the rebellions shows how employees might develop authenticity as a means of resisting organizational logics.

Authenticity forms an important cultural focus in late modern society in functional domains such as spirituality (Heelas, 1996), therapy culture (Illouz, 2008), consumer culture (Campbell, 1987) and work. Given that it is not an ontological feature, but a social value system, it is important to analyze how this cultural discourse is used in these diverse domains. In this study, the focus was on the new spirit of capitalism and its relation to authenticity, but Merton's anomie typology also holds promise for other cultural domains where authenticity is used. This raises questions that have potential for future research. The study did not encounter any participants who were outspokenly critical of the expressive courses themselves. All of them embrace mindfulness or OMD as a means to self-discovery. People critical of the discourse of self-discovery might reveal more about how mechanisms of control underlie the new spirit of capitalism in organizations. The category of retreatists was also not encountered in these particular case studies. Other case studies outside the capitalist mainstream might illustrate complete rejection of both expressive individualist beliefs and organizational utilitarian goals. Finally, the category of the rebellions was in this study found in the mindfulness case study that was unconnected to a particular organization, but further research might reveal whether this category also plays a role in courses within companies. This chapter has enabled initial exploration by means of Merton's typology of the very diverse applications of expressive individualism in the new spirit of capitalism.

NOTES

1.   This brings many paradoxes that characterize this 'culture of authenticity'. While authenticity is portrayed as exempt of social norms and conformity, 'being your-

self' becomes itself a collective norm in late modern culture, as can be seen in advertisements, social media or youth subcultures such as hipster culture. This implies that people can be socialized in this norm of authenticity, even though its most important belief is that we have to get rid of the alienating influence of socialization and 'just be ourselves' (see also Cortois, 2018).

2. The fact that this is a social expectation illustrates that being authentic paradoxically also is a social role in itself.

3. The relation between Romanticism and nature especially becomes apparent in the writings of Rousseau on the 'noble savage' (1754). In contrast to other social contract thinkers such as Hobbes, who views the state of nature as 'solitary, poor, nasty, brutish and short' and a 'war of all against all', Rousseau perceives this state as harmonious and has an optimist view on human nature. For him, society has a detrimental effect on the originally good and authentic nature of man, because it promotes envy and self-consciousness.

4. This business challenge consisted of an additional project to the usual tasks the managers had in their company. The project required them to be more creative, to come up with solutions to structural problems that the company had struggled with already and to go beyond their specific business expertise. It required them to work together with managers from other divisions of the organization and to align with the general business strategy. In a final phase, they had to present the outcome of this project to the board of directors.

5. To get an idea of the demographic background of the anonymously quoted interlocutors, we give the age and the (last practiced) profession or function in the company accompanied by a pseudonym.

6. No moral meaning is attributed to these symbols, certainly not in terms of one option being in any way better than the other. These symbols were used after Merton who also uses them, but he uses them in a different context, i.e. to analyze deviant behavior. In his analysis, the '+' is reserved for legitimate use of goals or means, and the '–' for illegitimate use, i.e. deviant, according to the general opinion. He relies here on institutionalized opinions of what is deemed legitimate and illegitimate.

7. The coaches suggested that while this critical reflection occurs in every company, it might happen more frequently in certain companies with conservative cultures. This observation suggests that the company culture might work as an intermediate variable that influences people in the application of the expressivist ethos in the company. Further research to the interaction between company cultures and expressive individualist trainings might shed further light on this.

8. This argumentation, however, completely puts the responsibility of finding the right position on the side of the individual, while we also saw that the company culture might have a negative impact on the employees. The coaches do not question the company culture and that there might also be some work on this side even when 'the right individual is on the right place'.

9. This label does not have a positive connotation, but merely indicates that these employees use the expressive ideology to question their current situation and to potentially change it in their own benefit. What they criticize is merely their specific context or the means to achieve their goals, but not the overarching neo-liberal goal of material success. In this regard, the label might be misleading since critique is not used as a challenge to culturally accepted neo-liberal goals. Instead, one might even claim that all things considered, these managers are the

least critical, because the ethics of authenticity makes them pursue their own interest even beyond alternative values such as loyalty to a company.

REFERENCES

Aldred, L. (2002). Money Is Just Spiritual Energy: Incorporating the New Age. *Journal of Popular Culture, 35*(4), 61–74.

Barker, K. K. (2014). Mindfulness Meditation: Do-It-Yourself Medicalization of Every Moment. *Social Science and Medicine, 106,* 168–76. https://doi.org/10.1016/j.socscimed.2014.01.024

Becker, G. (1976). *The Economic Approach to Human Behavior.* Chicago: University of Chicago Press.

Bell, E. & Taylor, S. (2003). The Elevation of Work: Pastoral Power and the New Age Work Ethic. *Organization, 10*(2), 329–49.

Bell, E. & Taylor, S. (2004). 'From outward bound to inward bound': The Prophetic Voices and Discursive Practices of Spiritual Management Development. *Human Relations, 57*(4), 439–66. https://doi.org/10.1177/0018726704043895

Bellah, R., Madson, R., Swidler, A., Tipton, S. & Sullivan, W. (2008). *Habits of the Heart: Individualism and Commitment in American Life.* Berkeley: University of California Press.

Bennis, W. (2009). *On Becoming a Leader: The Leadership Classic.* New York: Basic Books.

Boltanski, L. & Chiapello, E. (2005). *The New Spirit of Capitalism.* London: Verso.

Bröckling, U. (2015). *The Entrepreneurial Self Fabricating a New Type of Subject.* London: Sage.

Burke, V. & Collins, D. (2004). Optimizing Skills Transfer via Outdoor Management Development, Part II: The Client's Perspective. *Journal of Management Development, 23,* 715–28.

Burletson, L. & Grint, K. (1996). The Deracination of Politics: Outdoor Management Development. *Management Learning, 27*(2), 185–202.

Campbell, C. (1987). *The Romantic Ethic and the Spirit of Modern Consumerism.* London: Blackwell.

Carette, J. & King, R. (2004). *Selling Spirituality: The Silent Takeover of Religion.* London: Routledge.

Case, P. & Gosling, J. (2010). The Spiritual Organization: Critical Reflections on the Instrumentality of Workplace Spirituality. *Journal of Management, Spirituality and Religion, 7*(4), 257–82. https://doi.org/10.1080/14766086.2010.524727

Corner, P. D. (2009). Workplace Spirituality and Business Ethics: Insights from an Eastern Spiritual Tradition. *Journal of Business Ethics, 85*(3), 377–89. https://doi.org/10.1007/s10551-008-9776-2

Cortois, L. (2018). *Becoming an Individual: A Cultural-Sociological Study of Socialization into Individualistic Scripts.* Leuven: PhD dissertation, KU Leuven University.

Cortois, L. & Laermans, R. (2018). Rethinking Individualization: The Basic Script and the Three Variants of Institutionalized Individualism. *European Journal of Social Theory, 21*(1), 60–78. https://doi.org/10.1177/1368431017698474

Cortois, L., Aupers, S. & Houtman, D. (2018). The Naked Truth: Mindfulness and the Purification of Religion. *Journal of Contemporary Religion, 33*(2), 303–17. https://doi.org/10.1080/13537903.2018.1469276

Costea, B., Crump, N. & Amiridis, K. (2008). Managerialism, the Therapeutic Habitus and the Delf in Contemporary Organizing. *Human Relations*, *61*(5), 661–85. https://doi.org/10.1177/0018726708091763

De Keere, K. (2014). From a Self-Made to an Already-Made Man: A Historical Content Analysis of Professional Advice Literature. *Acta Sociologica*, *57*(4), 311–24. https://doi.org/10.1177/0001699314552737

Du Gay, P. (1994). Making up Managers: Bureaucracy, Enterprise and the Liberal Art of Separation. *British Journal of Sociology*, *45*(4), 655–74.

Ehrenberg, A. (1991). *Le Culte de la Performance*. Paris: Calman-Lévy.

Fleming, P. (2009). *Authenticity and the Cultural Politics of Work. New Forms of Informal Control*. Oxford: Oxford University Press.

Fleming, P. (2014). *Resisting Work: The Corporatization of Life and Its Discontents*. Philadephia: Temple University Press.

Fleming, P. & Sturdy, A. (2011). 'Being Yourself' in the Electronic Sweatshop: New Forms of Normative Control. *Human Relations*, *64*(2), 177–200. https://doi.org/10.1177/0018726710375481

Foucault, M. (2010). *The Birth of Biopolitics: Lectures at the Collège de France 1978–1979.* London: Palgrave.

Greeson, J. M., Webber, D. M., Smoski, M. & Brantley, J. (2012). Changes in Spirituality Partly Explain Health-Related Quality of Life Outcomes after Mindfulness-Based Stress Reduction. *Journal of Behavioral Medicine*, *34*(6), 508–18. https://doi.org/10.1007/s10865-011-9332-x.Changes

Hammer, O. (2001). *Claiming Knowledge: Strategies of Epistemology from Theosophy to the New Age*. Leiden: Brill.

Hanegraaff, W. (1996). *New Age Religion and Western Culture: Esotericism in the Mirror of Secular Thought*. Leiden: Brill.

Heelas, P. (1996). *The New Age Movement: The Celebration of the Self and the Sacralization of Modernity*. Oxford: Blackwell Publishers.

Heelas, P. (2003). Work, Ethics, Soft Capitalism and the 'Turn to Life'. In P. Du Gay and M. Pryke (Eds), *Cultural Economy: Cultural Analysis and Commercial Life* (pp. 78–96). London: Sage.

Illouz, E. (2008). *Saving the Modern Soul: Therapy, Emotions and the Culture of Self-Help*. Berkeley: University of California Press.

Islam, G., Holm, M. & Karjalainen, M. (2017). Sign of the Times: Workplace Mindfulness as an Empty Signifier. *Organization*. https://doi.org/10.1177/1350508417740643

Jones, P. & Oswick, C. (2007). Inputs and Outcomes of Outdoor Management Development: Of Design, Dogma and Dissonance. *British Journal of Management*, *18*(4), 327–41.

Kabat-Zinn, J. (1994). *Full Catastrophe Living: Using the Wisdom of Your Body and Mind to Face Stress, Pain and Illness*. New York: Random House.

Lash, S. & Urry, J. (1994). *Economies of Signs and Space*. London: Sage.

Mayo, E. (1945). *The Social Problems of an Industrial Civilization*. Boston: Harvard University Press.

Merton, R. K. (1938). Social Structure and Anomie. *American Sociological Review*, *3*(5), 37–45. https://doi.org/10.2307/2084686

Merton, R. K. (1968). Continuities in the Theory of Social Structure and Anomie. In R. Merton (Ed.), *Social Theory and Social Structure*. New York: Free Press.

Negri, A. & Hardt, M. (2000). *Empire*. Cambridge, MA: Harvard University Press.

Parsons, T. (2007). Individuality and Institutionalized Individualism. In T. Parsons and G. Sciortino (Ed.), *American Society: A Theory of Societal Community*. Boulder: Paradigme.

Parsons, T. and G. M. Platt (1973). *The American University*. Cambridge, MA: Harvard University Press.

Rose, N. (1989). *Governing the Soul: The Shaping of the Private Self*. London: Free Association Books.

Taylor, C. (1989). *Sources of the Self: The Making of Modern Identity*. Cambridge, MA: Harvard University Press.

Taylor, C. (1991). *Ethics of Authenticity*. Cambridge, MA: Harvard University Press.

Tipton, S. (1982). *Getting Saved from the Sixties: The Transformation of Moral Meaning in American Culture*. Berkeley: University of California Press.

Turner, B. S. (2005). Talcott Parsons's Sociology of Religion and the Expressive Revolution: The Problem of Western Individualism. *Journal of Classical Sociology, 5*(3), 303–18.

Vallas, S. P. & Cummins, E. R. (2015). Personal Branding and Identity Norms in the Popular Business Press: Enterprise Culture in an Age of Precarity. *Organization Studies, 36*(3), 293–319. https://doi.org/10.1177/0170840614563741

Wilson, J. (2014). *Mindful America: The Mutual Transformation of Buddhist Meditation and American Culture*. Oxford: Oxford University Press.

4. A 'juggly mummy's' life history of teaching yoga: embodied postfeminism and neoliberal spirituality

Amanda Peticca-Harris, Kseniya Navazhylava and Genevieve Shanahan

[At the meeting for the city recreation programs], I thought I want to sit at the table with yoga instructors because I want to know more about yoga. And as I sat there, one of the other yoga instructors said, "You know what I really hate? I really hate these people come teach yoga with no credentials." And I said, "Really? Why?" And she said they don't know what they are doing and they're going to put people at risk and everything else. And I said, "Yeah, but I'll tell you in India when they were doing yoga a few centuries ago, they didn't have a certification. Because yoga is a journey for me and for you. We are growing together. It's not about me teaching you, it's about me showing you, you doing it – and both of us learning. So, what do you need a certification for that for?' (Maria)

The first author was initially introduced to Maria through an extended interview that she conducted in the summer of 2015 as part of her doctoral research, a study that focused on the lived experiences of yoga teachers in North America. At the time of the interview, Maria was a divorced, 39-year-old mother of two children, aged 10 and 12. With a college diploma in social work, Maria found herself clocking into a nine-to-five job as a case manager for personal support workers focused on spinal cord injuries, supplementing her income by teaching yoga classes part time at a local gym (albeit, as the opening quote here reveals, without the recognized certification credentials).

Maria's interview struck us as being especially salient for exploring the relationship between spirituality and neoliberalism as it problematized many facets found within the discourse of yoga that highlight a dark side to New Age spirituality and wellness practice that, to date, is rarely expressed in the existing literature and popular media. Thus the aim of this empirical chapter is to illustrate, through the use of a life history approach (Tierney, 1998), the ways in which Maria navigates various experiences of metaphysical embodiment (health, illness, childbearing/childrearing) and the economic necessity of supporting herself and her family through paid body work, both in personal support work and her spiritual work as a yoga teacher.

To do this we follow the proposal that teaching yoga is a form of body work (Wolkowitz, 2002), labour that is done on one's own body as well as on the bodies of others (Twigg, 2010). Earlier body work studies have been primarily concerned with those who engage in changing the aesthetic appearance or overall well-being of bodies, including salon workers (e.g., Gimlin, 1996; Kang, 2003), massage therapists (e.g., Oerton, 2004; Sullivan, 2014), and fitness instructors (e.g., Maguire, 2008; Harvey et al., 2017). Yoga does not fit neatly into traditional conceptions of body work, though it does share some of the defining characteristics such as workers' employment experiences and challenges. This literature highlights that, across various occupations, such work can be dirty, disgusting, stigmatized, sexualized and undertaken in precarious conditions. Further, many of the challenges that body workers face are grounded in inherent inequalities that they endure based on gender, race and class. Few body work studies have examined these conditions from a postmaternal, whole-life perspective, or taken into account work–life balance or workers' competing family priorities and commitments, which may attract people to this form of flexible yet precarious employment. Given the disappearance of gendered, progressive policies oriented towards mothers in neoliberal economies, women workers face new ethico-political struggles in crafting their careers in contexts that have become anti-maternal, glorifying market work and devaluing family work (Stephens, 2012; Perrier & Fannin, 2017a).

Set against the broad backdrop of the research question 'How can gendered embodiment be understood in the context of neoliberal precarity?', the life history approach taken in this chapter provides the reader with a glimpse into a more holistic account of who Maria understands herself to be and the struggles, paradoxes and tensions she experiences within the discourse of yoga, especially while balancing the demands of teaching yoga as a source of income while simultaneously relying on it as a personal reprieve and health-management tool. In this chapter, we contribute to scholarship on embodied spirituality and postfeminism by exploring the ways in which Maria uses yoga to manage the challenges of neoliberal, postmaternal society, specifically in the contexts of health, family and work. At the same time, we demonstrate how this mobilization of spirituality reinforces neoliberal, postmaternal and postfeminist discourses, exacerbating the psychological ill effects of this context by individualizing responsibility.

YOGA AS A POSTFEMINIST, NEOLIBERAL, SPIRITUAL PRACTICE

Maria narrates her experiences of teaching yoga in part by drawing on a broader neoliberal, postfeminist agenda that disrupts the notion of the 'yummy mummy' (Negra, 2009), as she responds to contextual factors that enable her to spend a great deal of time in the home, caring for her two children. The 'yummy mummy' label comes from media studies (McRobbie, 2008) and describes a type of white, heterosexual, celebrity-influenced woman who, following success in her own career, has made a choice to retreat from the general labour market to combine motherhood and self-care with part-time or from-home work (Allen & Osgood, 2009, p. 5) and, importantly, enjoys it and is successful at it. As a cultural phenomenon represented in film, magazines, and now through various online platforms, the iconic 'yummy mummy' represents the 'good mother' as a consumer subject who acquires the highest quality goods for herself and her family (Fraser, 2013). This ideal of a middle-class woman who is able to devote significant time to parenting while at the same time being entrepreneurial in terms of crafting new arrangements for her professional activity also aligns well with the literature on 'mumpreneurs'. Nel et al. (2010) observe that these women forge a business model based on care and community building rather than necessarily prioritizing business profit. Mumpreneurship appears as a female response to unconventional economic spaces, such as family and community (Ekinsmyth, 2011), while at the same time connecting to women's traditional caring responsibilities (Lewis, 2014, p. 120).

These categories can be understood as aspects of postfeminism, more broadly understood as a discourse characteristic of the neoliberal era, in which responsibility for gender equality is individualized and cast specifically in terms of economic success, and a new feminine ideal of an entrepreneurial yet nurturing female subject is enforced both from without and within (Sullivan & Delaney, 2017; Baker & Kelan, 2019; Liu, 2019). It suggests that women 'should aspire to be "high commitment" wives and mothers who embody passion and glamour while climbing the corporate or entrepreneurial ladder' (Sullivan & Delaney, 2017, p. 837). Postfeminism as a discourse validates and supports postmaternalism, under which care work is marginalized, relegated to the private sphere and excluded as grounds for public support. Through postmaternal thinking, 'neoliberal policies transform social responsibilities for dependent others into "burdens" to be borne by individuals' (Perrier & Fannin, 2017a, p. 383), specifically women. In pursuit of 'having it all', and to support these care 'burdens', women are encouraged to engage in alternative entrepreneurial pursuits that can be balanced with care duties, such as freelancing, portfolio careers and mumpreneurship, with little recognition of the attendant economic risks (Sullivan & Delaney, 2017, p. 839). As in neoliberalism itself, agency is enshrined and structural constraints, including those of caring interdependence, are denied. As we go on to show, Maria's experience diverges from the postfeminist ideals of the mumpreneurial 'yummy mummy', as her status as a single mother excludes the possibility of choosing to retreat to work at home or a part-time job in order to spend more time with her children. Instead, she must negotiate between the demands of her family, a full-time job and yoga practice as an additional source of income.

We hone in on teaching yoga as a postfeminist, spiritual practice that reproduces and enhances neoliberal discourses in part because of its complexity and current popularity. The word yoga comes from an ancient Sanskrit word *yug* meaning 'to unite', or join together to create a balance between one's internal and external consciousness (Vivekananda, 2005). Yet, the contemporary practice of yoga as we know it today bears little to no resemblance to pre-modern Indian traditions, as Maria aptly points out, which were believed to emphasize stillness and meditation. Yoga now, in the West at least, invokes an image (or stereotype) of a sweaty, glowing, toned, spandex-clad, skinny woman performing a series of gymnastics-like postures, understood by yoga practitioners as a sequence of *asanas* that are tied together through *vinyasa* (movements), and are connected by a steady breathing technique (*ujjayi pranayama*).

The economic significance of yoga is striking. In North America alone, the yoga industry generates more than US$16 billion per year, through practitioners' spending on yoga classes, clothing, equipment and accessories (Yoga Alliance, 2016). The number of yoga practitioners in just the United States has increased to over 36 million, up from 20.4 million in 2012, with women representing 72 per cent of practitioners (Yoga Alliance, 2016). Much of the existing academic literature on yoga is related to its history or to the health benefits of regular yoga practice. For example, De Michelis (2004) reports that the focused gaze (*dristi*) and *ujjayi* breathing is believed to centre the practitioner's attention, with the effect of promoting health, stress reduction, authenticity, beauty and spiritual well-being. More metaphysically, traditional spiritual beliefs aligned with the yogic lifestyle presuppose a concern for connection and world harmony (Dagar et al., 2018), which in the East is traditionally understood as taking distance from the ego and its insecurities as a source of suffering. Subjectively, the practice of yoga is directed at letting go of the self-ego in order to build the self-spirit that has no 'I', that is distilled harmoniously in the surrounding context.

Despite its ubiquity, however, yoga remains relatively unexamined in organizational research. As suggested by Morley (2001), 'the academic analysis of yoga must extend beyond textual analysis and engage with the experience of practitioners' (p. 73), given that little is known about the work and identities of those who teach yoga, mostly, as in this case, who identify as being women. This is of particular surprise given that the yoga industry has boomed, and supply of yoga teachers has also increased. For example, in 2017, there were over 72,000 registered certified yoga teachers with Yoga Alliance, and there are two people interested in becoming a yoga teacher for every one teacher in the United States (Yoga Alliance, 2016), while many others are believed to teach without formal certification.

Yoga teachers most commonly work as independent contractors, sometimes working at yoga studios and gyms for group classes with zero-hour contracts, sometimes working in clients' homes for private sessions. Zero-hour contracts are increasingly common under neoliberalism (Standing, 2011, p. 42), constituting a type of flexible employment agreement that does not guarantee the worker any work, pay, professional progress or standard social package (Harvey et al., 2017). In this way, employers enjoy the ability to rapidly resize their workforce, while workers gain access to relatively informal, often part-time work that may fit more easily around care and other work responsibilities. As independent contractors, furthermore, yoga instructors can be understood as operating within the 'gig economy' (Friedman, 2014). Evoking the flexible yet inconsistent work of musicians (Harvey et al., 2017), gig workers perhaps enjoy greater control of their time and work practices, yet their exposure to the vagaries of the market is complete (Petriglieri et al., 2019). Additionally, in contrast to a prevalent discourse of emancipation, such flexible employment in fact demands a high level of emotional labour and commitment (Harvey et al., 2017), in this case commitment to practising, progressively developing and teaching yoga.

Here we posit that, when yoga becomes a part of a spirituality–economy nexus through incorporation into professionals' work and non-work lives, it facilitates the transformation of workers into entrepreneurial subjects who are personally responsible for their own employability and health (Godrej, 2017). Sullivan and Delaney (2017), in their study of the role of the evangelical Christian prosperity gospel in network marketing, identify a number of ways in which both neoliberalism and postfeminism can dovetail with individualistic spiritual discourses. The tying together of spirituality and entrepreneurship arguably deprives the worker of the ability to critique or complain – when a God/god is responsible for one's (potential) economic success, economic failure must be tied to the individual's spiritual or moral shortcomings. This corresponds with Godrej's (2017) claims that, while yoga has long acted as a means of spiritual self-discipline and self-care, under neoliberalism this technology of the self reflects an 'imperative – and responsibility – to maximize human vital capacity through self-management, investment in oneself, optimization of one's own well-being, and thus of one's future value' (p. 781). In its modern, Western forms, yoga is often individualized and couched in terms of personal responsibility for health, spirituality and fulfilment. The spiritual veneer of this type of yogic practice can even operate to displace ethical concern for the effects of neoliberalism, tempting the practitioner to view social inequality as the consequence of insufficient self-discipline (Godrej, 2017, p. 786). Economic subjects become loaded with full responsibility for their life history, and (perhaps ironically) the 'ego' becomes emphasized over the 'context'. Hence, we would argue that neoliberalism renders difficult the incorporation of a traditional yogic system of beliefs into one's lifestyle. The practice of yoga becomes an instrument to strengthen the self-ego in place of the self-spirit, focusing on 'me time', working on one's own body and making money from this process. This transformation can be understood as a response to neoliberalized economic conditions that dismantle traditional social support systems, as seen unfolding in four interconnected contexts: health, spirituality, family and work.

LIFE HISTORY METHODOLOGY

According to Watson and Watson-Franke (1985), a 'life history is any retro-spective account by the individual of his [*sic*] life in whole or part, in written or oral form, that has been elicited or prompted by another person' (p. 2). These life stories act as a meaning system from which an individual can interpret reality and act in a way that provides personal meaning (Peticca-Harris & McKenna, 2013). Life histories then act as self-narratives, which give shape to an individual's account of the relationships among events across time. In developing a self-narrative, the individual attempts to establish coherent connections among life events that are systemically related and unfold sequen-tially (Gergen & Gergen, 1986). Tierney (1998) suggests that the life-history approach enables a researcher to gain insights about both the comings and goings of a person's life and how they live. The life history thus acts as a portal into the life happenings of another person, providing a clear outline of key events and milestones. It also provides a more illustrative landscape, rich with descriptions that vividly paint the meaningful connections between these events. In this chapter, we provide a space for Maria's experiences to unfold sequentially, in terms of both the historical events as she recounts them, as well as the importance she attaches to these events in her interview. As such, we present the findings through various excerpts related to three broad but overlapping spheres that have shaped Maria's sense of self: yoga as it relates to health, family and work. We unpack these themes in the following section.

YOGA AND HEALTH: TAKING RESPONSIBILITY FOR ONE'S OWN MEDICAL SUPPORT

Maria's yoga practice can be traced back to the health ailments she experienced in her early 30s. Yoga became a home practice that enabled her to find relief from pain induced by tumours in her hips and helped to improve her mobility. As she recounts:

> I was a runner and sports in general was such a big part of my life and then I hit a wall because the tumor was above my hip and I've never been the same. And that was in 2009, and I've watched things decline like the lengths I could walk, or certain stretches. There are things I can't even do anymore with that leg. So, I see things happening to me and I have no other choice but to do yoga. You know? I felt pain. But I decided I wanted to feel better. When I do yoga, mentally, all my stress is gone, and my body doesn't hurt ... And yoga became the thing that actually kept me mobile. And then my passion for the yoga for my own health sort of transformed into helping other people get through health issues that I believe that Western medicine can never solve.
>
> I guess I don't believe in Western medicine because I don't even know much about it but I just feel like, okay I have an issue, you give me a pill, I go away. It doesn't solve why the issue ... like for example, these bone tumors. You can give me a painkiller, or you can give me, an injection like the one I got today. You're not doing anything to find out why are you actually developing this and maybe what can we do to stop that? Where, I feel like yoga is sort of addressing that piece like naturally I'm trying to help my body sort of eliminate certain things that I feel like I go to specialists, I've been to almost all of them in the city. I go to them, I waste half my day for nothing. Nothing they don't even, I have a broken hip and I have walked with a limp for like two years and you don't even offer me a cane. Nothing. Every person I go to, I go to physio ... they say well we can physio you until you're fixed. Well the surgeon, the surgeon says you're too young. I'm not going to fix you yet, you go to the doctor and well I'm not going to give you drugs because you will get addicted. And nobody wants to help because they can't figure out why someone under 40 has this issue. It's supposed to be an 80-year-old issue.

In this excerpt we see that Maria's foray into the practice of yoga emerged out of a desperation generated by lack of support from the medical community. Being batted around the Ontario healthcare system without much success or relief and feeling as though only her symptoms were being treated, she turned to yoga for physical, subjective and economic reasons: "I also needed [yoga] for my mental health. And I mean, I do it in my own house. I don't go to a gym. Mostly because I can't afford it and I don't have the childcare." Maria's connection with yoga is entrenched in trying to find her own solutions to her physical condition. She is agentic, trying to use her own athletic ability to remedy her body's physical and psychological trauma. Here, she is not teaching yoga only from an altruistic motivation to help others, as is often suggested in the existing body work literature (e.g., Lawler, 1997; McMurray, 2012). Instead, yoga is presented as a symbiotic practice whereby yoga teachers are able to take care of themselves, as well as others. Further, Maria's experience highlights the ways in which some individuals are bypassing the medical community and acting as their own health advocates by taking it upon themselves to find self-healing 'cures' rather than demand more of the medical professionals who are treating them.

While researchers have paid some attention to a shift towards non-allopathic or alternative medicalized remedies (see Fulder, 1996; Sutcliffe, 2003), it is rarely positioned in a way that foregrounds the failings of the medical community as a trigger for this shift in regime. Diminished trust in Western medicine produces an individualization of care, placing increased responsibility on the sick or injured to rise to the challenge and overcome their own medical adversity. This both represents a 'crisis of legitimization' within biomedicine and amplifies the alternative and holistic practices that are challenging it (Hancock et al., 2015). Twigg (2000) acknowledges that many self-care practices such as yoga are 'packaged in the language of therapy' (p. 390). This, in turn, aligns with what Furedi (2003) has termed 'therapy culture', in which North American consumers are taking a self-help or do-it-yourself approach to their overall health regimes.

A second important feature regarding Maria's own personal yoga practice is its place and space. While contemporary yoga is often depicted as happening in an urban yoga studio or as a home-based practice rooted in ritualized self-care (Valente & Marotta, 2005), Maria admits she practises at home due to the cost of studio-based classes (which, on average, run between US$12 and $20 per one-hour class – see NAMASTA, 2005). This economic situation is further exacerbated by the demands of her role as a single mother and a lack of access to affordable childcare.

We thus see how the spiritual practice of yoga can operate, within a neoliberal context, to facilitate the shifting of responsibility for health and employability from the state and employers to individuals. A working woman in the neoliberal age is encouraged to make time and space to heal herself rather than relying on the support structures of the family (in traditional patriarchal cultures), the state (in welfare-state cultures) or community organization (in feminist cultures). While postfeminism might read Maria's response as an entrepreneurial approach to her own health, her choice to grasp an opportunity for self-care is at the same time a reaction to the structural demands of the healthcare and welfare context. In this way, the spiritual focus within yoga on self-mastery and self-healing can function to obscure the ways in which community and state support are lacking.

YOGA AND FAMILY: CHOOSING AGAINST AUTHENTIC CONVERSATION ABOUT PRECARITY

In addition to coping with her physical condition, Maria also reveals that she has a conflicted relationship with her status as a single mother. She explains that at the same time as confronting the hip tumours, she was considering growing her family:

> I was approaching 35 or something and I was like wow, I want to have another kid. Doesn't look like I'm going to have the love of my life. I had a boyfriend. I was like I want a baby. I don't care if you stay, I want another baby. And we are still, like we have a good relationship, but we don't live together or anything. But yeah, I'm still alone with the kids.

With the perceived ticking of her biological clock, the desire for more children presented itself and she opted to have a second child in spite of her tentative and precarious relationship with her partner. Yet, as she reveals, the practicalities of her reality as a single mother make her day-to-day life very challenging at times:

> It kind of sucks because it's like, I would never in the world give up my kids, you know? They're the best things that ever happened to me but as a woman, you can pretty much kiss anything goodbye unless you have someone that's going to look after you, you know, give you a nanny and pay all your bills and everything and let you go do what you need to do for you. You're not going to fly. You have a ball and chain and then you're going to live with frustration. Just this morning, I was talking to Luke's dad, and I was saying I wish I could get to the point of enjoying [Luke's] company, I said but maybe it is the fact that he just prevents me from doing anything … even to go pee. I can't do that without being harassed, you know? You know but, and I have so many things I want to do. So many things. And I can't. Like, I want to teach myself how to play the guitar and I have reached a certain point and I would love to put some time into practice but I can't pick it up. As soon as I pick it up, it's taken away from me. People are grabbing it, people ask me questions – I can't do anything. So, I feel like I come home from work and I sit here trapped with all these things I would love to do and I can't. I'm trapped. But then if I feel like that then I'm a bad mother.

Here we see the tensions mounting as she discusses her day-to-day challenges, which again correspond to financial insecurity. Perceived as an ally in restoring damaged health as described earlier, here yoga and other leisure hobbies come into conflict with Maria's daily work and family routines. She recognizes the need to invest more time in order to improve, but her current family situation – a single working mother of two children – leaves no space nor time for individual non-organizational professional development. Family pressure to let go of these hobbies, and more specifically her own time, persistently push her towards questioning her ability to develop. Although Maria positions herself as independent and strong-willed, we see a glimpse of reliance, dependence and submissiveness as she regrets not having someone to pay her way. Here, as she vividly portrays the embodied reality of caring responsibilities and the struggle to balance the demands of work and motherhood, childbearing and childrearing are portrayed as an individual's responsibility rather than a social issue (Vair, 2013). We get the sense that she thought somehow it would be different than it is, that the rhetoric and reality of independent single motherhood don't quite align. In addition to having financial limitations, she also watches her own passions and goals stagnate due to the demands of rearing two children on her own. She shares that she feels trapped by her circumstances, despite the role her own choices have played in shaping these circumstances. Her success is externalized and conditional, rather than within her control:

> I feel like I do what I have to do to pay the bills and my kids have stunted me from any type of progression I would like to have in my life. I mean I can't even finish a thought if it's near 4-o-clock because I got to shut down and rush out to facilitate all of that and I can't take a course and I can't do really anything.

She blames her children for her lack of progress and, as the next section illustrates, this includes her employment opportunities. Yet, sadly, her desperation is further compounded by her feeling that she is not able to speak openly about the overarching fear of being judged as a bad mother and about the limitations that the choice she made in relation to kids has placed on her life. She disrupts the notion that motherhood is somehow a natural way of being, comprised of sacred relationships and an intense uncomplicated love for one's children (Thurer, 1994; Nelson & England, 2002). She discounts motherhood, which according to Vair (2013) reaffirms the undervaluing of women's care work, a key to subordination (p. 169), but in another light also signifies that she is trying to establish an identity separate from postfeminist ideals of retreatism into the home (Lewis, 2014). Most striking of all, Maria does not question social structures, but instead focuses on her own abilities to circumnavigate the challenges that the unforgiving and contradictory structures of home and work present (Peticca-Harris, 2016).

The possibility of an authentic conversation about the challenges and sacrifices of motherhood is thereby problematized in a neoliberal society, where self-actualization, especially in the form of professional development, is seen as the responsibility of the individual. A postfeminist mother has to contend with both generalized devaluing of care work and the absence of support for this work, and she searches for revaluation and balance in spirituality. The neoliberal reading of yoga emphasizes conversation with oneself directed at changing oneself, in place of an open conversation with society at large directed at changing the status quo. In this way, yoga as a form of neoliberal spirituality can be seen as silencing discussion of the struggles of working and caring in postmaternal society.

YOGA AND WORK: INCREASING FINANCIAL AUTONOMY, EXACERBATING STRESS

As a single mother, the ways in which Maria narrates her career opportunities are conditioned above all by the need to earn an income and support her family. For example, she states, 'What I feel in my life is that I work to make money and I do what I'm told. But it's very rare to do work that you feel passion for.' Primarily, she is speaking about her full-time role as a caseworker and she goes on to share:

> I made the decision to be a caseworker based on my financial need and not on my goals and desires. And when I saw the job itself and I was like, I don't want to do this anymore, right? Like manage case studies? I don't want to do this anymore. You know? I was kind of tired of that so the job itself, like if you look at the job description, it's not really interesting.

As mentioned, Maria supplements her income as a personal support worker by teaching fitness classes, most recently as a yoga instructor. Sullivan and Baruch (2009) suggest that some people hold multiple jobs in order to experience authenticity and express their whole and true self through work. While Maria does not frame teaching yoga as a passion or full-time professional pursuit, she does get personal satisfaction from teaching yoga:

> Yeah. I helped a lot of people in fitness, you know? Which is really weird because you wouldn't think so and it's not through fitness that you end up helping them. The yoga brings them for a certain thing, and you end up on a journey together, you know? And I think, remember I said some people like to help people … I think, and do well because I am able to guide them through other areas of life outside of yoga.

Although she finds her job as a case manager uninteresting, her desire to help people is evident. Yoga provides her with this platform. Additionally, it provides her some financial security: 'And you know, for me, the fitness, has always been the back-pocket job for today's labour market. So, whenever I experience layoffs, which is regular, then I have that in my back pocket, and I can survive while I look for work.' This 'back-pocket' job as a possibility to generate income demands entrepreneurialism and reflects a sense that one's well-being is one's personal responsibility, as suggested by Maria in earlier fragments. Harvey et al. (2017) suggest that such an understanding is currently promoted throughout the economy, with entrepreneurialism often presented as the only way to navigate precarity. Teaching yoga acts as an insurance policy for difficult financial periods, which she notes occur regularly. She is also able to sweeten the total compensation available to her:

> So right now, I'm only doing 2 classes per week. But I remember using that as a way to negotiate in my other role. Like, I remember somebody wanted to hire me and they said, you know, we can only pay you this much; I said, listen, I will work for you, but I need more money. So, what you're going to do, you're going to give me an hour off a week and I'm going to go teach fitness in that time under your time and get paid. That's how I will make it up.

Maria is not moonlighting as a yoga teacher until her 'big break', nor is she trying to experience meaningfulness through holding a second job as suggested by Caza et al. (2018), or even trying to become a hybrid entrepreneur (Raffiee & Feng, 2014). Instead, teaching yoga is a second job, a 'gig' alongside a broader series of other professional activities. Behind the allure of flexibility, teaching yoga on a part-time, zero-hour contract basis means that Maria is not guaranteed work or pay, and the employers (gyms and studios) retain full control over scheduling (Harvey et al., 2017). Maria uses teaching yoga to safeguard against the precarity of the broader labour market, yet the teaching itself is also fragile and insecure. While Maria treats yoga teaching as a back-pocket plan for times of financial insecurity, diversifying her income stream and exposure to risk, she also faces the possibility of compound risk:

> I have been teaching fitness for 12 years, but I just got the job because they hired me because I'm a really good networker ... I just know how to get jobs and they needed a yoga instructor and I said, I'll do it. And they said are you a certified teacher? I said no, but I'm a certified fitness instructor who has been practicing yoga for a decade and they said okay; I said, listen, send me in a class and if they don't like me, they'll fire me.

In sum, the practice of yoga for Maria is primarily about personal self-care and helping others, and secondarily about mitigating financial insecurity. Yet, despite the rhetoric of yoga as a coping tool for managing emotional and physical turmoil, we see that teaching yoga has itself become a source of stress, given the potential that her non-certified, zero-hour contract work might abruptly end, thereby exacerbating her financial insecurity. Of note, Maria's lack of formal certification illustrates the strength of the discourse of yoga and what teaching yoga *should* encompass. The lack of recognized training credentials acts as a driver of precarity for Maria. Instead of relying on the certification, Maria conceives of yoga teaching as a kind of intuitive care work, which is subject to relational rather than professional norms – shadowing, in many ways, the role expectations of being a mother. Yet, the caring, intuitive, bodily aspect of teaching yoga is undervalued by the market, just as her mothering labour is devalued and not treated as work.

We find, then, that teaching yoga is negotiated as a source of autonomy in a delicate balance between full-time employment, which is seen as valuable work, and motherhood, which is not. While neoliberalism demands that workers be proactive in finding non-traditional contexts for monetizing their extra-organizational skills, it positions care as intuitive rather than a professional competence. For instance, as Sullivan and Delaney (2017) note, precarious entrepreneurship is framed as women 'simply talking', backed up by the traditional gender roles of evangelical Christianity, thereby depriving workers of the possibility to question the individualized economic risk and potential non-remuneration of their work. Yoga as a spiritual practice that highlights altruistic giving and self-care is similarly instrumentalized in the compounding of feminized body work as devalued, contributing to a discourse that hinders opportunities for mobilization and further professionalization of care work. These discourses and material conditions shape a postfeminist self-identity as an improbable balance between seeking autonomy and coping with a lack of control over the conditions and organization of work.

DISCUSSION

Contemporary spiritual practices such as yoga are believed to foster a widening of connectedness, achieved through self-observation and personal awareness, leading to a feeling of interconnectedness with oneself, which is then extended to other people, nature, all living beings and the divine (Liu & Robertson, 2011). These practices include not only postures, but also meditation, mantras, breathing techniques, and even devotional practices such as signing the names of the divine (Corner, 2009). Yoga as a spiritual practice primarily emphasizes connectedness to one's own abilities, meditative states of mind and higher states of interconnected being, rather than to socially approved body ideals. This reflects the premises of postfeminism that decentralize ideas of femininity, and facilitate building a postmaternal, postfeminist community through teaching and sharing a practice (Perrier & Fannin, 2017b). In this chapter, we have observed how Maria negotiates and narrates alternative experiences that portray the practice of doing and teaching yoga in a different light, revealing how gendered embodiment can be understood in the context of neoliberal precarity.

We have emphasized how the context of the gig economy leaves little space for the universal interconnectedness, love and devotion central to the spiritual practice of yoga. Instead, we find that yoga as a practice, initiated as a form of self-care, is mobilized as an entrepreneurial endeavour out of economic necessity related to Maria's status as a single mother and, thus, her caring and financial responsibilities for others. She devalues her own maternal role and spiritual practice in a context of glorification of market-based work, which is often portrayed as entrepreneurial and independent (Harvey et al., 2017), thereby crowding out the non-financial and dependent work of caring, both within the family and in yoga teacher–student relationships. Maria is a single parent, trying to make ends meet and provide for her family, while overcoming her own physical health challenges. It is difficult to see the divine, spiritual interconnection between Maria and a universal consciousness as her narrative speaks more strongly to the painful aspects of embodiment, with accounts of her ill health, childbearing and childrearing, and struggles to financially support herself and her family. In contrast to the 'yummy mummy' image constructed in popular media accounts of 'mumpreneurs', the reality of the postmaternal economy epitomized by Maria's experience reveals a much darker but also paradoxically liberating picture: finding work that fits personal demands which are shaped by health limitations, tensions between family needs and economic pressures rather than a search for ideal bodies or transcendentality.

Maria's personal yoga practice has been a beacon of hope for her own physical ailments but teaching yoga is also presented as a fail-safe, back-up option that in itself poses risk in an oversaturated labour market. As such, although details from her life history suggest an alternative, darker side to the spiritual practice of yoga and its marketization, it remains difficult to problematize the divine practice, so that remains largely uncritiqued. Without critique, the precarious working conditions are sidelined under the veneer of unity and harmony. Notably, Maria does not identify as a 'yoga teacher', but rather as a fitness instructor who teaches yoga. This may reflect her lack of recognized certification credentials as a yoga teacher, intensifying her precarity in this role. In response, Maria seems to engage in complex identity work to maintain her insecure status and income stream. She positions herself outside of many of the spiritual aspects of the practice, emphasizing the physicality of the practice, for which she is qualified, thereby downplaying its transcendental characteristics. At the same time, she highlights the relational history of yoga, in which yoga practice is a journey undertaken side by side (Randall & Munro, 2010), aligning with ideals of postmaternal community building (Perrier & Fannin, 2017b), which are, nevertheless, devalued by the market. This careful balance of discourses – of marketable physical competence and extra-market relational activity – is clearly precarious.

In this chapter, we sought above all to get close to Maria's reality, the ebb and flow of her life, and some of the significant relationships and milestones that have impacted how she understands herself and yoga. The intention here was not to generalize from Maria's experiences, but instead to emphasize her specific and unique life history such that it might resonate with others. Maria's life history is far from the glossy 'yummy mummy' experience of home retreatism; rather she struggles with negotiating her identity rooted in the three main tensions discussed earlier: responsibility and growing structural demands for self-care; authentic discontent and pressure for self-balance through spirituality; and autonomy and lack of control over the organization of work. Through her lifetime journey juggling the conflicting demands of work, life and subjectivity, Maria develops a new form of subjectivity – that of a 'juggly mummy' – involving more agency than her earlier image of motherhood suggested, yet simultaneously one that is also more limited. Although Maria has agency and choice in how she opts to live her life, her choices are always constrained by both her circumstance and broader societal regimes of truth (Foucault, 1995) or discourses that shape what, who and how a person aspires to 'be' (du Gay, 1994; Peticca-Harris & McKenna, 2013).

These discourses are both resisted and reproduced here in this chapter. In writing about Maria's engagement and struggle with a postmaternal neoliberal economy, we – three feminist academics, variously approaching the biological milestone of 35 – find ourselves both empathizing with Maria's situation and questioning her decisions, perhaps in an attempt to secure our own autonomy by framing her struggles as the consequence of ill-considered personal choice (the splitting and blaming strategy described by Baker & Kelan, 2019). As illustrated by Liu (2019), academia can be a hotbed of postfeminist discourse, and our socialization within this discursive environment surely colours how we read the choices of other women. If the perfect postfeminist woman is 'ambitious, industrious, individualistic, yet soft, sweet, nurturing' (Liu, 2019, p. 30), then Maria falls short in her intimations of frustration with her kids and in the fantasy of being taken care of by a partner. Of course this idealized identity involves an impossible balance, and so the realization of one characteristic involves the negation of the other. We perhaps bristle, for instance, at the underemphasis on care for her elderly clients as a motivation in favour of economic hustle and self-actualization – there is not enough 'feminine' sweetness presented to make the 'masculine' ambition palatable, though the latter is demanded by the postmaternal economic regime that requires she financially support her children through work outside of the home.

More pernicious, perhaps, is the seductive pull of individualized explanations for her current predicament. We fear finding ourselves trapped and frustrated, and so assign personal responsibility to Maria, for example, for her choice to have a second child outside of the context of a stable relationship, obscuring the contribution of the postmaternal social structure. Indeed, this is a common postfeminist response to economic hardship, especially. Sullivan and Delaney (2017), for instance, find that successful network marketers 'rarely acknowledge structural constraints, such as a lack of social protections, and instead tend to retrospectively narrate that struggles stem from a deficient mindset' (p. 847).

In presenting Maria's story, then, we try both to personalize and democratize understanding of the neoliberal regime, highlighting the ways in which it simultaneously constrains and serves this particular working mother. Yet this democratization is a process, a movement towards a freedom that is never achieved (Rhodes, 2019). Her own narrative is a simplification of a full life presented through her own postfeminist lens, and we further simplify and interpret this narrative with the weight of our own baggage, self-recriminations and defensive othering.

Alongside this, we would like this chapter to contribute to ongoing discussions about reproduction of the neoliberal regime through spirituality by describing a scenario in which a practice that is generally presented as transcendental – or at least liberated, emotionally oriented and inwardly directed (Liu & Robertson, 2011) – serves instead as an attempt to overcome precarity. Although such spiritual practice can lead to transformation of the subject through developing an entrepreneurial stance, this transformation does not happen as a spiritual act of self-realization. Rather the spiritual practice becomes rationalized within a personal economic programme of emancipation within the constraining conditions of single motherhood. Yoga becomes an organizing and disciplining tool, which frames this transformation within a cultural ontology of responsibility for oneself, one's body, one's authenticity and one's employment. In this way, Maria is encouraged to take control of her body and her 'embodied competencies' (Warhurst et al., 2000, p. 4), with her physical capital (Shilling, 1991) as a competitive advantage on the market (Bourdieu, 1986). Similar to the fitness industry where employees are constructed as 'walking billboards' (Zeithaml & Bitner, 1996, p. 304) for the business, the practice of yoga allows for the commodification of Maria's physical presence through instilling the responsibility, entrepreneuriality and flexibility necessary for work in the gig economy. Engaging the concepts of 'deep health' (Sointu, 2006) and spiritual transformation, yoga transcends to deeper levels of self. Where yoga is practised as a means of taking responsibility for one's own health and well-being in the context of precarious labour, employers are relieved of their responsibility for workers' health. At the same time these gig workers seek to be more competitive at work and therefore available to join a company's workforce on demand – in other words, reproducing their post-maternal selves in a neoliberal context.

Liu and Robertson (2011) suggest that spirituality works through interconnections with a higher power, human beings and nature. We have engaged the logic of interconnection by following Maria's neoliberal self-transformation through three levels of self-identity: exploring how her self is redefined by yoga on the individual level in connection to her health and well-being; on the relational level in connection to her family; and on the collective level, through negotiating space for yoga as an economic and community activity.

We emphasize how relational and collective engagement shapes Maria's interpretation of yoga, a practice that is centred on oneself, as a means of organizing her life to address the challenges of precarity through ongoing negotiations with her community. With this insight we contribute to research regarding the neoliberal reproduction of self, with a focus on collective practices central for studies of spirituality and postfeminism.

We also add to postfeminist studies by nuancing the critique of the idea that women already have the required material resources within themselves to feel well (Gill & Orgad, 2015). Yoga as a social practice, contributed positively to Maria's construction of her own physical well-being and building postmaternal community through providing care to others. This, in turn, contributed negatively to her psychological well-being by revealing the tension between subjectivities oriented towards work and care, and by increasing the pressure felt to negotiate time and space between competing responsibilities. Therefore, we delineate a delicate balance between physical and psychological resources performed by working women within the discourse of 'feminist self-care' when it is translated as a source of income in a neoliberal economy.

There is clearly scope for further consideration of the dissolution of 'work' and 'care' as pure categories shaping self-identities in neoliberal economies. While our research questions the dual opposition of work and care (England, 2005; Zelizer, 2005) through nuancing the contexts of constructing oneself under pressure of precarity, more work needs to be done to explore postmaternal community building as a social practice of taking care both of oneself and others. Recognizing interdependencies and creating communities as alternative spaces for the renegotiation of women workers' identities as employed mothers are increasingly seen as ways to navigate postmaternal conditions in neoliberal economies (Gibson-Graham & Roelvink, 2010; McRobbie, 2013). Future studies could consider investigating the implications of yogic community building (and beyond into other spiritual practices) as altruistic care in the context of the traditional heteronormative family, as opposed to constrained care in the context of working single mothers.

REFERENCES

Allen, K. & Osgood, J. (2009). Young women negotiating maternal subjectivities: The significance of social class. *Studies in the Maternal*, *1*(2), 1–17.

Baker, D. T. & Kelan, E. K. (2019). Splitting and blaming: The psychic life of neoliberal executive women. *Human Relations*, *72*(1), 69–97.

Bourdieu, P. (1986). The forms of capital. In Richardson, J. (Ed.), *Handbook of theory and research for the sociology of education* (pp. 241–58). Westport, CT: Greenwood.

Caza, B. B., Vough, H. & Puranik, H. (2018). Identity work in organizations and occupations: Definitions, theories, and pathways forward. *Journal of Organizational Behavior*, *39*(7), 889–910.

Corner, P. D. (2009). Workplace spirituality and business ethics: Insights from an Eastern spiritual tradition. *Journal of Business Ethics, 85*(3), 377–89.

Dagar, C., Pandey, A., Navare, A. & Pandey, N. (2018). How yoga practices result in human flourishing. *Academy of Management Annual Meeting*, Chicago, 10–14 August.

De Michelis, E. (2004). *A history of modern yoga.* London: Continuum.

Du Gay, P. (1994). Making up managers: Bureaucracy, enterprise and the liberal art of separation. *British Journal of Sociology, 45*, 655–74.

Ekinsmyth, C. (2011). Challenging the boundaries of entrepreneurship: The spatialities and practices of UK 'mumpreneurs'. *Geoforum 42*(1), 104–14.

England, P. (2005). Emerging theories of care work. *Annual Review of Sociology, 31*, 381–99.

Foucault, M. (1995). *Discipline and punish: The birth of the prison.* New York: Vintage Books.

Fraser, N. (2013). *Fortunes of feminism: From state-managed capitalism to neoliberal crisis.* London: Verso.

Friedman, G. (2014). Workers without employers: Shadow corporations and the rise of the gig economy. *Review of Keynesian Economics, 2*(2), 171–88.

Fulder, S. (Ed.) (1996). *The handbook of alternative and complementary medicine.* New York: Oxford University Press.

Furedi, F. (2003). *Therapy culture: Cultivating vulnerability in an anxious age.* London: Routledge.

Gergen, K. J. & Gergen, M. M. (1986). The self. In Gergen, K. J. & Gergen, M. M. (Eds), *Social psychology* (pp. 62–89). New York: Springer.

Gibson-Graham, J. K. & Roelvink, G. (2010). The nitty gritty of creating alternative economies. *Social Alternatives, 30*(1), 29–33.

Gill, R. & Orgad, S. (2015). The confidence cult(ure). *Australian Feminist Studies, 30*(86), 324–44.

Gimlin, D. (1996). Pamela's place: Power and negotiation in the hair salon. *Gender and Society, 10*, 505–26.

Godrej, F. (2017). The neoliberal yogi and the politics of yoga. *Political Theory, 45*(6), 772–800.

Hancock, P., Sullivan, K. & Tyler, M. (2015). A touch too much: Negotiating masculinity, propriety and proximity in intimate labour. *Organization Studies, 36*(12), 1715–39.

Harvey, G., Rhodes, C., Vachhani, S. J. & Williams, K. (2017). Neo-villeiny and the service sector: The case of hyper flexible and precarious work in fitness centres. *Work, Employment and Society, 31*(1), 19–35.

Kang, M. (2003). The managed hand: The commercialization of bodies and emotions in Korean immigrant owned nail salons. *Gender and Society, 17*(6), 820–39.

Lawler, K. (1997). Pain assessment. *Professional Nurse, 13*(1 Suppl), S5–8.

Lewis, P. (2014). Postfeminism, femininities and organization studies: Exploring a new agenda. *Organization Studies, 35*(12), 1845–66.

Liu, C. H. & Robertson, P. J. (2011). Spirituality in the workplace: Theory and measurement. *Journal of Management Inquiry, 20*(1), 35–50.

Liu, H. (2019). An embarrassment of riches: The seduction of postfeminism in the academy. *Organization, 26*(1), 20–37.

Maguire, J. S. (2008). Leisure and the obligation of self⬚work: An examination of the fitness field. *Leisure Studies, 27*(1), 59–75.

McMurray, R. (2012). Embracing dirt in nursing matters. In Simpson, R., Slutskaya, N., Lewis, P. and Höpfl, H. (Eds). *Dirty work: Concepts and identities* (pp. 126–42). Basingstoke: Palgrave Macmillan.

McRobbie, A. (2008). *The aftermath of feminism: Gender, culture and social change.* London: Sage.

McRobbie, A. (2013). Feminism, the family and the new 'mediated' maternalism. *New Formations, 80*(80), 119–37.

Morley, J. (2001). Inspiration and expiration: Yoga practice through Merleau-Ponty's phenomenology of the body. *Philosophy East and West, 51*(1), 73–82.

NAMASTA (2005). *A growing profession: 70,000 yoga teachers.* Retrieved October 15, 2013, from www.namasta.com/pressresources.php

Negra, D. (2009). *What a girl wants? Fantasizing the reclamation of self in postfeminism.* Abingdon: Routledge.

Nel, P., Maritz, A. & Thongprovati, O. (2010). Motherhood and entrepreneurship: The mumpreneur phenomenon. *International Journal of Organizational Innovation, 3,* 6–34.

Nelson, J. A. & England, P. (2002). Feminist philosophies of love and work. *Hypatia, 17*(2), 1–18.

Oerton, S. (2004). Bodywork boundaries: Power, politics and professionalism in therapeutic massage. *Gender, Work and Organization, 11*(5), 544–65.

Perrier, M. & Fannin, M. (2017a). Refiguring the postmaternal. *Australian Feminist Studies, 31*(90), 383–92.

Perrier, M. & Fannin, M. (2017b). Belly casts and placenta pills: Refiguring postmaternal entrepreneurialism. *Australian Feminist Studies, 31*(90), 448–67.

Peticca-Harris, A. M. (2016). *Exploring the identities of North American yoga teachers from different perspectives on the self.* Unpublished doctoral dissertation, York University Toronto, Ontario.

Peticca-Harris, A. M. & McKenna, S. (2013). Identity struggle, professional development and career: A career/life history of a human resource management professional. *Journal of Management Development, 32*(8), 823–35.

Petriglieri, G., Ashford, S. J. & Wrzesniewski, A. (2019). Agony and ecstasy in the gig economy: Cultivating holding environments for precarious and personalized work identities. *Administrative Science Quarterly, 64*(1), 124–70.

Raffiee, J. & Feng, J. (2014). Should I quit my day job? A hybrid path to entrepreneurship. *Academy of Management Journal, 57*(4), 936–63.

Randall, J. & Munro, I. (2010). Foucault's care of the self: A case from mental health work. *Organization Studies, 39*(11), 1485–504.

Rhodes, C. (2019). Sense-ational organization theory! Practices of democratic scriptology. *Management Learning, 50*(1), 24–37.

Shilling, C. (1991). Educating the body: Physical capital and the production of social inequalities. *Sociology, 25*(4), 653–72.

Sointu, E. (2006). The search for wellbeing in alternative and complementary health practices. *Sociology of Health and Illness, 28*(3), 330–49.

Sullivan, K. R. (2014). With (out) pleasure: Desexualization, gender and sexuality at work. *Organization, 21*(3), 346–64.

Sullivan, K. R. & Delaney, H. (2017). A femininity that 'giveth and taketh away': The prosperity gospel and postfeminism in the neoliberal economy. *Human Relations, 70*(7), 836–59.

Sullivan, S. E. & Baruch, Y. (2009). Advances in career theory and research: A critical review and agenda for future exploration. *Journal of Management, 35*(6), 1542–71.

Sutcliffe, S. J. (2003). *Children of the new age: A history of spiritual practices*. London: Routledge.

Standing, G. (2011). *The precariat: The dangerous new class*. London: Bloomsbury.

Stephens, J. (2012). *Confronting postmaternal thinking: Feminism, memory, and care*. New York: Columbia University Press.

Thurer, S. L. (1994). *The myths of motherhood: How culture reinvents the good mother*. Boston, MA: Houghton Mifflin.

Tierney, W. G. (1998). Life history's history: Subjects foretold. *Qualitative Inquiry*, *4*(1), 49–70.

Twigg, J. (2000). *Bathing: The body and community care*. London: Routledge.

Twigg, J. (2010). Clothing and dementia: A neglected dimension? *Journal of Aging Studies*, *24*(4), 223–30.

Vair, H. (2013). The discourse of balance: Balance as metaphor and ideology. *Canadian Review of Sociology/Revue Canadienne de Sociologie*, *50*(2), 154–77.

Valente, V. & Marotta, A. (2005). The impact of yoga on the professional and personal life of the psychotherapist. *Contemporary Family Therapy*, *27*(1), 65–80.

Vivekananda, R. (2005). *Practical yoga psychology*. Bihar: Yoga Publications Trust.

Warhurst, C., Nickson, D., Witz, A. & Marie Cullen, A. (2000). Aesthetic labour in interactive service work: Some case study evidence from the 'new' Glasgow. *Service Industries Journal*, *20*(3), 1–18.

Watson, L. C. & Watson-Franke, M. B. (1985). *Interpreting life histories: An anthropological inquiry*. New Brunswick, NJ: Rutgers University Press.

Wolkowitz, C. (2002). The social relations of body work. *Work, Employment and Society*, *16*(3), 497–510.

Yoga Alliance (2016). *Yoga in America study*. Retrieved December 2017 from www.yogaalliance.org/Portals/0/2016%20Yoga%20in%20America%20Study%20RESULTS.pdf

Zeithaml, V. A. & Bitner, M. J. (1996). *Services marketing*. New York: McGraw-Hill.

Zelizer, V. A. (2005). *The purchase of intimacy*. Princeton, NJ: Princeton University Press.

5.   The commodification of re-sacralised work in the neoliberal era

Tom Vine

This chapter reflects on the disposition of some people to *pay* to work within an environment which promises a more authentic organisational experience to those typically associated with neoliberal norms. In 2010–11, I spent just over a year living and working in a New Age commune in Scotland, known as the Findhorn Foundation. While work at Findhorn is certainly a form of economic activity, it represents an extraordinary reversal of economic orthodoxy; the direction of monetary exchange is inverted and so participant-visitors pay to work for them. Notably, this represents a different category to voluntary work (where monetary exchange does not take place at all) or working holidays (where participants work – typically in 'natural', sustainable or communal contexts – in exchange for food and lodging). Findhorn's mantra is *Work is love in action!* We might interpret this from deeply cynical or critical perspectives and in so doing regard it as a deceptive mechanism for extracting value from gullible participants. From another perspective, however, that participants willingly pay to do this work suggests there is something about the work itself that they are attracted to; something which is lacking in their routine daily work practices. To this end, I tentatively interpret work at Findhorn as re-sacralised; a tonic for its conventional and de-sacralised rendering under neoliberalism. And, of course, there is a tension between this apparent re-sacralisation and its evident commodification, a tension which finds empirical echoes elsewhere in the literature (see, for example, Carrette & King, 2005).

The Findhorn Foundation constitutes an arresting example of how belief and spirituality inform our collective attitudes to work. Understood sociologically, *laboured work* is seen alongside *identity work* (Schwalbe & Mason-Schrock, 1996). While it is well documented that sources of economic identity have shifted from the arena of production (and particularly, the craft or experience of production) to the arena of consumption (see Bauman, 1998, for example), the culture at Findhorn is one in which excessive consumption is maligned (see Brierley's claims in Kay, 2001: 202, for example). Comparable findings have been reported from other New Age contexts (in their 2000 text, Prince and Riches explore attitudes to consumption and work in Glastonbury, for example). However, rather than offer re-sacralised work opportunities on a voluntary basis, Findhorn is unusual in that it has successfully commodified the re-sacralised working experience itself. Such is the salience of organisational identity, participants at Findhorn – many of whom lead itinerant organisational lives (see Vine, 2018) – are prepared to pay to participate in a working environment which, ostensibly at least, promises a re-sacralised – and purportedly more authentic – organisational experience.

The Findhorn Foundation is sometimes described as a commune. Its members, however, prefer the term 'community' or 'intentional community'. Established in 1962, the founders' vision was life premised on spiritual and ecological sensitivity. It was modest at its inception – just a single caravan and a small vegetable garden – but over the years it has spawned a much larger community. It is now home to approximately 300 people, most of whom work for the community either directly or in the form of related business ventures providing both conventional and esoteric products and services for the thousands of visitors it receives each year.

The Findhorn Foundation is the largest intentional community in Europe and remains a strong brand within New Age circles (for a systematic discussion of the New Age, see Heelas, 1996). Visitors to the community typically enrol on group-based residential programmes, each of which has a particular focus. These include 'Experience Week' (an introductory programme which offers participants a taste of community living, and is a prerequisite for other courses); 'Ecovillage Training' (a practical course for planning and constructing settlements with a firm emphasis on sustainability); and 'Spiritual Practice' (a course for honing meditative and related techniques). In addition to these specialist programmes, Findhorn also offers a number of residential workweeks on which participants work alongside community members on dedicated cleaning, maintenance, building and horticultural projects. Of my six residential visits to Findhorn, three were on such programmes. These included Experience Week, a workweek with the homecare department and a workweek with the maintenance department.

Although full immersion is impractical (and, given the potential for institutionalisation, not always advantageous), I was able to dedicate a full year to my ethnography. Over the course of this period, my stays with the community ranged in duration from four nights to two weeks. I lived and worked alongside community members, and maintained regular contact with participants on email forums throughout the entire period. Significantly, with the exception of the long-term residents, who constitute a minority, this sporadic participation is not dissimilar to how the majority of participants experience Findhorn. For a more detailed discussion of the ethnographic approach adopted, see Vine (2018).

RE-SACRALISING WORK AT FINDHORN

My first encounter with the community mantra, *Work is love in action!*, came on the very first day of my first visit to Findhorn (enrolled on Experience Week, a group-based residential programme designed to give participants a taste of community living). We had each received a paper copy of the timetable for our coming week, on which the mantra appeared. The timetable itself is worthy of comment. Although based on a fairly generic (and typed) template, it was extensively personalised. For the most part it was handwritten and, in places, illustrated charmingly. The document represents a creative take on what is essentially a bureaucratic artefact. From this first encounter, I read and hear the phrase uttered almost daily throughout my year's research. As a management academic accustomed to 'management speak', vacuous mission statements and hyperbole-ridden recruitment brochures, claims such as these are met with scepticism. I wrote in my field notes that day: 'As we all perused the timetable, I looked carefully at the faces around the room in which we had all assembled. I wanted to see if any of my co-participants were similarly taken aback at the phrase: "work is love in action". If they were, they didn't show it.'

I had expected our 'off-duty' conversations later that evening to reveal a semblance of cynicism. None did. It was with some surprise, then, that when I did eventually hear a comment in this vein, on a later visit, it was from Anna, one of the 'focalisers' (Findhorn describes focalisers as supervisors who ostensibly practise responsibility without authority): 'Sometimes I can't believe people come all the way to northern Scotland to clean for us, and they *pay us* for the privilege!'

Anna simultaneously acknowledged the absurdity of the arrangement and yet at the same time, her gesturing towards the glowing faces assembled around the table at which we sat, unequivocally implied she suspended her disbelief on the basis of the satisfaction participation affords. I was compelled to ask one of my co-participants, Sarah, how she felt about paying to work. She commented simply: '£95 for a week's holiday is good value!' Of course, in the event, the cost is much greater once you take into account travel to and from Scotland (in Sarah's case, from Germany). However, it is interesting that Sarah described this week as a holiday, thus aligning the experience to more typical working holidays despite the fact that participants on working holidays do not normally *pay* to work.

In a book published by Findhorn Press, ex-Findhorn resident, Carol Riddell, describes the principle of 'Work is love in action!':

> The Findhorn Foundation lifestyle is not retreatist. We consistently aim to present the 'good news' of our Self-discovery and to maintain it in our daily practice as a working community. We are exploring a new, positive meaning in work – not

only in what is done, but in how it is done and the way it is shared with others. We express this by the phrase 'Work is love in action!' To begin to experience work in this way is often very revealing for our guests, who discover that they can find satisfaction in tasks they previously regarded as menial and mundane. As currently dominant social desires to maximise material gain and output are superseded and people become used to working in an economy of sufficiency, our perspective on work, which includes discussion and mutual sharing, decentralisation and democratisation of authority, could gradually transform working life. Changed attitudes to work are not a means by which greedy employers can extract more output from individuals. (Riddell 1991: 58)

During the 'sharing' session (the concept of 'sharing' has a special significance at Findhorn; it is explored in more detail further on) on the evening of our first day in our work departments during Experience Week, without exception every participant had reverence for the work we had undertaken that day. Janine, one of the first to speak, commented thus: 'At home I hate cleaning! I absolutely hate it! But here ... the whole experience [is] magical! And why? Because here we work *together* [and] it is done with *love.*'

Janine, it transpired, had established a 'sharing' template for others to follow. Almost every contribution that evening followed this same format. At home, participants reported that domestic tasks were undertaken out of necessity, but here – because they were 'done with love' – they took on a special and rewarding significance. In the book *Growing People*, community member Johnny Brierley (2001: 203) comments that a concern for global longevity 'is manifesting itself in the grudging "greening" of business'. However, he continues, '[w]e are now ready to start the next major shift which is to experience business as a sacred space and give meaning to the oft quoted phrase that "our work is our love made visible"'. For Brierley, then, an ecological conscience in business is only the beginning. The difference between business and work notwithstanding, Brierley offers further insight:

> From the perspective of our Essential Nature we will naturally create work that is life enhancing and inspiring, rekindling a sense of meaning and purpose in our collective lives ... At the root of the problem is the rise of materialism, defined as the denial of a spiritual reality behind our material reality. So 'Business for Life' [a conference organised at Findhorn] focused our attention on how we mend the rift, how we could marry spirit and matter and so have our material and spiritual needs fully realised... The Conference ... was never meant to be 'business as usual'. We recognise there is still a large gap between right livelihood and much of our current business practice [at Findhorn]. Our subtitle was to re-consecrate our work. This acknowledged that we needed to re-embrace the spiritual reality and purpose directing our lives. (Brierley 2001: 202)

Brierley's concerns in respect of 'materialism' resonate with Bauman's (1998) concerns in respect of identity-inspired 'consumption'. Crucially, their proposed solutions are comparable too. While Bauman proposes the decoupling of work from its economic value in the interests of securing what he refers to as an 'ethics of workmanship', Brierley advocates the re-consecration of work. Indeed, from 'work is love in action' through 'work is our love made visible' to 'the re-consecration of work', there are myriad discursive devices supporting the claim that working for the Foundation affords a fundamentally different experience of work to that conventionally recognised. Rhetoric aside, there is a discernible attempt on the part of Findhorn to continually reinforce the notion of work as spiritually significant above and beyond these carefully packaged and marketed soundbites.

For my third and fifth visits to the community, I enrolled on dedicated 'workweeks', working for the homecare and maintenance departments, respectively. The homecare working week was advertised as: 'Sprinklings of Light: Spring Cleaning at the Park'. I was struck by the accompanying marketing material that promised the following: 'We will work together as a group, cleaning and cleansing both ourselves and the spaces used by our guests and community on outer and inner levels.'

On the first day of that workweek, I recorded the following in my field notes: 'Assembled in the community centre, we are asked to close our eyes, in expectation of "a little surprise". Upon opening our eyes, we see in front of each of us a small bucket (each labelled with our names) containing a pair of rubber gloves, a cloth, a bottle of Ecover cleaning liquid, a chocolate and a hand-written scroll. Mine says, "Your work this week will bring pleasure. Thank you."' This 'little surprise' elicited shrieks of delight from my co-participants. And beyond these small gestures, there are broader attempts to re-sacralise work. Over my year in and out of the field, I compiled a list of practices which I identify as evidence of this re-sacralisation. These include: (1) the processes of 'attunement' and 'sharing'; (2) the fact that the preferred approach to particular work tasks is often inefficient; (3) the conscious attempt to provide all participants with a feeling of usefulness; and (4) the recognition that work has a dualistic function. Each is explored below.

Work and the Processes of 'Attunement' and 'Sharing'

The process of 'attunement' is a central part of life at Findhorn. My ethnographic observations reveal that there are three elements to attunement. First, it is seen as a means of 'holding the energy' (it is worth noting that energy is a pervasive motif in New Age discourses, and represents the focus of a pending publication). Second, it constitutes a mechanism for allocating specific work tasks. Third, it offers a forum in which participants are encouraged to 'share' their daily experiences.

Typically, when a group at Findhorn assembles they 'tune in'; when they depart – even temporarily – they 'tune out'. Responsibility for attunement sits with the focaliser; although individual participants may, on occasion, be asked to lead the attunement process once familiar with its mechanics. There is a strict code for attunement. Participants sit or stand in a circle (over the course of my research I attuned with large groups of as many as a hundred or so, and on a couple of occasions, with just one other person). Each participant proffers to their neighbours their right hand palm up and their left, palm down. The rationale offered for this was twofold. First it minimises hesitation; second, it means that each person simultaneously holds another's hand and has a hand held by another. During an informal chat in the hot tub on a later visit, I was told that this technique also facilitates a smoother and more efficient 'flow of energy' between bodies. Participants normally keep their eyes closed during the attunement process. Once the focaliser decides that the attunement is complete he or she will indicate this by gently squeezing their neighbours' hands, each of whom then squeezes the hand of the person next to them and so on until all assembled are aware that the process is complete.

Since there is an overriding emphasis on working as part of a group, attunement thus becomes a fundamental aspect of work at Findhorn. It is used on a community-wide basis to underscore planning and strategy, but it is also used at a more prosaic level to pair participants with work departments, roles and individual tasks. My first encounter with attunement was during Experience Week:

> We had gathered in the main meditation sanctuary at Cluny Campus. We stood in a circle and were instructed to close our eyes ... A list of work departments was then read out – garden, homecare (house-keeping), kitchen and maintenance – after which we had been instructed to mull over the options. The list was then read out a second time, and we were encouraged to raise a hand when we felt 'drawn' to a particular work department. Once the attunement process was complete the four lists of names corresponding to each of the four departments was read out by way of confirmation.

I was aware at the time that the focaliser reading out the list of work departments only moved on to the next work department once sufficient numbers had been recruited for the department in question. The fact that participants were meant to wait until they felt 'drawn' to a particular work department before raising their hand meant that the focalisers would not find themselves in an uncompromising situation where they read out a work department only to be greeted suddenly with ten or so upheld hands. The mystique in which the process is enshrined is thus preserved. In an earlier academic account of Experience Week, Sutcliffe (2000: 222) suggests that attunement at Findhorn therefore helps resolve 'a potential clash between organizational requirements and existential agenda'. Although I sought to maximise my faculties of perception in the interests of efficacious autoethnography, I found myself selecting rather than being drawn towards. I attuned to work in the garden. Collectively, however, through this process of attunement, we were assigned in equal measure to each of the four work departments. Although now 'attuned' to our particular work departments (in which we would remain for the duration of the week), we soon discovered that our working days would be framed by further attunement. Irrespective of the department I worked with over the course of my research, we attuned as a department at the beginning of each day, before and after lunch, and at the end of each day. The first daily attunement also served the purpose of allocating specific tasks (on a number of occasions, where several people were assigned to a particular task, where appropriate, they further attuned to decide how to break down the task into subcomponents).

Attunement also usually incorporates what Findhorn refers to as 'sharing'. Prior to (or immediately following) the described ritual which involves closed eyes and held hands, sharing provides an opportunity for participants to say as much or as little about their state of mind or their experiences from the current or previous day, or their anticipations for the day ahead. It usually takes the form of the spoken word, but on occasion I witnessed participants singing or dancing, by means of alternative expression. By way of initiating the process, one of the focalisers usually begins by saying a few words. They then nominate either the person to the left or right of them, and the sharing proceeds either clockwise or counter-clockwise around the assembled circle. Sharing is thus an interesting means through which conventional notions of hierarchy (in this case, in terms of voice or opinion) are challenged. On many occasions these attunement sessions lasted over half an hour and never did I witness anybody urged to 'be brief'. Each person is permitted as much time as they require. On the second work day of the maintenance workweek, I made the following entry in my field notes:

> During our pre-work sharing, Rochelle commented: 'I was really inspired by the talk at the Community Meeting last night … I realised then that yesterday … I wasn't consciously working "love in action". I loved working with the group but wasn't focusing on working with love.' There were tears in her eyes as she said this and she stared into the light of the candle that flickered in the centre of the table around which we were all congregated. We were silent. I glanced at the focalisers, Harvey and Bud, but they too were focused on the candle. I felt a bit uncomfortable but had realised by now that sharing wasn't really a time for dialogue but was rather intended as a space for each of us to express ourselves without constraint of time or emotion. Eventually, Rochelle continued. 'Today' she said 'I must be sure I am working love in action'. We each continued to share in turn. Further round the circle, it was Dawn's turn to share. Like Rochelle, she too was crying. Through her tears she gestured, however, that she did not wish to speak this morning. Once the sharing was complete we together blew out the candle. As seems to be tradition in the

maintenance department, the extinguished light was 'sent' as a blessing to a worthy cause. On this occasion Harvey wished for us to send the light to a 'successful morning' ... and he quickly corrected himself ... 'well, successful in a spiritual sense ... in terms of work as love in action' ... and Bud added 'yes, successful in the proper sense of the word'.

There are several interesting observations to glean from this particular episode. First, attunement – in its guise of sharing – helps re-sacralise work by establishing an emotional association between the group members. The very fact that Rochelle was stirred emotionally to the point of tears is testament to the effectiveness of this process. Second, that Rochelle chose to speak about her apparent inability to work 'love in action' on the previous day, demonstrates the reflexive function of the attunement process. Third, that Rochelle spent a considerable amount of time sharing (even though much of it was spent in complete silence) whereas Dawn chose not to speak at all, demonstrates both that attunement democratises voice and opinion but that it is also considered non-mandatory. Fourth, that Harvey chose to 'send the light' to a 'successful' morning demonstrates that he was responding to the emotional desire of his participants (specifically Rochelle). As focaliser, through the process of attunement, Harvey had effectively garnered an understanding of Rochelle's needs beyond the confines of her economic utility. Fifth, that both Harvey and Bud sought to clarify the meaning of success within Findhorn circles, reinforces the fact that successful work at Findhorn does not necessarily correspond to successful work in conventional contexts. In this way, both the frequency and time allocated for attunement, as well as the ritual's defining characteristics, signal to participants that diligence is preferable to pace, and that efficiency should remain subordinate to efficacy. Indeed, inefficiency is a celebrated characteristic of work at Findhorn, the focus of the next section.

Work and Inefficiency

Ostensibly, the working day at Findhorn is 9am to 5pm but in practice it is considerably shorter. There are morning and afternoon breaks, both of which are officially 20 minutes but in reality tend to be half an hour each; there's an hour and a half for lunch and at least half an hour of the rest of the working day is spent attuning and sharing. The following entry from my field notes made during the maintenance workweek illustrates this point: 'I heard our focalisers calling to each other. Bud said "Harvey, hurry up! It's lunchtime." I glanced at my watch and saw that it was only 12.15; lunch didn't officially start for another quarter of an hour. I pointed this out to Bud. He looked round, and said with a matter of fact tone, "Yes, but we have to tune out."'

On the many days I spent working for the community, never did we actually work more than five hours in a single day: there is no expectation at all to work a 'full' eight-hour day. To the extent that this can be regarded as inefficient in terms of labour utility, then so too can the work methods. Although none of those I encountered over the course of my research expressed discontent at the fact they were paying for the 'privilege' of working for the Foundation, personally, I did feel uneasy about the arrangement, not because I didn't wish to work but because initially at least I couldn't help feeling manipulated. As Experience Week progressed and I later garnered further work experience on the two workweeks, I found the arrangement easier to stomach because I came to realise that the work methods at Findhorn were so at odds with conventional ideas of efficiency. I felt, therefore, that any underhand attempt to extract surplus value from paying participants would invariably have tightened up on fairly straightforward notions of task efficiency. Later in the year I read Riddell's account of Findhorn's approach to work and agreed with much of her deliberation:

> Visitors who come to the Findhorn Foundation full of notions of business efficiency and 'modern management methods' are often taken aback by the slowness, complexity and apparent vagueness of our decision-making processes ... The pace of life here raises questions about the wider civilisation of which management techniques are a part. Does a society organised for the maximisation of production create relaxed, harmonious and holistically developed human beings? All the evidence says no. On the contrary, stress levels are high and stress-related disease is endemic. Individuals are alienated from their jobs, working rather for their pay packets than because what they do satisfies them. This is widespread disillusion and purposelessness. (Riddell 1991: 94)

Indeed, within every one of the work departments conventional notions of efficiency were implicitly rejected. I attuned to the garden department during Experience Week. Over the course of the week, I helped plant seedlings, weeded vegetable patches and on the last day helped harvest. From a conventional perspective, each of these tasks was conducted inefficiently. On the day I was planting seedlings, I made the following entry in my field notes:

> This morning I attuned to work with Claude and Emma. We were transplanting parsley seedlings from a single tray to a tray with separate chambers. I asked Claude why the seeds were not planted directly into single chambers. 'We plant them together because they like to sprout next to their brothers and sisters.' When attuned to weeding later in the week, I was given a brief pep talk by one of the more experienced gardeners. 'You are welcome to wear gloves, Tom, but most of us here working at the garden choose not to. This is because we can connect more fully both with nature and with the task. We pick weeds one at a time between thumb and finger. We have respect for the weeds, because we know [through the process of composting] we will eat them one day.'

Broadly speaking, there are resonances here with Fournier's (2008) research on economic de-growth. The specific point about connecting more fully both with nature and with the task is fundamental in terms of the re-sacralisation of work. In *The Craftsman*, Richard Sennett (2008: 149) suggests that 'the hand is the window on to the mind'. He continues: 'We have trained our hands in repetition; we are alert rather than bored because we have developed the skill of anticipation. But equally, the person able to perform again and again has acquired a technical skill, the rhythmic skill of a craftsman' (178). In one respect, then, work at Findhorn reflects that of the traditional craftsman in that it combines a focused, assiduous mind with diligent, precise hand movements.

On the Friday, we all harvested. I attuned to harvesting broad beans. My field notes for that day read as follows:

> Today was our final day in our work departments. I attuned to join Tracey-Unity [she tells me that Tracey is her given name, and Unity her spiritual name] and Yuuka harvesting the broad beans. Each Friday all the crops which are ready to harvest are collected and then distributed across approximately 180 vegetable boxes and delivered to customers in the local area, as well as supplying the various kitchens at the Findhorn Foundation. The entire harvesting process was inefficient. In addition to the regular attunements, we harvested broad beans in accordance to a sliding scale of crop size. This essentially meant harvesting the entire patch multiple times, each time picking beans which were sufficiently large to meet the current round's requirements (which decreased each time round until the focaliser was satisfied that we had picked enough beans to meet the requirements of that particular week's order).

In this way, then, whereas a more conventional approach to harvesting might have expressed concern at such a laborious method and have instead closely assessed the yield during the process of picking, at Findhorn, sensitivity to the ripeness of the crop and diligence of the harvesting took priority.

Work in the homecare department was comparably 'inefficient'. On Monday of the homecare workweek, I 'attuned' to clean windows:

> I was given a generic spray bottle with 'Organic vinegar and water' written in black marker pen across the side. I ask which cloth to use for the windows, but am told newspaper is best (there were plentiful old copies of the *Guardian* newspaper for this purpose). It transpires – I think – that the print assists in the cleaning process. The smell of vinegar is pungent – I prefer Windowlene!

The following afternoon:

> Although yesterday and this morning I have ongoing problems with the spray bottle, it is only now that I discover that the clogging is not because of a fault with the bottle. Jeff, one of our focalisers, tells me the organic vinegar/water mix we are using to clean the windows has a tendency to clog the plumbing in the plastic spray

bottles because there is significant sediment build-up. Apparently the non-organic fortified alternative doesn't clog.

I discussed the situation with Zoë, with whom I was working. She had come across the problem before on previous workweeks. She explained that I must regularly remove the pump mechanism inside the bottle and rinse it in water. I did as instructed. At lunchtime, I happened to be talking to another of the participants, Sarah (who was also cleaning windows), and she confirmed that she too had been rinsing the mechanism in her bottle regularly. It didn't seem to bother either of them in the slightest, and yet it frustrated me. I couldn't see the logic in using *organic* vinegar for something as trivial as cleaning windows, particularly as it made the process more time consuming. But Sarah brought my concerns into relief: 'We're not cleaning,' she corrected me, 'we're sprinkling light.' It wasn't until later on in the week that Jeff, one of our focalisers, saw me rinsing the pump mechanism that I witnessed a semblance of rebellion. It was, however, palpably comic. Jeff commented: 'I go to Tesco to buy non-organic vinegar for precisely this reason! [He laughs raucously.] In fact, I have to confess that I visit the "evil empire" pretty regularly for cleaning products … various bits and pieces. I'm also always on the lookout for when the local whiskies are on offer [he winks]. I refuse to pay £28 for a bottle!' At this point, and in a mock display of surreptitiousness, Jeff passed me a spray bottle which contained fortified rather than organic vinegar. On a fairly rudimentary level this anecdote demonstrates that humour is a part of life at Findhorn. More significantly, however, this can be seen as a small act of subversion or resistance. Furthermore, while research in more conventional workplace settings typically documents subversion or resistance among those in the junior shop-floor ranks, here it was the party with elevated authority – the 'focaliser' – who sought to transgress this expectation.

Towards the end of that week, I was seconded to work in the kitchen. The entire kitchen facility was undergoing its annual spring clean. It was clear that a lot of work was required and by the time I arrived, there were close to 20 people already working. I was eventually introduced to the kitchen focaliser:

Tom: Hi, I'm Tom. I was sent by Jeff to help out in the kitchen… What would you like me to do?

Jayne: Well, er [thinking carefully], we have already attuned to the tasks this morning …

Tom: Well, I don't mind what I do.

Jayne: What would you like to do?

Tom: I honestly don't mind; I'll help out anywhere.

Jayne: But what would you *like* to do?

Tom: Ah … I can help clean the floor.

Jayne: OK, yes, then do that.

Despite the fact that there was a lot of work to do (which is why I was seconded from homecare to the kitchen in the first place), Jayne was evidently
uncomfortable *allocating* me a task. On the one hand, this demonstrates the
importance the process of attunement holds for its participants. Jayne didn't
want to *assign* me a task, presumably because this would undermine the very
premise of attunement. Interpreted another way – and to the extent attunement
represents ritualised procedure – it demonstrates a reticence to step outside the
delineated processes in which work is framed at Findhorn.

The last of the departments I worked with was maintenance. Prior to attending the maintenance workweek, I had arranged to meet up with Sofie in the
Netherlands who was one of the co-participants I had met and got on well
with during the homecare workweek earlier that year. I explained to Sofie that
I was soon to be back in Findhorn on the maintenance workweek. Sofie was
evidently excited by the prospect:

> I attuned to maintenance last year … of course, it is a very male department, but
> I didn't mind … In fact, I couldn't believe how *inefficient* [she placed a keen empha-
> sis on the word] it was … we decided one morning to so do some painting, got there
> [to the site which required painting] and realised we didn't have any brushes! And
> then one time we got to a bathroom to do a plumbing job, and realised we didn't
> have the right equipment for that either! Mind you, Sprinklings [of Light] was the
> same wasn't it? Jeff [one of our focalisers] would say: 'we can work this afternoon,
> or have the afternoon off … whatever you feel like doing!' [Sofie laughs out loud.]

Sofie's comment about the gender bias in the department is interesting. She
implied that 'efficiency' is traditionally a male characteristic and yet for her,
the very first thing she said of the department was that it was both male and
inefficient. To some extent, my own ethnographic experience on the maintenance workweek supported this. Of the five participants, four were male and
all but me were over the age of 50. Two were in their late 60s, one of whom
had a back problem. It reminded me very much of the British sitcom, *Dad's
Army*. Physically, only two of us were really suited to the work, but this didn't
seem to worry our focalisers. Over the course of the week, we moved bricks,
scaffolding, furniture, sheds and demolished an old static caravan. We each
did what we could, even though for some of the less able among us this meant,
for example, carrying one brick at a time from one site to another. On the very
first day of the workweek, and prior to actually beginning any work, one of our

focalisers, Harvey, took us to Universal Hall (one of the principal communal buildings at Findhorn) and recounted the story of its construction in the 1970s, paying particular attention to the varying quality of the external stonemasonry: 'You will notice on this wall [gesturing] that the gaps between the stones are quite large.' Moving round the building, he continues: 'Here [gesturing] they [the gaps] are smaller – the stones have been cut more precisely.' Moving further round: 'Here [gesturing], they are smaller still. The workmanship is incredibly good, and note the ornate patterns [gesturing].'

It transpires that the first wall he showed us was built by hired professionals. As the community watched the professionals work, they were convinced they could do a better job and so decided to finish the work themselves. The second wall demonstrated their early attempts, and the third and final wall their workmanship once they had gained significant expertise. The anecdote is interesting for a number of reasons. First, although Harvey is careful not to lead interpretation of this sequence of events, it is clear that it demarcates a difference between conventional mainstream work ethic and the community work ethic. Second, it bolsters the contention that at Findhorn efficiency holds less import than diligence. Work at Findhorn is an expression of human spirit. Diligent, careful work is an expression of *love* – for self, planet and community; it is a kind of worshipful act to which traditional models of efficiency, productivity and accounting are unable to sustain. Third, since Harvey told us this story at the beginning of our workweek, it served as an example from which we were expected to take methodological inspiration.

Work and a Sense of Usefulness

During the homecare workweek, I took the opportunity to spend some time chatting to the staff in the Visitors Centre at the Park Campus. The Visitors Centre dispenses key information about the Findhorn Foundation, conducts tours of the campus and stocks an array of fliers advertising various services and local attractions. The Centre's manager, Ronnie, wanted to talk about retirement as he had just turned 60: 'As more and more members near retirement age, my concerns – and those of the community more broadly – are what to do with us "elderberries". The problem is further complicated by the fact that, since Findhorn is a multinational community, not everybody is entitled to a pension.' He then supplemented this concern with another: 'We also need to ask ourselves how we can ensure older people are made to feel useful.'

Ronnie's comments helped make sense of behaviour I had observed in Luke, one of my co-participants that week. At 69, and the eldest of those enrolled on the homecare workweek, Luke always seemed to volunteer to do extra work while the rest of us were drinking herbal tea, playing cards or napping at the end of the working day. Luke had been retired for nearly a decade now, lived alone and didn't engage much socially in his home town of Hull. Findhorn workweeks (of which he tells me, he enrols on 'almost all of them') allow Luke to demonstrate that he is still capable of contributing in terms of labour. In one respect, Findhorn represents an ideal environment in which retired and older people *can* work. As we have seen already, conventional notions of efficiency are rejected in favour of a sacralised approach to work. In a mainstream employment context, younger workers regularly constitute a more 'efficient' solution to the problem of labour. Not only do they traditionally cost less, but they are assumed to be capable of meeting ever more demanding schedules and work expectations. To the extent, then, that older people represent 'inefficient' subjects, they are commensurate with the work culture at Findhorn. Another of the participants on the homecare workweek, Cherie, a retired nurse, made an interesting comment: 'I get the impression that [our focalisers] are struggling to find me things to do.' Throughout the week, Cherie was on dusting duties. She was a short lady in her late 60s and clearly lacked the physical strength to manage certain tasks and so the duty to which she was attuned was most appropriate. The focalisers were thus both accommodating of senior participants who were determined to prove their mettle (such as Luke) and sensitive to the physical limitations of those who didn't (such as Cherie).

During the maintenance workweek, our group met with Alfie, one of the community's managers. Steve, one of our group who was reaching retirement age himself, initiated the conversation.

> **Steve:** Is there a retirement age in the Foundation?
>
> **Alfie:** A hundred and twelve [the group laughs raucously]. You only get a pension if you've got a letter from your mum [more laughter]. [Adopting a more serious tone:] the national retirement age applies but if somebody wants to work on we consider extending it … but the retirement age is actually a big thing to me and it's something that we're looking at now because the community is getting older … How can we make a difference between someone who has been here for twenty years and somebody who has been here for two years? They're both fully committed, their energy and their heart is in the right place … how can we say to one you can stay but you can't …
>
> **Tom:** What's the experience from other communities round the world?
>
> **Alfie:** In other countries age is kind of respected and it isn't necessarily respected here.

Alfie raises two pertinent points. First, he emphasises the fact that (having existed for close to a half century) the Findhorn community is now an aging community. Alfie tells us it will not be long before the older members of the community require full-time care, akin to that provided in mainstream nursing homes. This brings into sharp relief the mentality espoused by 'living in the present' and helps reinforce the rationale behind an apparent drive towards a more carefully formalised and proceduralised organisation. Second, Alfie draws upon the cultural distinction between the West and East as regards perception of older people. He thus sees Findhorn as consistent with Eastern traditions of respect, just as it is inspired by Eastern spirituality. Ronnie's earlier reference to the community's older members as 'elderberries' implics a comparable, if light-hearted, perspective. Steve asks another question:

Steve: Because of their age, [is it right to assume] they can't necessarily put in the same input as anyone else?

Alfie: Whether they can stay or not is not based on their input ... no, if somebody has been here and they've done the [required] length of service ... I don't know what that is because that's one of the questions that we're looking at now ... it doesn't matter if they can only work a day a week or can't work at all ... I think we've got ... yeah, Felix who looks after the transport ... is sixty-seven. Jimmy, who's one of the hardest workers, is seventy-one ... so it's not about the age ... if the Foundation can support them it will support them ... but [equally] we've got an aging community ... what we gonna do about it? Can we provide ... elders' housing? ... and how do we keep them integrated? How do we make them feel of value? And how do we get the Foundation to recognise that value?

At this point Alfie's comments echo those of Ronnie. Not only is Findhorn thinking proactively about the future and the means by which the organisation will support retiring individuals in terms of both resources and the provision of care (which mainstream society does), but it is asking how it might instil in these individuals a sense of self-worth and means of making them feel useful (which mainstream society doesn't). In this way, work (as 'usefulness') is considered an essential part of being, irrespective of age.

Work as Dualistic

On the Findhorn website, the page advertising the details of the homecare workweek included a number of quotations from participants from previous years. One of these read as follows: 'This isn't an ordinary spring clean; it is a grand opportunity to clear out "old baggage" on all levels ... don't miss it. Work is love in action!' (Linda, 2009, Spring Clean participant). Findhorn recognises a dualistic nature to work. For Linda, not only was she spring cleaning the various facilities at Findhorn, but she was spring cleaning herself (or clearing out old baggage, as she puts it). Crucially, the phrase 'Work is love in action!' intonates this too. The sharing session described earlier in which Rochelle was moved emotionally is of fundamental importance in terms of understanding the extent to which work at Findhorn might be regarded as dualistic. Rochelle commented during her sharing that although she worked hard, she'd realised retrospectively that 'I wasn't consciously working "love in action"'. Later that same day, and as sensitively as I could, I asked Rochelle what she meant by not consciously working love in action. 'It may sound stupid, but yesterday I wasn't focussing fully ... I was working hard but I wasn't working within my heart.' We embraced. Rochelle started crying. To her, the Findhorn tradition of *Work is love in action!* was to be taken very seriously. Her sincerity was testament to how the work can (and ought to) double as a form or expression of love. By way of interpretation, work might be seen dualistically as both *laboured work* and *identity work*. Although no other participants appeared as emotionally stirred as Rochelle, over the course of my research I gathered further evidence of work as a form of identity expression over and above its immediate (conventional) purpose. Shortly after the homecare workweek, I received the following email from Sofie, who I worked alongside that week: 'I thoroughly enjoyed the Cleaning Week and as sometimes happens, I did not really realise [this] until it was over. I truly treasure that experience, the laughter, the fun, the cleaning, the chats ... Was great meeting you there.' At first glance, her second sentence might seem absurd: 'I truly treasure that experience, the laughter, the fun, the cleaning ...'; *the cleaning*? A conversation I had with Sofie during the workweek itself helps lend clarity to this comment. During our lunch break, Sofie comments that her work colleagues back at home expressed disbelief that she was to be working on her holiday. I suggested that, perhaps, the utility comes from participating in a community, but Sofie said: 'It is actually about serving others; it's about the sense of service.' She placed great emphasis on the words. She continued: 'Until money becomes a factor, people work for the sake of service, but once money is involved they begin to watch how much work they are doing and assess its value in terms of money ... Inevitably,' she continued, 'you do less work and demand more money.'

For Sofie, then, work at Findhorn has a non-monetary rationale. She described this in terms of service. Service is here considered as fundamentally social ('serving others') whereas monetary exchange is regarded as asocial. Work at Findhorn has a double purpose. It is a form of labour with a certain utility, but in serving, Sofie reconnects with a pre-modern form of work 'experience', an experience and feeling her mainstream job at home does not offer. For Alvesson et al. (2008: 15), identity work is 'the ongoing mental activity that an individual undertakes in constructing an understanding of self that is ... positively valued'. By serving, as opposed to simply working in the interests of remuneration, Sofie thus identifies within herself positive value. In another email, this time from Andy, whom I'd also met on the homecare workweek, a similar sentiment is conveyed. Since our time on the homecare workweek, Andy had been working in the maintenance department (although on a separate programme to me): 'I "worked" in maintenance, though it was really just pure fun for me.' That Andy chooses to use inverted commas when typing the word 'worked' is revealing. Andy acknowledges that he was working in the conventional sense of the word, but that he enjoyed it so much compels him to abstract the word from its taken-for-granted meaning (and conventional implications).

In each of these cases, we see evidence that work at Findhorn constitutes a supplementary purpose. For Rochelle, when suitably focused, her labour is an expression of love. For Sofie, labour is an expression of service. For Andy, labour is an expression of fun. It is this conceptualisation of labour above and beyond its usual interpretations (necessary, paid, disagreeable, etc.) that constitutes for participants at Findhorn what Schwalbe and Mason-Schrock (1996) refer to as 'subcultural [collective] identity work'. Subcultural identity work is 'the work people do together to create the signs, codes, and rites of affirmation that become shared resources for identity-making' (121, emphasis added). While the signs are formed from the discourse emphasising, for example, love (Rochelle), service (Sofie) and fun (Andy), the code is captured in the oft-quoted phrase 'Work is love in action!'; and the rites of affirmation are the related processes of attunement and sharing. Most significantly, however, work is always undertaken in groups. This therefore reinforces the 'togetherness' necessary for subcultural identity work. There is significant metaphorical mileage in the fact that Experience Week and the departmental workweeks – as well as a whole array of residential programmes centred on specific spiritual, therapeutic or ecological techniques – are described as workshops on the Findhorn calendar. Although some of these workshops do not involve work (in its conventional rendering), participants on any given workshop live, attune, share, eat and socialise together. The principle of 'workshop' here abstracted from its historical association with manufacture, is entirely commensurate with the concept of 'identity workspace'. Petriglieri and Petriglieri (2010: 45) suggest that 'by definition individuals cannot conduct identity work in isolation'; it must instead be 'facilitated by a holding environment that supports the individual in the cognitive, emotional, and social process of elaborating, experimenting with, and consolidating the meanings associated to the self'. Workshops at Findhorn, it seems, constitute holding environments of this nature; indeed, the entire Findhorn community more generally might legitimately be regarded in this way: 'In order to see whether it is true that the ultimate knowledge of Love lies within you, try adopting the same methods as those who have already discovered it. You will find that you get the same results. The Findhorn community is an ongoing workshop in which this "experiment" is being practised' (Riddell 1991: 25, emphasis added).

CONCLUDING THOUGHTS

The case of Findhorn reveals something remarkable about the relationship between belief and spirituality on the one hand, and economy and work on the other. The social, spiritual and anthropological dimensions of work are consciously rekindled and celebrated at Findhorn. To this end, Findhorn encourages its participants to re-evaluate their attitudes to work, to view work as 'love in action'. This re-sacralisation is not without tension. The surreptitious – if humorous – use of non-organic vinegar in window-cleaning spray bottles is one example of tension. On occasion, too, I witnessed procedural disagreements about how best to carry out particular tasks. However, these constituted minor and, perhaps, inevitable pockets of resistance, none of which tainted the overarching tradition of work within the community which prioritises diligence, tolerance and an understanding of personal limitations. At Findhorn, work represents both a form of labour on the one hand, but also a physical and emotional space for subcultural identity re-creation. In this sense, Findhorn is an example *par excellence* of Petriglieri and Petriglieri's (2010) 'identity workspace'.

However, this re-sacralisation comes at a price: participants must pay to experience work at Findhorn. It is difficult to see how the practice of paying for the privilege to work could have arisen outside of neoliberal discourses. Indeed, it would be disingenuous to overlook the fact that Findhorn depends on mainstream society for its economic survival, not least in terms of providing an ongoing supply of disillusioned 'workers' in search of – and willing to pay for – a re-sacralised work experience. Furthermore, at some point Findhorn must have realised it could commodify and make money by offering participants a taste of work life in the community; ironically, this is itself characteristic of a neoliberal mind set, and so invites a more pertinent question. We began this chapter by commenting on the extraordinary reversal of economic orthodoxy evidenced at Findhorn. The question is, are we likely to see this practice expanded into more prosaic organisational life in the future? If the central tenets of neoliberalism continue to dominate, the answer is most probably yes. However, broader indications suggest that this may take place in a very different context. One example is the evolving nature of internships. In their study of newspaper reportage of interns and internships, Schuer and Mills (2016) note that a common motif is of the overworked intern. They comment, thus:

> Within the *New York Times* articles, descriptions of interns carrying heavy workloads and working long hours as a part of the internship (i.e. being overworked) were characterized as the way in which these young people could 'pay their dues'. For instance ... interns were advised to put in the long hours of an internship or to

serve multiple internships as a way of demonstrating their qualification and preparation for a 'real' job.

Will we eventually reach a point where the 'payment of dues' includes actually paying for the privilege of the intern experience in the first place? Internship places are typically competitive; a logical – and neoliberal – conclusion of this is that some candidates may be prepared to pay for a sought-after internship experience. After all, the experience will likely enhance a candidate's résumé which, in turn, can legitimately be expected to help secure paid work in the future. In the final analysis, and spiritual aspects aside, a desirable experience of work is no different to any other desirable experience, be it a treatment at a hotel spa or a ride in a hot air balloon: all can be commodified, packaged and sold to the highest bidder. As an academic schooled in a critical tradition of scholarship where we are expected to find fault with organisational configuration and to reveal subtle mechanisms of control that underlie apparently good intentions, it is tempting to do precisely this in respect of Findhorn. In the event, however, I am compelled to conclude differently: I thoroughly enjoyed living and working at Findhorn and my overwhelming impression is that most people fortunate enough to share the experience do so too.

REFERENCES

Alvesson, M., Ashcroft, K. & Thomas, R. (2008) 'Identity Matters: Reflections on the Construction of Identity Scholarship in Organization Studies', *Organization*, 15(1), 5–28.

Bauman, Z. (1998) *Work, Consumerism and the New Poor*, Buckingham: Open University Press.

Brierley, J. (2001) 'Business for Life: Re-consecrating Our Work', in K. Kay (ed.), *Growing People: People's Personal Experience at the Findhorn Community*, Hong Kong: Pilgrim Guides.

Carrette, J. & King, R. (2005) *Selling Spirituality: The Silent Takeover of Religion*, London: Routledge.

Fourner, V. (2008) 'Escaping from the Economy: The Politics of Degrowth', *International Journal of Sociology and Social Policy*, 28(11/12), 528–45.

Heelas, P. (1996) *The New Age Movement: The Celebration of Self and the Sacralization of Modernity*, Oxford: Blackwell.

Kay, K. (ed.) (2001) *Growing People: People's Personal Experiences at the Findhorn Community*, Hong Kong: Pilgrim Guides.

Petriglieri, G. & Petriglieri, J. (2010) 'Identity Workspaces: The Case of Business Schools', *Academy of Management Learning and Education*, 9(1), 44–60.

Princes, R. & Riches, D. (2000) *The New Age in Glastonbury: The Construction of Religious Movements*, Oxford: Berghahn.

Riddell, C. (1991) *The Findhorn Community: Creating a Human Identity for the 21st Century*, Findhorn: Findhorn Press.

Scheuer, C. & Mills, A. (2016) 'Discursivity and Media Constructions of the Intern: Implications for Pedagogy and Practice', *Academy of Management Learning and Education*, 15(3), 456–70.

Schwalbe, M. & Mason-Schrock, D. (1996) 'Identity Work as Group Process', *Advances in Group Processes*, 13, 113–47.

Sennett, R. (2008) *The Craftsman*, London: Penguin.

Sutcliffe, S. (2000) 'A Colony of Seekers: Findhorn in the 1990s', *Journal of Contemporary Religion*, 15(2), 215–31.

Vine, T. (2018) 'Home-Grown Exoticism? Identity Tales from a New Age Intentional Community', in T. Vine, J. Clark, S. Richards & D. Weir (eds), *Ethnographic Research and Analysis: Anxiety, Identity and Self*, London: Palgrave Macmillan.

6. Enchanted gardeners in urban food gardens: a case study of Khayelitsha, Cape Town

Darlene Miller

URBAN FOOD GARDENS: A RADICAL SPIRITUAL CHALLENGE TO 'BIG FOOD' REGIMES

In South Africa, our past has produced a disconnection from the land and, through this dispossession, a conflicted relationship with productivity. Creating hope in conditions of barbaric exclusion – such as the neo-liberal exclusion experienced by urban unemployed youth in Africa – is a rebellious act. I propose here that food gardens may be a point of reconnection with the soil – and the land – from which we have been disconnected through dispossession. In this sense, acts of self-governance become a form of activism, expressed at both the individual and collective levels: individual, in the sense of the forms of self-discovery and alternative aesthetics; collective as a new food movement with an economic outcome in food subsistence.

Radically rupturing with global food scripts engineered by transnational food corporations, I argue that there is potential for reclaiming governance of the body in the act of local urban food production. Our situated knowledge derives from indigenous knowledge of how to work the land, how we represent and name the land and the deep forms of spirituality and animism that accompany such indigenous knowledge of the land.

Thus urban food gardens have the potential to be spaces of healing that open up opportunities for new knowledge creation. Through urban food gardens, youth have the potential to direct both their economic subsistence income strategies as well as political activism. Such alternative food movements are at the core of challenging what is produced, how it is produced and for whom it is produced. While in the global North, food movements include the Slow Food Movement and 'locavores', the dominant food movements of the global South focus on food sovereignty.

In light of the links between food sovereignty and indigeneity, this chapter also links indigenous and endogenous knowledges. Endogenous knowledge refers to the new cultures and new ideas of personhood arising around food. In Khayelitsha, a South African township, young men are seeking to make gardening 'cool' to attract young people into food production. In the poor, (still) black townships of South Africa, endogenous knowledge involves navigating the politics of the township terrain and working within the geographies of township life. Ikhaya Garden is a case study of a food alternative based at a local township school, and there is much that we are able to learn from the politics of resistance that emanates from this garden.

The first section of this chapter counterposes the global context of elite consumption to the social plight of unemployed young men. The personhood of food producers is also tied to a new politics of food, in which youth mobilisation around subsistence food gardens becomes a counter to the fast-food cultures of frenetic urban lifestyles. In this sense their connection with the garden represents a radical spirituality. The second part of the chapter discusses the methods of the research as a 'food journey' with the assistance of a Western Cape food cooperative (Harvest of Hope) and a local township tour agency (Uthando). The third section presents the case study of the 'cool gardeners' in Khayelitsha, and the spiritual radicalism of these 'enchanted gardeners' as they disavow state, capital, religion and dominant food regimes. I then conclude with a discussion of the spiritual significance of the urban food garden as a stable ecosystem and a space of repossession.

ELITE CONSUMPTION AND ANGRY YOUNG MEN

'Angry Young Men' by Mtini

Angry young men
with fists raised
ready for extreme sports
we see them on the news
in the streets
and the siren systems
sound their pleading on the borders
screaming for hope
not to be alienated from the earth
Angry young men
will jump off bridges
ram into cars
strap on the suicide bomb
purposefully start wars;

they lost the ability
to rule their families
respect their women
build their houses …
their seed is raping the earth
leaving them blind
Angry young men will mobilise the secrets of their hearts
In order to find anchors for their roots.

There is a relentless despair that governs neo-liberal everyday life, a space of hopelessness that engulfs the psyches of those who have not 'made it' or succeeded. The end of Apartheid opened the path for elite transition (Bond, 2014), in which a small minority of black South Africans could become a part of the accumulating classes. The global context of neo-liberal transition coincided with our democratic opening in 1994 and, as celebrity culture and politics exploded internationally, rapid accumulation and upward class mobility became a new reality for black South Africans – but only for some.

Neo-liberal accumulation continued the marginalisation and exclusion of the majority of black South Africans who remained in the black ghettoes of Apartheid. Succeeding financially became visually accessible to South Africans in both urban and rural areas, connected to television sets, in the images of new glossy black public officials who could be seen everywhere in public life. But as this sensibility of neo-liberal success took root in our country after democratic transition, so too did the realisation of many that the promised 'rainbow nation' was an illusion for most, black and white, in different ways. Black youth, facing unemployment rates of around 40 per cent in South Africa today, were definitely part of those excluded from neo-liberal capitalism.

In this neo-liberal context, young men are treated as a social problem. As global governance systems enter a phase of dangerous transition – with competing hegemonic poles, demographic explosion and global migrations – these angry young men feed into global problems of unemployment and socio-political instability. Black youth in South Africa are part of this global phenomenon. The logic of the Fourth Industrial Revolution, as many term the new digital stage of capital accumulation, creates a global surplus labour force, an army of unemployed that the economy cannot absorb. Structural unemployment has become a feature of many societies across the globe. While being young is associated with strength, vitality and virility, for many of these discarded youth, the space of economic exclusion that they inhabit is a place of desolation and despair.

South African state policy reflects the shift from social welfarism and social democracy to neo-liberal concepts such as 'resilience' (Chandler & Reid, 2016). The approach advocated to young South Africans is to pursue social entrepreneurship. Neither capital nor the state provides youth with viable employment opportunities, therefore youth are encouraged to engage in start-up enterprises. For the 'enchanted gardeners' in the Cape township of Khayelitsha, however, a different path of personal and social activism has emerged.

Unemployed young men are mostly uninterested in agricultural livelihoods. Obstacles to the participation of young and male urbanites in small-scale agriculture and rural development are well documented. For example, De la Hay and Beinhart (2017) recently documented the paucity of labour, especially young people, for agricultural subsistence farming in the Eastern Cape of South Africa. Peri-urban and urban agricultural initiatives face resistance from young urban poor whose expectations are shaped by global consumptive imaginaries. With elite consumption visible through multiple media sites, including social media and television, interest in agricultural development amongst urban youth is low. Environmental conservation initiatives sometimes also conflict with local farming practices, such as the conservation of wild animals that threatens domestic farming and therefore livelihoods.

While mass food production and supermarket distribution provide the bulk of vegetable needs, food consumption and distribution increasingly includes small-scale urban vegetable production. In South Africa, some food gardens have linked up with the Slow Food Movement that espouses a transformative food ideology and builds awareness of the relationship between food, the environment and the individual. A key objective of this environmental movement in South Africa and elsewhere is food security.

The study presented here shows that these forms of political and economic empowerment in urban food gardens are organic and driven from below, unlike state-led policy initiatives that are generated at the national level with variable success. Current social policies promote particular narratives of employment, seeing young black men as part of a reserve of labour, or alternately as potential entrepreneurs. None of these narratives necessarily address unemployment or the precarity of urban youth, but in some ways, the new young township farmers are social entrepreneurs as envisaged in these social policies. However, our evidence shows that these food movements are not engaging with the state – neither their radical food activism nor their local economic activities attempt to harness state support for their valuable entrepreneurialism.

INDIGENEITY AND THE POLITICS OF FOOD

The global food regime continues to produce food insecurity and also results in land grabs, climate change and food waste (Blay-Palmer, Sonnino & Custot, 2016; Rama, 2015). The food sovereignty movement has risen in response to some of these challenges, suggesting that food production and distribution should be localised to limit the influence of markets on food (Pimbert, 2008; Windfuhr & Jonsén, 2005). As Grey and Patel (2015) point out with reference to Canada, food sovereignty movements are sometimes closely linked with movements to promote indigenous rights. In former colonies, colonisation has impacted on how colonised people see themselves, as well as their understanding of the world around them and their role in that world. In order to understand the personhood of food producers, we need to look towards both the indigenous knowledge of tradition and the new endogenous knowledge or post-colonial urban life.

In South Africa, colonialism led to huge changes in the food system. The Xhosa culture of self-reliance was destroyed through cattle killing related to the prophesies of Nongqawuse (Peires, 1989). In this tale, a young woman is held responsible for the starvation of Xhosa people. The tale is also linked to the loss of women's power and their confinement to private spaces, while men were left to dominate public spaces (Thorpe, 1996). Colonialism therefore had to destroy women's power to make men dependent on colonial markets for survival (e.g. working in the mines and for white farmers). The struggle for food sovereignty is also therefore 'the continuation of anti-colonial struggles in ostensibly postcolonial contexts' (Grey & Patel, 2015, p. 433) – while at the same time, the patriarchal models developed under colonialism persist today (Gqola, 2015). Furthermore, in the post-colonial era, indigenous knowledge often runs counter to formal (colonial) education; for example, a Nigerian study found that environmental knowledge was negatively associated with formal education and wealth (Makinde, 2016).

Nevertheless, women's knowledge has lived on through folk tales told to children as they are growing up. Folk tales include knowledge of food production (Hobongwana-Duley, 2015), provide moral guidance and a sense of cultural belonging to children and youth. Despite the ongoing sharing through folk tales about food, indigenous foods are rarely cultivated and are only collected in the wild, even though many are highly nutritious (Jansen van Rensburg, Vorster & Adebola, 2014). New means of survival go alongside food transitions which include increased fat and carbohydrate intake (Bourne, Lambert & Steyn, 2002) and the promotion of urban food gardens to alleviate food insecurity (Battersby, 2013). The new urban lifestyles and food cultures, alongside traditional knowledge passed down through women, create particular ideas of personhood in township youth.

Urban food gardens around the world are often seen in light of their economic potential to address food access (e.g. Beery et al., 2014; Kuhnlein et al., 2013; Shrivastava, Shrivastava & Ramasamy, 2014; Tagtow, 2016). However, both indigenous food consumption and urban food gardening also have socio-cultural (Battersby, 2013; Cutter-Mackenzie, 2009) and spiritual connotations (Panelli & Tipa, 2009; Woodley et al., 2006). This complex understanding of food and food practices has been little explored in the literature on indigeneity (Grey & Patel, 2015). Despite the dearth of literature, Panelli and Tipa (2009) point to ways that understanding the socio-cultural and spiritual aspects of food can contribute to well-being, aside from a purely medicalised health perspective.

Food stability may also be understood as a form of body security, in which food is not just linked to health, but also to 'well-being', which links 'calmness, health, happiness, food products, positive emotions and satisfaction with specific aspects of life' (Ares et al., 2015, p. 304). Even in urbanised contexts, food carries socio-cultural values. For example, a South African study found that in townships high meat consumption was associated with a high socio-economic status, and specific types of food are also used in celebratory, spiritual and funeral rituals (Puoane et al., 2006). Similarly, a study in India found that wealthier people were more likely to eat at Western-style fast-food restaurants (Aloia et al., 2013). These examples show that food culture is essentially linked to displays of personhood – showing who one is through the consumption of specific foods.

In South Africa, vegetable gardening in homes, schools and clinics has been widely promoted as a way to address community nutrition needs in urban gardens (e.g. Altman, Hart & Jacobs, 2009; Cilliers et al., n.d.; Drimie & Ruysenaar, 2010; Faber et al., 2002; Faber, Venter & Benadé, 2002; Faber, Witten & Drimie, 2011; Karaan & Mohamed, 1998; Malan, 2015; Modi, Modi & Hendriks, 2006; Nemudzudzanyi et al., 2010; Webb, 2000). Urban gardening can transform unused land into viable and sustainable areas for food production, but to improve the reach of urban gardening initiatives, urban planners need to become involved in planning for urban agriculture (Eigenbrod & Gruda, 2015; Zeeuw & Drechsel, 2015). Apart from off-setting food expenditures and creating jobs, urban gardens can be places where people come together, helping to strengthen social and cultural ties (Ackerman et al., 2014) and address the social ills associated with alienation. The environmental impact of food gardens, including on climate change, is also an important consideration (Ackerman et al., 2014; Dixon et al., 2009).

Battersby (2013, p. 457) argues that 'the limited engagement with social aspects of urban agriculture has meant that the practice has tended to be viewed in overly economistic and utilitarian terms', with the social and community benefits being ignored or seen as secondary. In the context of food sovereignty Grey and Patel (2015, p. 438) have pointed to the sacred qualities of food: 'sacredness does not merely congeal in particular spaces, but is a quality of the totality of the natural world – including all of the life-forms that provide sustenance and frame trade networks'. Understanding about what is sacred also contributes to people's understanding of themselves as persons and community members.

RESEARCHING THE HARVEST OF HOPE IN A FOOD COOPERATIVE AND NON-PROFIT ORGANISATION

In 2015 I searched for a local food cooperative from which to source my vegetables for personal consumption. I located a food cooperative called Harvest of Hope which distributed vegetables in brown bags in suburbs of the Western Cape province in South Africa. The pattern of distribution followed the racial geographies of the city; the suburbs were on the white and middle-class side of the Cape railway line. Food bags were delivered to homes; signed-up consumers paid online and collected the vegetables from the designated home once per week. The service was efficient and the food bag held five to seven different vegetables each week. Quality was good – the vegetables were fresh and nutritious, facilitating the preparation of tasty meals.

An interesting dimension of the distribution practice was the insertion of photos of both the vegetable garden and the gardeners who had provided the vegetables. Unlike the alienating practice of supermarket food shopping, the source of the vegetables was provided with the fresh produce. I visited Harvest of Hope's distribution hub and offices and joined the local trip that they used to supply.

While conducting this local tour, I wondered about the racialised dimension of the non-governmental organisation's activities, in particular the patterns of consumption of the food produced by local gardeners. To what extent, I wondered, was the food alienated from its local environment, providing sustenance for those on the 'other side of the line' – the old Apartheid geographic divisions. Through snowball interviews, I was directed to the case study for this research, Ikhaya Gardens. The tour operator recommended that I direct these questions at the two gardeners who run the Ikhaya Food Garden.

'Science-Citizen' and Feminist Research Methodologies

This research project was based on feminist research principles. First, the 'researcher–researched' divide was disrupted in various ways. For example, the two research subjects, the community gardeners, were included in the composition of the research team. An effort was made to disrupt the power relations in which university academics gather knowledge from local respondents with no accountability to those constituencies. Workshops were held in which theoretical principles of the project were explored and understandings of food governance were shared.

A documentary was produced to enable development of a learning tool based on the activities of the garden and to expand its reach. The two gardeners were the key narrators in the documentary. This endeavour to link university-based science and citizen activities is part of the co-design of knowledge, in which communities and scientists recognise their joint contributions to the knowledge project in the making. Feminist methods of action research were also adopted through these learning activities and the production of the documentary for advocacy purposes. This project thus entailed a form of 'Mode 2 knowledge' (Krop & Blok, 2011).

The thoughtfulness, consistency over time and care given to the project by its founders made it a 'best practice' case study. The responses of Ikhaya gardeners to my preliminary questions about township consumption of the food produced in their garden was insightful and influenced my decision to choose Ikhaya as the key case study at this point in my research. They had opted out of Harvest of Hope, explaining that the garden needed to be a dedicated supplier for Harvest of Hope if you were one of their suppliers. The goal of Ikhaya, on the other hand, was for the garden to serve the community in different ways, either through the sharing of food produce from the garden or through the educational activities provided to the learners at the school. This suggested that, unlike the Harvest of Hope suppliers, Ikhaya gardeners would not have a regular source of income and cash for various urban needs, but for these gardeners cash income was not the main concern. This in itself was an unusual choice for youth who lack opportunities for formal employment and income.

Writing under neo-liberalism cannot be an act of intellectual subordination to neo-liberal indicators under new public management at universities. Writing has to be an act of radical rupture and continuous self-discovery, in which we dare ourselves to be enchanted. If the dominant space of governmentality enforces pragmatism, our task as critics of neo-liberal subjectivity is to find our true selves, and express those true selves relentlessly and implacably. We have to find our way out of disillusionment, disenchantment and despair and reach for the light, and this gleam will find the new young poets and prophets who will break through the greyness of practicality, and become our new spaces of enchantment and delight. In this sense our work is a spiritual journey.

These 'enchanted gardeners' became a site of reconnection for me as a South African researcher and lecturer upon whom the weight of new public management falls. It allows me to engage with and simultaneously side-step the external dictates on our writing, and to find the places of 'writing ourselves'. With this writing reconnection comes the political reconnection with dispossessed identities, finding our own histories in the midst of a continuous evacuation and hollowing out of who we are as the peoples of South Africa: 'The intention is not to wake up one day and decide to be gardeners, but to answer the calling. In the townships, gardening was never abnormal unless you were working in a white man's garden. It is not a matter of looking backward, but forward, within the cracks of coolness and fashion and bling. Today, this could be a different type of person: cool gardeners' (Xolisa and Athenkosi, Ikhaya Food Gardeners, Second Food Research Team Workshop, WSG, Johannesburg, May 2017).

THE 'COOL GARDENERS' AND IKHAYA AS A NEW FOOD MOVEMENT

Khayelitsha, the urban township where the food gardeners live and grow their gardens in the grounds of township schools, covers an area of about 47 square kilometres. It is situated 30 kilometres from Cape Town's city centre, and is the fastest growing and third largest black township in South Africa, with a population estimated around 2.5 million. Racialised geographies of Apartheid endure in these black urban spaces, in which white South Africans predominate in middle-class suburbs closer to cities and economic hubs, while black working-class South Africans are displaced in residential spaces far away from such urban hubs.

Cape Town, on the other hand, is branded as a global city, with rapid urbanisation and high-tech development, a popular tourist waterfront and an expanding foreign elite citizenry from different parts of the world. To work and/or reside in and near the city is to be included in the neo-liberal spaces of high gloss and neo-liberal success.

The relationship between physical territoriality and food security (enmeshed with food sovereignty) is a central analytical nexus. As sovereignty, security is a generic concept. It is adaptable to a multitude of aspects and can be entangled with a mosaic of contexts or sectors. In that sense, security is about sustainability in safety – that is the durability of a particular ecology of life, of living or being. This utopic quest for a stable ecology includes our relationship with our own planet – a relation which is multi-dimensional in all kinds of ways. One of the most important facets of this human–planet relationship is built around the accessibility, production and provision of food. Subsequently, the primary role that Earth plays in the processes of production of nourishment stimulates a human emotion or feeling to perceive the planet as a 'mother' – an entity that constitutes a key actor and catalyst in the sustainability of existence. Something we refer to as being or living on Earth. Hence for many communities around the world, Earth – this time perceived as Land – is a cornerstone of being, for building a home, establishing villages and communities and building massive social structures such as kingdoms, states or empires.

Within such a perspective, the way that land is organised – its geographical stratification and spatial configuration – constitutes not only the material space as we know it but also an array of contained socio-political discourses and praxis. Such geo-social structures can also be viewed as a container. In those containers exist, in the case of the developing world, what Derrick Gregory refers to as the Colonial Present – that is the discursiveness of praxis in time and space.

In that sense, these particular spaces are a constitutive part or a segment of particular security apparatuses, thus regimes, that can constitute an analytical entry point – as is the case in the urban township of Khayelitsha in South Africa. Today, a constellation of regimes of conduct and circulation constitute what we refer to as securitisation. The analyses of the food security dimension of any peculiar security regime/apparatus can lead to a better understanding of the role or agencies of the food activists in such socio-political strata – in this case the small food producers of urban gardens.

In the current context, 'Big Food' and its interface with the distribution, circulation and accessibility of quality food deeply impacts the growth of local food production and the potential expansion of new networks of food production. Local food gardens often aim to break the alienation of farm to table, side-stepping the large-scale intermediaries of supermarket chains. But the food distribution of urban food gardens is on a scale that does not radically alter the political economy of food production and distribution. More importantly, agri-food and the current food regime are major contributors to global warming through pesticides. Genetic modification of food also makes the food regime vulnerable to biological distortion. Organic farming is a potential counter to such environmental degradation (although it is not without its own environmental challenges). The governance of organic and local farming can provide important environmentally sustainable nodes for food production and distribution.

In the particular case of South Africa, black land loss means that township youth – especially young black men – are disconnected from the land's productive abilities and its healing potential. In a recent event in Johannesburg, South Africa (Africa Day, 2016, Wits School of Governance), the former president Thabo Mbeki challenged South African students of the decolonisation movement when they insisted that they wanted to take back the land that had been stolen from them by white colonisers. But what would you do with the land, provoked ex-president Mbeki, knowing full well that the urban youth in his midst were the subjects of (post)-modernity who had long lost their connections with rural life and the soil. The students' rejoinder was less than clear.

THE GARDEN AS A STABLE (SECURE) ECO-SYSTEM

Ikhaya is a Xhosa word meaning home. Ikhaya is a community food garden based at Isikhokheli Primary School in Khayelitsha. The food garden is a small L-shaped piece of land in the school grounds and works as a not-for-profit community activity. The vegetables produced in the garden are utilised for both the education of learners at the primary school where the garden is based as well as for consumption. The harvest of the garden is seasonal and is not sufficient for subsistence. As produce is generated, pots of food are made; bunches of vegetables are given to mothers in the community. No payment is required but small donations are often given as a token of gratitude. Various donations have been given to the garden, including a water borehole, a container for their offices and a table tennis board. The garden includes vegetables, edible flowers and indigenous plants and trees. Disused vehicle tyres have been adorned as seats and makeshift pot plants.

The garden was started in 2010 by two gardeners who were part of a poets' collective:

> Within the whole movement that was happening of arts in the streets and in our neighbourhood there was a huge need for the practical element so that's how I and the group that was already active with the arts and the poetry, got to the point whereby we started the garden and then from there got to the point where we were sharing knowledge through the arts. It felt only right to share knowledge in the garden as well.

They saw that the field in the school was filled with litter and was not being used; they approached the school's principal about starting a garden in the 10 by 15 square metre area. The principal agreed and provided water for the garden while the youth cleared the rubble and started growing on the site. Learners from the school attend the garden after school a few times during the week. Some of these learners have begun to make their own gardens at home, drawing on what they have been taught by the young gardeners at Ikhaya Garden.

Food activism today forms part of the struggle for a reconnection with the Earth in a context of post-colonial dispossession and the reassertion of autonomy over our bodies. This awareness of nature dawns on the gardeners as they first experience this connection with the Earth:

> I started with a garden at home. Then I came across the Abalimi tour. It was great; it was inspiring. I then decided I would work with Mama Bokholo at Nyanga and soon after decided to start my own garden. I saw the need in our own community and saw things that I had never seen before, like Nature. I then spoke to the principal where this garden is: she loved the idea.

While urban gardening has been present in South African townships in the past, urban densification has reduced the presence of these gardens as supplementary household incomes. The urban food garden movement led by black township men defies dominant forms of political economic organisation as well as urbanisation trends. Transnational agri-food systems have reduced our ability to govern our own bodies (for example, managing the amount of fat and sugar in our food). Body awareness through urban food gardens promotes a form of autonomy and self-awareness that challenges the alienation produced by Big Food systems.

Ikhaya is a form of food activism that advocates a different politics of the body. Food gardens based at schools in Khayelitsha demonstrate that new forms of body subjectivity arise through participation in the urban food gardens. The gardeners advocate against the loss of agency over our food consumption, for example, they rail against carcinogenics in braais (called 'shissanyamas' in South Africa). They have a vision of a nutritionally sound community that participates in growing their own food, while developing cultural activities around environmentally sound food production.

Young people are constantly cajoled in townships to apply for jobs and engage in self-promotion. X describes the futility of these endeavours:

> Young people in Khayelitsha are so much pressured. They have the pressure of going to school, graduate, don't get a job, some of them they pass matric and they can't continue further, others they drop out because they don't connect with the education they are getting. Because some of the young people, you go home, your parents are telling you to get a job but you keep applying with CVs, you don't get a job.

Production and distribution systems for urban food gardeners are located in racialised geographies of Apartheid and post-Apartheid South Africa. Due to Apartheid social engineering, Khayelitsha is on the edge of Cape Town and not well integrated into the vibrant city economy. These racialised geographies have a direct bearing on the limits and prospects for young people. The spatial containment of the black township is characterised by one of the gardeners as 'living in a box':

> Young people in Khayelitsha as well they are living in a box: they watch too much TV and they want to practice what they see on TV. So you find some of the youth they are living an American dream, you have everything but you have nothing where they dance and sing their troubles away but in the morning you will hear that someone is dead from that dancing. All these shebeens and all these drug spots are run by gangsters so if the community is run by gangsters young people need to find a remedy for themselves.

These new food movements espouse a radical politics of nutrition and body awareness. They mobilise through township social events that bring food, poetry and music together. Local cultural events called 'Impilo', meaning food market, are organised on weekends in which soup is made from recycled food such as vegetables and poetry is performed and music is played. These events are also called 'disco soups'.

Through these events they present the garden as a central element in their township ecosystem that promotes a stable ecosystem for young people in the midst of the township's unstable systems of life. 'Making gardening cool' for young people and young men in particular is a key objective for the young gardeners. Young people, school teachers and learners are drawn to these events in which the garden plays a central role:

> In terms of the achievements there's many that we can go through but just to highlight a couple of few very simple achievements is having to ignite the interests of the teachers since they are the first role models to the kids who already are in the school since they see them on a regular basis and longer hours so having to capture their interest not just in terms of having to observe or view the garden but having to want to engage with it on a practical level, whether it's wanting to request a specific herb or plant that they want to use or ask questions based on what's happening in the garden. So for me that could have been one achievement that stands out because through that achievement we have had a domino effect of many more achievements in terms of interest and engagement from the community.

Food gardens in South Africa have particular racialised and gendered attributes: food gardens and local markets are associated with white environmentalists, while community gardens are often maintained by older black women who have retired and have time on their hands for daily gardening. The difference in these local school-based gardens in Khayelitsha is that they are led and maintained by self-employed black youth who self-identify as activists that bring community awareness, particularly to young learners at the school:

> The relationship with the learners has been amazing from day one. The kids came in running, and they came to ask what were we exactly doing. When we told them that we were planting food they thought we were crazy. So we embarked on a journey with them from that moment to actually educate ourselves and prove that food really comes from the soil because they thought food comes from the shelves.

These gardeners are 'food activists' as they mobilise around social issues, but with food as a key organisational objective and instrument. Organisational links have developed between the Khayelitsha food gardeners and the Slow Food Movement in Italy, as well as the food sovereignty movement in South Africa. However, there has been some dissatisfaction with their engagement with some of these movements and the emphasis on rhetoric rather than more work on growth of food gardens. There is also some sense that their relations with the Slow Food Movement was somewhat instrumental given their 'authentic' township roots, so they have drifted away from this movement.

What is profound about the food gardeners is how they break through the most desolate and abandoned socio-economic spaces to find meaning in this space of neo-liberal abandonment. As 'the market' excludes many South African black townships from economic integration, an act of profound rebellion against this marginalisation, such as the creation of food gardens, entails reconnection with the land, new and different economic meanings, deeper understandings of the conditions of neo-liberal exclusion for young, black, working-class South Africans and, despite all of this, the possibility of beauty. Through these rebellious acts of economic self-activity, a space of hope and enchantment emerges: 'We are more focused on education; we are more focused on bringing back the dignity of the people, the independence. We are more focused on self-reliance where we say that you can feed yourself from the small soil that you have, so we're more about expanding the knowledge of growing.'

Ikhaya is also a model for 'water-wise' gardens. Cape Town as a city was hit by crippling drought in 2017 and 2018. Many food gardens were devastated. Ikhaya's mixture of vegetables and indigenous plants helped to sustain the garden through the droughts. While the vegetables died off, the soil was held together by indigenous succulents that continued to pass nutrients into the soil during the drought. When the drought subsided, the soil was able to regenerate and the vegetables grew again. This mixed form of gardening thus allowed Ikhaya to sustain itself through the serious water shortages experienced in Cape Town:

> Since we all know there has been a water drought in Cape Town, it has been a crucial element but not detrimental. I would say we have done the best to sustain our garden and it has survived through that era of drought. Lucky for us we have quite a magnificent garden with a lot of diversity in it. It has been much more [sic] easier for us to go through this very stressful era of drought here.

When the gardeners speak of their garden, it is with a spirit of hope and enchantment:

> The garden has been life: it has been an amazing life because you don't find that type of life in the townships but with the garden, is where you find the real things, that life does really exist. It is not a myth but life is in existence through the plants, through the trees, through the flowers and the vegetables, it's life.
>
> Never forget why you started something. It might be gardening or something totally parallel towards gardening, and never lose who you are and whatever you are doing what you are doing, and always stay true to yourself and the core reason of doing what you do, and most importantly, always enjoy it.

Our fieldwork suggests that new forms of land usage and food regimes, and new kinds of personhood, are both possible and necessary to confront these systemic challenges. Through an integrated local development approach that is simultaneously articulated at the regional and continental levels, innovative forms of food production and personhood, articulated in new food movements and urban gardens, can provide a template for advocacy by national, continental and global institutions. Prevailing food governance systems may enhance or limit the expansion of these particularistic food initiatives.

The revitalisation of small-scale agriculture should not be understood as a return to the past. For multiple reasons, the old forms of subsistence agricultural production have limitations in the current global context. These limitations have been established in a number of scholarly works and investigations. But the urbanised food growers that are springing up in different regions of the world present alternative forms of subsistence agriculture.

CONCLUSION: THE GARDEN AND SPIRITUALITY AS A SPACE OF REPOSSESSION

> The garden is a platform for spiritual and practical knowledge creation and circulation. The practicality alluded to here is about the knowledge useful to the mechanisms and strategies of survival of individuals or people under a subjecting regime of exploitation. Such an approach, as assumed by this project, subsequently allows for knowledge to emanate in the form of a new discourse; rooted in both indigenous and western epistemologies. Thus, by making going to a garden to initiate a transformative (spatially and psychosocially speaking) journey of learning by entering a hub of knowledge, the garden becomes a space of contextuality, an empirical ground of knowledge and praxis. (Rebecca Pointer, Project Assistant, WSG Food Research Team, 2018)

When we think about the term 'gardener' and what being a gardener means, we are taking on a project of personhood. In that sense, the project is redefining gardening as a project of dignity, opting out of consumerism and entrenching non-colonial civility: 'A garden is able to cultivate and facilitate the development of strategies for circumventing the existing geographies and regimes of dispossession by allowing a form of articulation of local and endogenous knowledge and practices. In this way, endogenous praxis gets connected to indigenous knowledge' (Rebecca Pointer, Project Assistant, WSG Food Research Team, 2018).

We find a continuum of spirituality in the way that the different urban small food farmers or gardeners connect with the soil in different contexts. A new way of centring the planet in the construction of our livelihoods may be in evidence as we endeavour to produce and consume in a sustainable fashion. Small-scale initiatives can thus provide prescient ontological insights that draw on past heritages and indigenous knowledges, while simultaneously looking forward to alternative food systems that nourish, enrich and revitalise our bodies rather than degrade our bodies.

New forms of food governance thus require a break with the ethos of secular rationalism that uphold modernity's attachment to aggressive mechanisation. The quest for appropriate technologies and local self-reliance can build more stable ecologies within our food systems. Such a quest need not be a utopian endeavour but can be part of an organic movement for food autonomy and self-reliance. While this quest links to the movement for food sovereignty, the Earth Connections envisaged in this project imagine a different politics of the body that moves beyond left-wing patriarchal modes of engagement (Miller, 2016).

These new visions for change are premised on existing conditions for change rather than promoting a utopian experiment; the 'small-scale agriculture' movement is growing in multiple forms. What is required is an interrogation of how these small-scale forms may articulate in a more democratic and forceful way with Big Food (agri-food) monopolies. Re-establishing control over our bodies and reconnecting with planet Earth is the antidote to alienation and supermarketisation of our food regimes. To build resilience in the face of climate change, food insecurity and chaos in global governance systems, a radical transformation of our food regimes through a small-scale revolution led by food movements globally is necessary, including the incorporation of digitally distributed templates for self-sufficiency and autonomous food production. While no panacea for youth unemployment, these new food activists can potentially break the narrative discourses of young black men as societal problems and see that young people are a solution to the systemic ills that we have created.

To be an 'enchanted gardener' is to be a life giver. As a gardener, one wants to see himself or herself as a nurturer of the soil. But such a nurturing needs to be decoupled from stereotypes of angry young (black) men, both in policy discourse and political praxis. 'Enchanted gardeners' are agents of beauty and purveyors of healing cultures of work and thought.

ACKNOWLEDGEMENTS

Thank you to the National Institute for the Humanities and Social Sciences and Wits University for funding this research, and the core team members, Dr Babalwa Magoqwana and Dr Gary Gabriels, for their inspiration and intellectual support. Thanks to Wits School of Governance at the University of Witwatersrand for hosting the project, a piece of action research with the Khayelitsha gardeners to generate new knowledge on urban food gardens in South Africa. Special thanks go to the project team for creating a truly enlightening and enchanting learning experience: the researchers and gardeners came together to challenge rational, Western, neo-liberal ideologies and let the spirit of earth connection generate new and decolonised forms of knowledge: Mouctar Diallo and Rebecca Pointer for insightful interventions at the start of the project; the videographers, Bridget Thompson and Abdul Cadir Ahmed Said, and their short documentary film, *Ikhaya*, produced jointly with the principal investigator Darlene Miller; Kemantha Govender and Lerato Mtambanengwe in their communications and event support; Mtini Michael Du Plooy for his project poem reproduced here, and his painting *Angry Young Men*, which encapsulated some of the enchantment we were trying to access and generate, as a counter to neo-liberal disenchantment.

REFERENCES

Ackerman, K., Conard, M., Culligan, P., Plunz, R., Sutto, M.-P. & Whittinghill, L. (2014). Sustainable food systems for future cities: The potential of urban agriculture. *Economic and Social Review*, 45(2, Summer), 189–206.

Aloia, C. R., Gasevic, D., Yusuf, S., Teo, K., Chockalingam, A., Patro, B. K. & Lear, S. A. (2013). Differences in perceptions and fast food eating behaviours between Indians living in high- and low-income neighbourhoods of Chandigarh, India. *Nutrition Journal*, 12, 4.

Altman, M., Hart, T. G. & Jacobs, P. T. (2009). Household food security status in South Africa. *Agrekon*, 48(4), 345–61.

Ares, G., de Saldamando, L., Giménez, A., Claret, A., Cunha, L. M., Guerrero, L., … Deliza, R. (2015). Consumers' associations with wellbeing in a food-related context: A cross-cultural study. *Food Quality and Preference*, 40, Part B, 304–15.

Battersby, J. (2013). Hungry cities: A critical review of urban food security research in Sub□Saharan African cities. *Geography Compass*, 7(7), 452–63.

Beery, M., Adatia, R., Segantin, O. & Skaer, C.-F. (2014). School food gardens: Fertile ground for education. *Health Education*, 114(4), 281–92.

Blay-Palmer, A., Sonnino, R. & Custot, J. (2016). A food politics of the possible? Growing sustainable food systems through networks of knowledge. *Agriculture and Human Values*, 33(1), 27–43.

Bond, P. (2014). *Elite transition: From apartheid to neoliberalism in South Africa*. London: Pluto Press.

Bourne, L. T., Lambert, E. V. & Steyn, K. (2002). Where does the black population of South Africa stand on the nutrition transition? *Public Health Nutrition*, 5(1a), 157–62.

Chandler, D. & Reid, J. D. M. (2016). *The neoliberal subject: Resilience, adaptation and vulnerability*. London: Rowman and Littlefield.

Cilliers, S. S., Siebert, S. J., Du Toit, M. J., Barthel, S., Mishra, S., Cornelius, S. F. & Davoren, E. (n.d.). Garden ecosystem services of Sub-Saharan Africa and the role of health clinic gardens as social-ecological systems. *Landscape and Urban Planning*.

Cutter-Mackenzie, A. (2009). Multicultural school gardens: Creating engaging garden spaces in learning about language, culture, and environment. *Canadian Journal of Environmental Education*, 14(1), 122–35.

De la Hey, M. & Beinart, W. (2017). Why have South African smallholders largely abandoned arable production in fields? A case study. *Journal of Southern African Studies*, 43(4), 753–70.

Dixon, J. M., Donati, K. J., Pike, L. L. & Hattersley, L. (2009). Functional foods and urban agriculture: Two responses to climate change-related food insecurity. *New South Wales Public Health Bulletin*, 20(2), 14–18.

Drimie, S. & Ruysenaar, S. (2010). The integrated food security strategy of South Africa: An institutional analysis. *Agrekon*, 49(3), 316–37.

Eigenbrod, C. & Gruda, N. (2015). Urban vegetable for food security in cities: A review. *Agronomy for Sustainable Development*, 35(2), 483–98.

Faber, M., Phungula, M. A., Venter, S. L., Dhansay, M. A. & Benadé, A. S. (2002). Home gardens focusing on the production of yellow and dark-green leafy vegetables increase the serum retinol concentrations of 2–5-y-old children in South Africa. *American Journal of Clinical Nutrition*, 76(5), 1048–54.

Faber, M., Venter, S. L. & Benadé, A. S. (2002). Increased vitamin A intake in children aged 2–5 years through targeted home-gardens in a rural South African community. *Public Health Nutrition*, 5(1), 11–16.

Faber, M., Witten, C. & Drimie, S. (2011). Community-based agricultural interventions in the context of food and nutrition security in South Africa. *South African Journal of Clinical Nutrition*, 24(1), 21–30.

Gqola, P. D. (2015). *Rape: A South African nightmare*. Johannesburg: MF Books Joburg.

Grey, S. & Patel, R. (2015). Food sovereignty as decolonization: Some contributions from Indigenous movements to food system and development politics. *Agriculture and Human Values*, 32(3), 431–44.

Hobongwana-Duley, H. Y. (2015). Exploring indigenous knowledge practices concerning health and well-being: A case study of isiXhosa-speaking women in the rural Eastern Cape. PhD, School of Education, University of Cape Town. Retrieved from https://open.uct.ac.za/handle/11427/15555

Jansen van Rensburg, W., Vorster, H. & Adebola, P. (2014). Delving in the past: Unearthing the diversity of traditional vegetables in South Africa (pp. 267–74). Presented at the XXIX International Horticultural Congress on Horticulture: Sustaining Lives, Livelihoods and Landscapes (IHC2014): 1102.

Karaan, A. & Mohamed, N. (1998). The performance and support of food gardens in some townships of the Cape Metropolitan Area: An evaluation of Abalimi Bezekhaya. *Development Southern Africa*, 15(1), 67–83.

Kropp, K. & Blok, A. (2011). Mode-2 social science knowledge production? The case of Danish sociology between institutional crisis and new welfare stabilizations. *Science and Public Policy*, 38(3), 213–24.

Kuhnlein, H. V., Erasmus, B., Spigelski, D. & Burlingame, B. (2013). *Indigenous peoples' food systems and well-being: Interventions and policies for healthy communities*. Rome: Food and Agriculture Organization of the United Nations.

Makinde, O. O. (2016). Evaluating indigenous environmental consciousness with residents of Ogbomoso in Nigeria. *Journal of Geography and Regional Planning*, 9(5), 87–103.

Malan, N. (2015). Urban farmers and urban agriculture in Johannesburg: Responding to the food resilience strategy. *Agrekon*, 54(2), 51–75.

Miller, D. (2016). Excavating the vernacular: 'Ugly feminists', generational blues and matriarchal leadership. In S. Booysens et al. (ed.), *#FeesMustFall Student Revolt,*

Decolonisation and Governance in South Africa. Johannesburg: Wits University Press.

Modi, M., Modi, A. & Hendriks, S. (2006). Potential role for wild vegetables in household food security: A preliminary case study in Kwazulu-Natal, South Africa. *African Journal of Food, Agriculture, Nutrition and Development*, 6(1), 1–13.

Nemudzudzanyi, A. O., Siebert, S. J., Zobolo, A. M. & Molebatsi, L. Y. (2010). The Zulu muzi: A home garden system of useful plants with a particular layout and function. *Indilinga African Journal of Indigenous Knowledge Systems*, 9(1), 57–72.

Panelli, R. & Tipa, G. (2009). Beyond foodscapes: Considering geographies of indigenous well-being. *Health and Place*, 15(2), 455–65.

Peires, J. B. (1989). *The dead will arise: Nongqawuse and the great Xhosa cattle-killing movement of 1856–7.* Indianapolis: Indiana University Press.

Pimbert, M. P. (2008). *Towards food sovereignty: Reclaiming autonomous food systems.* London: International Institute for Environment and Development.

Puoane, T., Matwa, P., Hughes, G. & Bradley, H. A. (2006). Socio-cultural factors influencing food consumption patterns in the black African population in an urban township in South Africa. *Human Ecology*, 14(special issue), 89–93.

Rama, R. (2015). Foreign multinational enterprises in the food and beverages industries of the BRICS. In W. Naudé, A. Szirmai & N. Haraguchi (Eds), *Structural change and industrial development in the BRICS* (pp. 294–323). Oxford: Oxford University Press.

Shrivastava, S. R., Shrivastava, P. S. & Ramasamy, J. (2014). Formulating a comprehensive strategy to counter the menace of malnutrition in developing countries. *Archives of Medicine and Health Sciences*, 2(2), 266.

Tagtow, A. (2016). Food security and urban agriculture. In *Sowing seeds in the city* (pp. 11–22). New York: Springer.

Thorpe, S. (1996). Women and power in African traditional religions: Nongqawuse and the Mujaji. In C. C. Landman (Ed.), *Digging up our foremothers: Stories of women in Africa.* Pretoria: University of South Africa Press.

Webb, N. L. (2000). Food-gardens and nutrition: Three Southern African case studies. *Journal of Family Ecology and Consumer Sciences, Tydskrif Vir Gesinsekologie En Verbruikerswetenskappe*, 28(1), 62–7.

Windfuhr, M. & Jonsén, J. (2005). *Food sovereignty: Towards democracy in localized food systems.* Bradford: ITDG Publishing.

Woodley, E., Crowley, E., de Pryck, J. D. & Carmen, A. (2006). Cultural indicators of indigenous peoples' food and agro-ecological systems. San Francisco: SARD Initiative commissioned by FAO and the International India Treaty Council, pp. 1–104.

Zeeuw, H. de & Drechsel, P. (2015). *Cities and agriculture: Developing resilient urban food systems.* New York: Routledge.

7. Citizens for Ghana and the kingdom: Christian personal development in Accra

Anna-Riikka Kauppinen

INTRODUCTION

Ghana's capital Accra has seen a boom in markets of personal development. In recent years, the industry has been characterised by Charismatic Christian discourses of the making of the competitive citizen-subject, which propose deeper Christian faith results in economic prosperity and national economic development. Adopting a long-term historical perspective on personal development in Ghana where "character building" closely dovetails with nation building, I explore the industry through the lens of young Charismatic Pentecostal media practitioners who produce spiritually motivated personal development programmes. Situated in a context where the popularity of Charismatic Pentecostal Christianity has risen hand in hand with post-1990s currents of neoliberal economic transformations, they frame personal development as a spiritual regime that enacts productive citizenship in Christian terms. Somewhat at odds with critical scholarship on personal development as a medium of neoliberal governmentality that shifts responsibility for social change from the collective to the individual, the young entrepreneurs in question view Christian faith as a revolutionary force in advancing Ghana's economic position. In dialogue with recent debates on the depoliticising effects associated with the globalisation of therapeutic industries of personal development, I draw attention to a multiplicity of historical macro-regimes, post-colonial African nation building in particular, that make personal development a distinctive global scene at the interface of "the world" and God's kingdom.

IN ACCRA

Timothy asked me to meet up with his team in one of Accra's few public libraries on a Saturday morning in 2014. He was a very busy man. In addition to his full-time day job in a marketing company, he was an entrepreneur and the leading force behind PEDNET (Personal Development Network) which he had started together with his friend Johnny when they were university students. PEDNET was "a network of affiliated initiatives committed to renewing paradigms and inspiring people to develop their leadership potential." In short, they organised various types of personal development programmes. That morning's meeting was to discuss the arrangements for their upcoming event called FENIX (Financial Excellence Summit) that focused on financial management and principles of investment. The main speaker of the summit was set to be Timothy's close mentor and a well-known Ghanaian Charismatic Pentecostal public speaker, Reverend Albert Ocran from the International Central Gospel Church (ICGC), that Timothy also attended. ICGC was one of Ghana's largest Charismatic churches and famous for its message of entrepreneurship and African economic development (De Witte 2012). Besides weekly sermons, its various Christian motivational speeches circulated via a variety of media, including media broadcasts and Christian self-help books by Mensa Otabil, the founder of the church that comprised nearly 700 branches in Ghana, and in several other countries across Africa, Europe, and the United States (see De Witte 2003). Similarly to the inspirational public figures at ICGC, Timothy was motivated to encourage others to pursue ambitious life goals, which, according to PEDNET's vision, would contribute to Ghanaian national development.

As we were about to start the meeting, Timothy's assistant and teammate Aisha explained to me, the new visitor, the rationale behind the organisation: "PEDNET is a Christian oriented group, so we want to enlighten and motivate. Whatever information we give out, we have Bible quotations supporting it." For instance, the FENIX seminar on principles of investment drew on Matthew 25: 14–30. The scripture tells the parable of a master and three servants, who the master entrusts to handle his money. The ones who invest wisely and grow the capital receive praise and more responsibility, while the one who buries the coins to the ground is condemned to darkness. Next to verses from the New Testament that encouraged investment and capital growth, Johnny added that FENIX also drew on scriptures that teach patience as investment practice, such as Ecclesias 11: 1: "Cast your bread upon the waters, for you will find it after many days."[1] When Timothy joined us, he specified that PEDNET's main goal was to "change the Ghanaian mind-set" and push people towards a new horizon of hope: "You live somewhere where in one circle, all is bad, there is no hope. Then you go to another circle, and there is hope … You see, in this part of the world, we look up to the government, my uncle, my husband. We don't take responsibility for our finances. But even Jesus said, you can't serve both God and money. You must have control of your finances." Enabling Ghanaians to "take control" of their lives, including personal finances, was a persuasive goal of this personal development initiative. In Timothy's and his associates' understanding, educating the Ghanaian public[2] on skills such as financial management contributed to *both* their professional *and* spiritual progress, and consequently, the wider national development. Ultimately, taking control of one's finances was not just a route to economic prosperity, but made the believer a better Christian. Pursuing excellence was hence a Christian duty that glorified God while "adding value" to the nation as a whole. Above all, personal development was not merely a secular enterprise geared towards the production of economically productive individuals on the journey to discover their "authentic selves" (Foster 2015, 2016; Guignon 2004), the kind of self that does not depend on others, including the divine. Rather, the very production of personal development programmes for largely professional and tertiary-educated audiences, such as FENIX, was biblically justified and thus drew the participant closer to the realm of the divine.

This chapter explores personal development through the lens of Ghanaian Christian visions of productive citizenship, namely, ideas on the kind of citizens who contribute to national development. I approach the industry of personal development from the perspective of one highly visible group of its cultural producers: Charismatic Pentecostal young, markedly middle-class entrepreneurs whose object of labour is to inspire others. By cultural producers, I refer to social actors who, while having privileged access to new mediums of creative expression due to their structural position in the local class hierarchy, also "negotiate the constraints of the particular material conditions, discursive frameworks, and ideological assumptions in which they work" (Mahon 2000: 468). Studying this negotiation provides valuable clues to alternative histories and genealogies of personal development from an Africanist perspective. While a growing, critical scholarship has focused on Western consumers of self-help (Davies 2015; Illouz 2008), which Foster (2016) sees as part of a broader neoliberal project of commodifying personal authenticity for capitalist ends, I shift the gaze to the concrete work that goes into the creation of cultural products of personal development in urban Ghana. Drawing on historical sources of the social meaning of "character building" in Ghana, and ethnography on the making of Christian personal development,[3] I show how post-colonial African economic transformation can be cast as a collective Christian responsibility. Among Timothy and his peers, while being themselves both consumers and producers of personal development, this work involved close attention to qualifying their self-help books, events, and programmes as "Christian," while ensuring that this work results in "national impact." In this regard, deepening one's faith is a vital medium of producing competitive subjects who can have an impact on the national scale.

In Ghana, as in various parts of post-colonial Africa, the kind of economic transformations seen in the past 30 years have been characterised by neoliberal currents of state privatisation and the influx of global flows of capital accompanied by political liberalisation. In some sense, the emergence of Charismatic Christian personal development in Ghana may seem like a logical corollary to neoliberal economic transformations, proposing that Charismatic Pentecostal Christianity has become the kind of "new spirit of capitalism" that ultimately "justifies engagement in capitalism" (Boltanski & Chiapello 2005a: 8). Christian personal development, on the surface, indeed seems to harness religious texts and other forms of spiritual engagement for personal productivity and capital accumulation, which relegitimises capitalism in a Christian guise (Boltanski & Chiapello 2005a). However, in this chapter, I make a somewhat different argument and focus on the ways in which Christian personal development indexes a novel type of political project in a context where locating politically meaningful action has become increasingly hard to discern (Salmenniemi 2019: 14). From the Africanist perspective, the range of institutions and sets of actors that shape public and political life has greatly diversified following the post-1980s structural adjustment programmes (SAPs) that paved the way for neoliberal economic transformations. As James Ferguson (2006: 86) argues, currently, "the cast of relevant political actors extends far beyond the roster of national governments and political parties" in various African contexts. Given this potential for alternative forms of political engagement (see also Piot 2010), throughout this chapter I suggest that the making of Christian personal development in Ghana engages its producers into particular politics of citizenship enacted through the guise of capitalist practice. The industry they are engaged with seems to promote seemingly neoliberal ethics of the self, including efficiency, excellence, honesty, and courage to invest and take risks. However, instead of concluding that the personal development boom in Ghana is ultimately evidence of the commodification of Charismatic Pentecostal Christianity into neoliberal forms, which Comaroff and Comaroff (2009) have termed "Divinity, Inc.", the case of Christian personal development points towards a multiplicity of historical macro-regimes that shape new forms of subject making, including Ghana's post-independence trajectory of nation building.

At the core, this chapter is about the concrete entrepreneurial, reflexive work that goes into qualifying personal development as a "Christian" endeavour that draws on a biblical source and yields national impact, while drawing on a longer genealogy of personal development and politics of citizenship in Ghana. By focusing on the practice of producing and running Christian personal development programmes, I show how Christian modes of address crucially shape the form and content of personal development as a distinctive kind of global scene ripe for comparative analysis.

ACCRA'S MARKETS OF PERSONAL DEVELOPMENT: A BRIEF OUTLINE

Personal development, in both its Christian and seemingly non-religious guises, was a ubiquitous feature of Accra. Massive billboards displayed upcoming programmes on business-planning skills, financial management, career progress, and entrepreneurship at busy traffic junctions; some of these programmes were church-based events that incorporated an explicitly spiritual element, others were organised by global brands such as Google, Ghanaian state agencies, or international and local non-governmental organisations. Ghanaian diaspora returnees were also active voices in the scene. They often drew on their experience abroad to inspire their audiences to reach towards "global standards," or to "change the economic story of Ghana," as Robert Klah declared in the opening event of *Ghana's Next Young Entrepreneur* competition in August 2013. Local newspapers frequently advertised programmes of personal development, such as one-day workshops on "business grooming," "image-management," and "professional branding." Personal development crept into daily life in various other urban spaces: when commuting in the city's most popular form of public transport, a crowded minibus *trotro*, passengers could be seen reading the Bible and a book on personal development side by side, perusing hard copies or reading passages on their smart phone screens. Besides global best sellers, such as Dale Canergie's "How to Win Friends and Influence People" and titles such as "Think Big and Grow Rich" that were regular offerings among local book sellers on the street, explicitly Christian self-help books authored by Ghanaian and Nigerian pastors were also carried in purses and pockets. Personal development had also its distinctive sound-scape – radio and TV stations broadcasted inspirational messages from Ghanaian and Nigerian pastors and young motivational speakers. Timothy, for instance, had a bi-weekly "Life Sense Hour" at a private radio station, where he addressed topics such as effective communication and true financial freedom, often backed up by quotations from the Bible.

*****

How has personal development emerged as a vibrant market in urban Ghana? On a global scale, the globalisation of industries of personal development has been connected to the mass-mediatisation of the "therapeutic ethos of the self," which followed the post-1980s transition from industrial production to advanced, service-intensive capitalism (Illouz 1997, 2008). This type of capitalism is characterised by the "prominence of service and information sectors, move from mass-production and mass consumption to flexible production and specialised consumption, and the centrality of lifestyle in class groupings"

(Illouz 1997: 12). In this kind of economy, bettering the self through personal development indexes competitiveness and agility in conditions of flexible capitalist production (Harvey 1990). As Abena, a young professional friend of mine who had participated in a personal development seminar run by Timothy's mentor Albert Ocran, stated, personal development programmes "added value" to herself as both a person and a professional. Instead of hierarchically organised large firms that used to commit the employee through the promise of financial security and guaranteed trajectory of career progress, contemporary capitalism is organised according to constantly shifting dynamics of social networks and what Boltanski and Chiapello (2005b: 165) call "projects." Personal development programmes hence increase one's "employability" on the journey of moving from one project to another (Boltanski and Chiapello 2005b: 166, see also Precarious Workers Brigade 2017).

While the public sector in Ghana has traditionally stood for the kind of hierarchically organised world of work described by Boltanski and Chiapello (e.g. Lentz 2014), the rolling back of state institutions after the 1980s SAPs has shifted the emphasis of the professional labour market to the private sector. The role of the private sector, including the presence of foreign multinational corporations, has become more visible especially in the capital Accra following the country's transition to democratic rule in 1992 and the liberalisation of the media and the public sphere. Currently, global media flows and rising skyscrapers offer new imaginaries of potential selves, identities, and "projects" to engage in. While Ghana never experienced mass-scale industrialisation and, similarly to various other post-colonial African economies, remains dependent on exports of raw materials for foreign exchange (Whitfield 2011), services and knowledge-intensive industries have emerged in major urban centres. However, the amount of professional jobs these industries and multinationals create does not match the amount of qualified candidates graduating from Ghana's numerous public and private universities each year. As a result, Ghana has a large tertiary-educated labour surplus and high figures of graduate unemployment (for Sudan, see Mann 2014). In this context, the boom in personal development makes sense. Given the historically salient desire for professional jobs and formal education in Ghana (e.g. Skinner 2009), personal development programmes offer an affordable means of lengthening the CV with additional qualifications given the intense competition for white-collar jobs.

The creation of Ghana's educated labour surplus is one effect of the kind of neoliberal economic policies that have shaped Ghana's political economy following the implementation of International Monetary Fund-administered SAPs in the 1980s. These programmes were designed to "modernise" the economy and were instituted as the condition of International Monetary Fund loans to relieve the debt crisis that various African countries grappled with after the 1970s. The SAPs introduced stringent austerity measures and transference of various state functions to other agencies, such as international and local non-governmental organisations (Ferguson 2006; Piot 2010). This is where the boom in personal development seems to connect most clearly with neoliberal economic policy-making: instead of setting demands on the national government, the programmes set demands on the individual to take responsibility, or "control" as Timothy's PEDNET framed it, of financial success and daily economic survival. In this sense, personal development becomes understood as a product of neoliberalism that transfers responsibility of economic organisation from a larger polity to the individual and extends the capitalist logic of accumulation to the management of previously unexplored arenas, including spirituality (cf. Berardi 2009).

However, to unpack a longer genealogy of personal development in Ghana, that starts way before the post-1980s currents of neoliberal economic trans-formations, it is important to understand the distinctive trajectory of framing Ghanaian citizenship after the country gained its independence from Britain in 1957. Within Ghana's post-independence economic and political trajectory, the very idea of personal development, if understood in the sense of "character building" and acquisition of new skills, has been closely tied with ideologies of national development. After declaring independence Ghana turned to state socialism, which rendered the state as the primary agent drawing the contours of public discourse. As Jeffrey Ahlman shows (2017) in his study of social and public life under Ghana's first president Kwame Nkrumah, the immediate post-independence era of the late 1950s and early 1960s saw the establishment of various politically motivated youth training programmes that became inte-gral to framing the public ideal of productive citizenship. Led by Nkrumah's Convention People's Party (CPP), organizations such as the Ghana Young Pioneers formed an integral aspect of the party's efforts to inculcate socialist work ethic through "building the character" of the youth, which included learning ideas of anti-imperialism, anti-capitalism, and African liberation. These programmes, unlike earlier programmes introduced during the British colonial era such as the Boy Scouts, focused primarily on ideological instead of physical training. The Young Pioneers, for instance, attended after-school classes to learn songs and recitations that emphasised Nkrumah's message of "collective national self-help and individual responsibility." As former partici-pants to these programmes reminisced, "the building of a young girl's or boy's character was as much a civic initiative as a personal one." Consequently, "[T]he youth came to model for all Ghanaians the requisite respect for work, commitment to timeliness, patriotism, and obedience necessary in a modern, postcolonial socialist state" (Ahlman 2017: 102). Beyond the youth that pro-grammes such as the Ghana Young Pioneers targeted, another objective was to build the character of Ghanaian workers. Controlling the meaning of work formed an integral aspect of this second stream of character-building discourse led by CPP's socialist party apparatus – work became construed in moral terms, the kind of activity that "link[s] all Ghanaians together in a program of cooperative development … The worker was to be the engineer of the nation, as he or she overcame individualism, personal avarice, and mentality of the colonial economy to labor for the collective good" (Ahlman 2017: 146–7). The character of the worker, in this case, was tied to patriotism and a concept of labour of which the primary objective was to contribute to the economic modernisation of Ghana.

Although organisations such as the Ghana Young Pioneers do not at first sight seem like typical personal development programmes, their emphasis on character building as a civic duty is an important historical starting point for the present analysis. Ahlman's insightful historical material suggests that there is a particular genealogy of comprehending the very idea of character building in relation to Ghana's nation building. Fast-tracked to Accra's contemporary public culture of personal development, questions emerge on the shifting dynamics of public discourse as to who, and for what kind of entity, does one seek to "better the self" for? While taking up roles formerly occupied by the colonial administration, Nkrumah's CPP sought to own the codes of representing ideal citizenship across generations. Encouraging the citizen to "better the self" was essentially a call to participate in the new independent state. However, as Ahlman notes (2017: 145), CPP's efforts collided with long-standing Ghanaian values of independence and ownership of one's labour, of which the primary purpose was to contribute to the glory of one's kin group. This was a particularly salient value among the demographically dominant Ashanti ethnic group. Therefore, to frame acquisition of new skills and work itself as a contribution to the nation state generated conflicts within families, trade unions, farmers, mining workers, and other occupational groups who weighed their multiple allegiances. At the core, as Ahlman remarks, CPP's era was a particularly "hopeful" era compared to some of the subsequent decades – the building of new infrastructure and acquisition of new roles and structures of access through CPP's programmes generated a sense of a nation that was robust and moving fast forward. Character-building programmes, which could be considered as the cultivation of a particular kind of "spirit" of productive citizenship along Nkrumahist lines of African liberation, were an integral aspect constituting this hope.

Next, I introduce a major shift that occurred in public discourses of personal development coming towards the 1990s, which has been increasingly characterised by the popularity of Charismatic Pentecostal Christianity in Ghana.

BETTERING THE SELF FOR GOD: CHRISTIANITY
AND NEOLIBERALISM IN GHANA

As described earlier, personal development has become a clearly discernible market in urban Ghana following the post-1990s currents of political democratisation and neoliberal economic transformation. While personal development stood for "character building" in state-administered citizenship programmes, contemporary markets of personal development display a variety of voices and emphases. Particularly visible voices in this scene are Charismatic Pentecostal institutions and actors. From the 1990s onwards, Charismatic Pentecostal churches have assumed many of the roles and functions that were previously performed by the state. In this section, I describe some of the dynamics that have contributed to the popularity of Charismatic Pentecostalism in Ghana and introduce the Charismatic Pentecostal cultural producers of personal development I worked with. Christian personal development aptly encapsulates the parallel trajectories of neoliberalism and Christianity in Ghana, which, I would suggest, are not independent variables but mutually intersecting transformations. As Meyer (2007: 12) argues: "Pentecostalism appears to be entangled with a culture of neoliberalism to such an extent, that it is impossible to still confine religion to a separate sphere ... and investigate the relation between religion and economy in instrumental terms." This interface of Christianity and neoliberalism has rendered personal development a distinctive kind of Christian scene of self-transformation, which, I argue, enacts post-colonial African nation building and productive citizenship in Christian terms.

Charismatic Pentecostalism first entered the Ghanaian religious landscape in the 1920s as a result of mission work by American evangelical Christians. Many of Ghana's influential indigenous Pentecostal churches, such as the Church of Pentecost, split from their foreign counterparts and became independent Pentecostal congregations (Asamoah-Gyadu 2005: 97). Newer Charismatic Pentecostal "one-man" churches, as they are locally called, namely churches set up by individual Ghanaian pastors, started to gain mass popularity during the 1980s. These churches were characterised by a rich ritual life, such as faith healing and deliverance from different types of afflictions (Asamoah-Gyadu 2005). This ritual space provided an opportunity for congregations to express their struggles and dissatisfaction with the hardships that structural adjustment and austerity measures had imposed on everyday life, which effectively positioned Charismatic Pentecostal churches as the counterforce to Jerry John Rawlings' military state of the 1980s (Meyer 1998). Moreover, they attracted audiences with a style of worship that is cunningly intimate in its address and engages all the senses in prayer and worship (De Witte 2008; Meyer 2004). On a broader scale, their popularity also benefited from access to new broadcast technologies facilitated by the liberalisation of the public sphere in 1994 (De Witte 2008). After decades of state censorship during Rawlings' military rule in the 1980s, Ghanaian Charismatic Pentecostal pastors, comparably to their American evangelical counterparts, enthusiastically embraced broadcast media for spreading the gospel. As a result, Christian sounds, images, and visions of future filled the airwaves. As Meyer (2004, 2015) remarks, the Ghanaian public sphere became effectively "Pentecostalite" in the sense that Charismatic Christian modes of address crept into other fields of popular culture, such as popular cinema. Christianity became a form of public culture that was somewhat at odds with Habermasian visions of a liberalised public sphere dedicated to secular, rational-critical debate of public affairs (Meyer 2004); instead of relegating religion to the private sphere, the transition to democracy rather heightened the public presence of religion in Ghana.

Besides their public role, Charismatic Pentecostal institutions and actors have also become highly visible in the economic sphere and organisational settings. As Asamoah-Gyadu (2005) observed in the case of "prayer vigils" organised to save the national flight carrier Ghana Airways, Charismatic Pentecostal leaders and lay believers seek to connect the scripture, and Christian ritual practice, to address concrete daily problems, such as poor public-sector productivity. As a result, "publicly Christian" actors in Ghana, also beyond pastors, have acquired a prominent voice in the discourse of national economic growth, seeking to frame a Christian spiritual regime as integral to success and a competitive future (cf. De Witte 2012), of which codes were earlier owned by agents of the Ghanaian state apparatus. While the popularity of Charismatic Pentecostalism has been recognised as a response to the effects of neoliberal economic privatisation (Comaroff 2009), another line of argument concerns the social productivity of Charismatic Pentecostalism itself as a site of value creation (Robbins 2009). Haynes (2017) frames this social productivity of Charismatic Pentecostalism in the Zambian Copperbelt as the value of "moving by the spirit." In her framework, religious self-cultivation along the Charismatic Pentecostal spiritual regime of prayer, fasting, and reading the scripture is not merely an instrumental vehicle to attain economic rewards through miracle and tapping into God's abundant resources, which has also been called "rice Christianity" (Robbins 2009: 57). Rather, a multiplicity of what Haynes (2017) calls "metrics" exist that index the value of "moving forward," including charisma and grace that in the Copperbelt exist in productive tension with the value of economic prosperity.

Taking a cue from Haynes' notion of the multiple kinds of metrics that can index "moving," or what for the present analysis could be called personal development, it is useful to consider what the "Christian" component of personal development in Accra could stand for. The explicitly Christian, predominantly male producers of personal development, such as Timothy, had a distinctive discourse of Ghana as a nation. They characterised the country as a "challenging business environment" that was crippled by high-level corruption, everyday bribery, and a general lack of "appreciation of rules and regulations," as Timothy put it. Their solution was to advance an idea of Christian reform in the Ghanaian marketplace.[4] This reform started from the reformation of the workforce: they needed to internalise "Christian values" and knowledge of the scripture to understand that their work lives were an integral aspect of their spiritual lives. As Richard, who similarly to Timothy organised personal development programmes, described, "people are one person in church and another one at work." The purpose of Christian personal development was to overcome this separation between faith and work, and cultivate a new kind of professional subjectivity.

However, instead of merely emphasising individual success, such as attaining economic prosperity, uniting work and faith stood for becoming better Christian persons, and consequently, a better nation, the kind of nation that could rise in the scale of successful national economies. According to Richard this progress could only occur through changing the "negative mind-set" of Ghanaians. "In Ghana here, there is too much talk of the devil. Why do we talk so much of the Devil when we all say God reigns supreme?" Indeed, in Ghanaian Christianity the imagery of the Devil has occupied a prominent position since the early missionary history, which also partly explains the contemporary success of Charismatic Pentecostalism. This strand of Christianity takes seriously the presence of evil spirits and offers a number of ritual solutions to spiritual afflictions, which connects with a longer genealogy of accounting for evil spirits in Ghanaian indigenous religions (e.g. Meyer 1999). Yet, Charismatic Pentecostal media entrepreneurs such as Richard and Timothy wanted to shift public attention away from "the Devil-mindset," which they saw prevalent in the majority of Ghanaian churches, and orienteer the believer towards God's grace. They believed that personal development programmes had the power to refocus the mind towards what Richard called "positivity" and Timothy as "hope," which ultimately led to national development. They were convinced that a "better Ghana" could be achieved through the cultivation of "better Christians."

The Charismatic Pentecostal entrepreneurs such as Timothy and Richard typically led registered enterprises that organised fee-paying events of personal development in Ghana's largest cities characterised by vibrant student populations, such as the capital Accra, Kumasi, and Cape Coast. Through producing programmes of personal development they aspired to generate spaces, or what Timothy had called "circles of hope," where novel conditions of possibility emerged. They explicitly distinguished themselves from what Richard called "the temple approach." Instead of churches, they primarily operated in what they called "the marketplace," while they remained active participants to their

Charismatic church communities and received advice and mentorship from their pastors. They also cultivated a particular kind of Charismatic Christian, masculine entrepreneurial style, which was in line with contemporary currents of self-fashioning. Following the 1990s currents of economic privatisation, entrepreneurship became a valued style of life (Shipley 2009), which contrasted with Jerry Rawlings' military regime when private businessmen and women were regarded with suspicion. In popular cultural representations, this entrepreneurial style was mediatised through the image of a young, sleekly dressed cosmopolitan male figure who has the authority to speak in public and challenge existing power dynamics[5] (Shipley 2013). In a comparable manner, Timothy and Richard aspired to distinguish themselves as a more "radical" alternative to the highly influential Charismatic Pentecostal "celebrity" pastors such as Mensa Otabil (see also De Witte 2011a), who were authoritative voices in the Ghanaian Christian public sphere. Religious leaders mainly "spoke from the pulpit," while Richard and Timothy aspired to create "impact in the marketplace," which eventually translated into Ghana's economic transformation. Their "product," instead of sermons and church buildings, was personal development. The purpose of personal development was to offer participants concrete tools to bridge the gap between work and faith, and direct attention away from the Devil into spaces and circuits of future transformation.

I will next turn to one event of personal development organised by Richard's company, Divine Media. In offering a description of the event, I pay attention to the prominent place given to the cultivation of a particular kind of spirituality as the key component of the competitive subject, and the role of Christian ritual in facilitating this transformation.

AT THE EVENT: ANOINTING THE COMPETITIVE SUBJECT FOR A BETTER GHANA

In March 2014, Richard and his media company Divine Media organised an event called "Spiritpreneurship Summit." Richard had started the company a few years back and had grown it into a media outlet of which a flagship product, a Christian lifestyle magazine called *Kharis Magazine*, was distributed to various institutions in and around Accra and Kumasi. The magazine was also part of the Christian personal development scene. The articles advised on acting as a true Christian in different spheres of life, such as marriage and work life. The magazine also included interviews on successful Christians whose lives served as inspirational examples for the readership. In a comparable manner, the main purpose of the Spiritpreneurship Summit was to offer these concrete tools for improving one's Christian lives, as Richard had outlined earlier. The stated purpose of the summit was to "raise Christian entrepreneurs" to act both virtuously, and productively, in business. In

Richard's vision, the summit would spark a "marketplace revolution" in Ghana by bringing together both leading corporate leaders and young graduates and entrepreneurs, who were the most common participants to the personal development scene in Accra. In Richard's view, his fellow young peers had to recognise that they could not simply "wait for jobs." They had to create one through entrepreneurship, and the Spiritpreneurship Summit was to offer "the spiritual edge" to do so. At first sight, this appeared wholly compatible with neoliberal economic subject making – to outsource responsibility of economic change, such as job creation, from the state to the individual, whose spirituality served as an economically productive force. However, as I explore here, the Spiritpreneurship Summit incorporated a strong discourse of Ghana's nation building, while it also devoted considerable time on the ritual "anointing" of the entrepreneur. The ritual element incorporated into the event served as the most important component of the making of the competitive subject who was tasked with the duty of Ghana's economic transformation. This points at the alternative "metrics" (Haynes 2017) and signs of personal development, which the ethnographic focus on the production of personal development programmes reveals.

When filming the promotional video of Spiritpreneurship Summit by the poolside of a hotel two weeks before the event, Richard pitched the event as follows: "Spiritpreneurship Summit is a platform for redefinition of business and work attitude. So we can redefine the nation." Echoing Nkrumah-style narratives of productive citizenship, redefining Ghana called for a particular kind of character building – entrepreneurs who had redefined their attitude to work through deepening their Christian faith. In order to reach towards this goal, Richard gave the platform to a handful of senior corporate leaders who in his assessment had managed to combine faith with work. He had approached a number of professionally acclaimed figures, all of them chief executive officers (CEOs) and managing directors of private companies, including real estate, banks, insurance companies and recruitment firms, who he called "marketplace apostles." One of the speakers of the summit, Mr George Addison, was the managing director of a well-known insurance company who had also authored a Christian motivational book. He explained to me his motivation to accept the young entrepreneur's request to dedicate one of his Saturdays to their programme: "As Christians, we are the salt and light of the society. We preserve, you know the way that salt is used to preserve food? As believers, we are this light, so you should not give up and leave to go to some foreign country. We complain Ghana is hard, Ghana is this, Ghana is that, but no, as Christians, we don't leave. You should not give up and complain, but make the difference." Perhaps counterintuitively, Mr Addison considered the summit an occasion to make a patriotic statement of Christians as the ones who "stay," and hence dedicate their life to the transformation of Ghanaian society. In another interpretation, his statement also implied that "true Christians" distinguished themselves from those Ghanaians who left Ghana for greener pastures abroad, including the metropoles of former colonial powers. While he did not comment on the structural inequalities underlying foreign migration as most often the only feasible means of significant economic progress for the majority of West Africans (e.g. Piot 2010), he seemed to propose that as middle-class and elite, structurally privileged Ghanaians, their duty as Christians was to stay.

As another important aspect of the spiritual transformation that this personal development event would facilitate, before the event Richard and his teammates had heated discussions on the role of "anointing" in the Spiritpreneurship Summit. The day before the event, we went to check the venue, a conference room of a centrally located upscale hotel. Besides praying in the room to dedicate the space to the hands of God ahead of the event, Richard and his teammates had a final meeting about the running order. They were discussing how much time they should dedicate to the anointing service. Nestor, Richard's closest associate, said: "Delegates, they come to learn, but they need the spiritual edge." For Richard, the anointing service was the primary highlight of the event. In Ghanaian Charismatic churches, anointing typically stands for applying olive oil to the believer's head in order to transmit divine blessings, such as healing and special powers from the Holy Spirit (De Witte 2003: 187). Richard and Nestor stated they wanted to reserve the maximum amount of time for "divine impartation." Jerry, the master of ceremonies of the event, complained that making everyone come to the front stage for anointing takes too much time. Richard objected, saying, "But what if people want that contact? ... It is important!" Nestor sighed, "Ah, democracy takes time," and proposed that we do the anointing "fast fast." Towards the end of the meeting, they finally agreed to take the oil out. The meeting finished with a long Charismatic-style prayer, which committed the space, the organisers, the audience, the families, and everyone involved in the organisation, into the hands of God.

As I arrived at the summit the following morning, Richard was running up and down, making sure everything was in place. The event was sold out, but contrary to Richard's objective of attaining CEOs of big businesses, the participants were mostly young men and women. The presence of more senior corporate professionals would have enabled to "take Spiritpreneurship to the corridors of power," as Richard whispered to me as we were about to sit down.

The event started with a long prayer and worship. We sang English gospel songs and engaged in intermittent prayer to dedicate the event in the hands of God, while we waited for all the speakers to arrive. When most people were seated, Richard started by speaking about the motivation behind the Spiritpreneurship Summit. "I was always sad seeing Christians compartmentalize themselves. They have their church-self and business-self, and this does not connect." The summit would bridge this gap and bring about a "revolution" in the Ghanaian marketplace. The summit was just the beginning of what Richard called a "movement," that would eventually take over the whole of Ghana, and in the long term, the whole of Africa and beyond.

The running order was a sequence of motivational speeches by the CEOs and Christian exemplary leaders, presentations from sponsors funding the event, and occasional music. Alongside Mr Addison and two other senior executives, Richard and his peers eagerly awaited the arrival of Dr Davidson, whose performance was expected to "electrify" the whole event. This real estate mogul was fast becoming one of Accra's best known "Christian businessmen." He had developed a school of economic theory that he called "Christian business spirituology," which he had printed on a background prop mounted to a visible spot in the conference room. During his speech, he gave a passionate account of the power of spiritpreneurship that centred on the idea of making a difference in Africa:

> Time is not on our side in Africa, because of technology and infrastructure. But we will give you the secret. We teach you the principles of seed and harvest, and it also applies to food and health, how to use resources. Africa is one of the most difficult places to work, because of human capital. Human capital has innate cultural inertia that we teach you to break down. So you join the global workforce! Holistically, use your spirit, soul and body in your business. Business is God's automated machine to fight poverty on Earth, especially in Africa. We have no excuse in Africa. It is the time of spiritpreneurship. Unearth the radical secrets in the Bible. What our forefathers in the Bible did, we are also able to do. Abraham, Job, Isaac, they were all spiritpreneurs! Like, Job sold houses. Churches don't sell houses … Now there is a model that you have to be a pastor to prosper. No! Adam was not a pastor! … Did you know that 67 percent of you is supernatural? And only one third is your body? Most of the time we depend on our body resources and neglect the power of spirit and our soul. The energy in you is more than 1000 times the nuke that was blasted in Hiroshima!

Dr Davidson's speech was a spectacular performance to the young aspirant entrepreneurs and professionals in the audience. Similarly to Mr Addison's remark earlier, his speech centred on the message that they could realise their dream in Ghana, and become successful on Ghanaian soil. Ghana was a "challenging environment," but they had all the power to succeed in growing their business with the help of God, given that "67 percent of their body was supernatural."

While Dr Davidson focused on the productive potency that inhered in one's spiritual power, the speech by Mrs Ellen Hagan, a well-known female CEO of her own recruitment firm, centred on the art of living "holy lives" in the Ghanaian marketplace. She talked about the ability to resist corruption and bribery that Christians had to confront on a daily basis. In her register, spirituality in business was cast in terms of piety and ethical self-cultivation, which eventually led to Ghana's economic transformation: when someone offers a bribe, one has to cultivate the character to refuse and thus lead by example, which eventually would change the mindset of the perpetrator himself. These kinds of decisions stood at the bottom of Ghana's economic progress: once Christians experienced true unity between their "church-selves" and "business-selves," as Richard put it, Ghana would rise in the global world order. Although the term "citizenship" was not explicitly used, the plea for leading "holy lives" in the marketplace was essentially a plea, as in Dr Davidson's speech, to contribute to Ghana's nation building.

Anointing service followed the speeches. To my surprise, although the production team had agreed otherwise the previous day, they decided to do a full anointing service with oil. The ushers, recruited from a Christian modelling agency Cross Walk Models, brought in small bottles of olive oil. One of the speakers, who was both a pastor and bank manager and served as the chief administrator of the anointing, stated: "This is ordinary olive oil, but we are going to make it into a blessed olive oil through our prayers." The ushers lifted the oil bottles up and kept them above their forehead as everybody prayed to bless the bottles. Next, they went around the room giving a drop of oil to each participant. The speakers advised the audience to apply the oil to their head, neck, hands, and especially feet, which were the foundation of their entire being. The audience followed the instructions. When everyone had applied the oil, we engaged in a fervent prayer that evolved into speaking in tongues. This was the visceral moment of opening the body to flows of spiritual power (De Witte 2011b), which took place in a markedly professional platform. This opening of the body was a crucial moment of allowing the Holy Spirit to take control of one's spirit, which could yield positive transformation in one's work, business, and eventually, in Ghana as a nation.

The use of anointing oil in a motivational event intended for raising a group of qualitatively different present and future professionals and businessmen can be taken as a technique of evoking divine presence. This called for material mediators (e.g. Engelke 2007), while Richard, Nestor, and Jerry debated how much time they could afford for this mediation. As their debate preceding the event shows, convincing the audience of the power that inhered in their spirit was one of the summit's key rationales. Given their existing observations on the Ghanaian professional world characterised by the separation of work and faith, and the limited capacity of Ghana's numerous churches to enact economic transformation, personal development in this event required a number of conduits through which to enable access to spiritual power. Anointing by olive oil was indeed the highlight of the summit and provided a physically felt experience of spiritual force. The use of oil mediated the flow of the Holy

Spirit, which facilitated self-transformation of the participants after hours of listening to speeches by veritable Christian exemplars of professionalism.

But what, ultimately, had been the "effect" of this personal development event? This turned out to be a key question for Richard and his team, which further engaged with the complex interface of Christianity, spirituality, and nation building in the era of neoliberal economic transformation.

AFTER THE EVENT: CALCULATING "IMPACT"

The cultural producers of personal development in Accra were constantly mindful of the question of "impact." They expected their work, the production of personal development programmes, to be more transformative than preaching to the congregation from the pulpit. Yet, as I attended the post-event review meeting with Richard, Nestor, and their brand strategist George, the question of impact encapsulated the ambiguities that inhered in the very idea of Christian personal development as the vehicle of nation building.

The meeting took a form of direct feedback that Richard recorded with his iPhone, structured around a set of questions that they had agreed on beforehand and which we would all brainstorm together. The first question was about general impressions. George started with praise: "The event captured the inaudible language of the heart, it was pioneering, it was a game-changer." He also esteemed that Dr Djangbah's presentation had been particularly powerful, judged by the visceral reactions from the audience. Next, we talked about the audience itself. As expected, Richard and his team had expected more high-profile business people to attend. "We wanted Christian business leaders, but didn't quite get that. We couldn't draw that many long standing leaders to come and share their experiences." This was a problem in terms of taking the message to the "corridors of power," as Richard had mentioned already at the event. These were the corridors where key decisions were made, namely, the kind of decisions that concerned the entire nation and had the highest impact. They brainstormed possibilities for ensuring that the event was advertised in appropriate corporate platforms in order to attract more senior participants in the following year.

The team also had a long discussion on the purpose of the Spiritpreneurship Summit: "We want to achieve something that goes way beyond motivation," Richard defined it. George added: "Yes, we want to create a new spiritual culture." They were also mindful of the fact that personal development had become a commodified industry, especially in the United States, as George described. "This is why people think that motivation is just about money. But we want to have a bigger impact." Indeed, this "bigger impact" had to do with changing the "spiritual culture" of Ghana – to charge a fee in order to give a "feel good" sentiment for the largely middle-class participants was simply not enough, and did not justify the dignity of their labour. At the core, they wanted to have a way to measure how the participants had been "affected" beyond that momentary feel-good sentiment. This was a difficult task, since they had not obtained direct feedback during the event. "We don't want people to just come to the event, be motivated, then go home and nothing happens," Richard said. We came up with the idea of getting testimonies from a sample group of participants that described how they were applying the principles of spiritpreneurship in their daily lives. Richard took meticulous notes. They also contemplated the possibility of making participants share business cards under the umbrella of the event. The idea was to create something "corporate, to go home with a sense of belonging," as Richard put it.

Lastly, we discussed the appropriate format for the future. Nestor and Richard proposed to host monthly meetings. George was hesitant, arguing that monthly meetings made the event too ordinary. Richard and Nestor defended the frequency due to "impact," since monthly meetings would enable partici-pants to have a continuous journey of self-transformation. They finally settled for a future strategy of an annual big summit that "fulfills a certain need, and activates the dreams," as Richard put it. The monthly meetings, for one, would break down to basics what Richard called "biblical economics." They were essentially Bible study seminars that focused on the economic principles of the Bible. Besides enabling participants to "live holy lives," studying the Bible from an economic perspective tapped into the competitive potential that adhered in their spiritual power, collective reading itself being a form of spiritual practice in Charismatic Christianity (Kirsch 2001).

Attending the review meeting was an important lesson on how personal development came to be qualified as "Christian" endeavour. Richard and his team clearly recognised that personal development had become a market that one could economically benefit from, given the demand for these programmes in a context of youth unemployment, including the kind of middle-class grad-uates that fee-paying events such as the Spiritpreneurship Summit attracted. The team shared a sense of responsibility for ascertaining that the programmes they produced had an "impact," which in the Charismatic Pentecostal church services often took the form of a testimony. The participant would testify through a personal story how the sermon one had listened to, anointing one had received, or prayer one had recited had concretely influenced one's life, for instance, in the form of a job opportunity, resolved conflict, or healing from an illness. The future plans for sourcing these testimonies was an important aspect of producing personal development. However, the suggestion to follow up on the journey of their participants was not merely to obtain the kind of endorse-ments that brought credibility, and more demand. Ascertaining impact was rather their Christian responsibility. They held the responsibility of making an impact on the spirituality of others, while continuing to align their own work and faith with God's will.

At the same time, the speeches in the Spiritpreneurship Summit of spearheading Ghana's economic development, and Richard's pleas towards "redefining the nation" through spiritpreneurship, echoed some of the discourses of citizenship that were already present in Nkrumah's citizenship programmes. In the review meeting, the question of impact was also a question of transformation on a broader scale – namely, making Ghana the kind of nation that was recognisably "Christian." Christian personal development generated the kind of citizens who felt responsibility towards God and thus "enacted" Christian faith across different spheres of life. This enactment of faith eventually contributed to Ghana's nation building, which Mr Addison had expressed in the metaphor of Christians as the "salt and light" of the society who stay put in Ghana. This is why impact mattered – impact was not only about personal economic prosperity or the accumulation of "spiritual points" for one's own salvation. Christian personal development was a spiritual practice geared towards the making of a respectable sovereign nation.

GOD'S CITIZENS: CONCLUDING REMARKS

In this chapter, I have discussed the broader implications of the booming markets of personal development in Ghana, and suggested that Christian personal development enacts citizenship in Christian terms in the post-1990s era of economic privatisation. Contrary to the post-independence era when codes of citizenship were defined by mass political parties, the key players spearheading new discourses of citizenship are Charismatic Pentecostal actors and cultural producers such as Richard and Timothy. They are motivated by an ideology of born-again Christians as the "salt and light" of society whose evangelical duty is to spread the message of ambition and excellence. This duty is conceptualised both in terms of religious adherence and productive citizenship – becoming a better Christian through personal development ultimately leads to Ghana's economic growth and national development. While Christian personal development seems to share much affinity with neoliberal virtues of self-presentation, detailed ethnography of producing the content and form of personal development programmes attests that there is more at stake. While neoliberalism often appears as the primary historical macro-regime that explains a number of cultural and social phenomena (Pedersen 2011: 30), Timothy's and Richard's efforts encapsulate a more complex genealogy of personal development in Ghana. This genealogy brings the trajectory of neoliberal economic transformations in dialogue with long-standing efforts of post-colonial African nation building, which has been facilitated through enticing citizens to take up particular regimes of character building.

Moreover, the precise role of spirituality and "deeper" Christian faith as the key component of personal development calls into question some of the key assumptions of neoliberalism itself. In the narratives of personal development that combine spirituality with Ghana's nation building, much emphasis is placed on developing the kind of spirituality that is adequately aligned with God's will and purpose. Drawing on the ethnography of Islamic human resource management programmes in Indonesia, Rudnyckyj (2010) has termed this emphasis on spirituality in settings of economic production as the shift from "faith in development" to "developing faith." In this reading, the key medium of personal development is collective participation in Christian praise, worship, and anointing. This kind of self does not seek to detach into an autonomous entity that exists loosely of the divine power – the power of the individual self is not enough to make an "impact" on a wider scale. Ghana needs divine power, and not only through the making of economically productive subjects through spiritual means, but through reconfiguring the entire idea of what kind of action qualifies as "productive" – as Dr Davidson argued, "67% of the human being is supernatural." Christian personal development programmes are one example of this realisation of one's supernatural potency and alignment of the self with divine force. The ethnography of Christian personal development in Ghana contributes to current efforts to decentre Western-focused theories of neoliberalism that often assume the free market, efficiency, and cost-benefit calculation as the building block of neoliberal governmentality. In this process, cultural producers such as Timothy and Richard are co-analysts and conceptual innovators in the effort to theorise neoliberalism, capitalism, and cultural change "from the south" (cf. Comaroff & Comaroff 2016).

Christian personal development represents a novel configuration within Ghana's political economy. Far from a politically disengaged form of self-cultivation symptomatic of the fragmentation of social political effort under conditions of neoliberalism (Salmenniemi 2019), the production of Christian personal development engages the entrepreneur in a project of *shared* character building, which in Ghana entails a long-standing history. The focus on spirituality, and the kind of selves, relationships, organisations, and national economies shaped as a result, can ultimately serve to revise some of the key tenets of neoliberalism and unearth distinctive genealogies of the making of the competitive subject.

NOTES

1. English Standard Version: www.biblegateway.com/passage/?search= Ecclesiastes+11&version=ESV, accessed 18 April 2019.

2. Ghana is a majority-Christian country, although statistics of religious affiliation are an object of constant public debate. The Global Religiosity Index conducted in 2012 reveals that 97 per cent of Ghanaians identify themselves as religious. Christians comprise close to 70 per cent of the population, while Muslims count as 16 per cent. Charismatic Pentecostals are around 30 per cent, other Protestant denominations such as Methodists and Presbyterians at 18 per cent, and Catholics at 13 per cent. The number of Ghanaians engaged in indigenous forms of worship, which includes consulting fetish priests, is difficult to count due to the fluid ways in which Christianity can blend with forms of indigenous religiosity, especially in rural regions (Meyer 1999). Moreover, the Ghanaian Muslim coalition frequently states that the total number of Muslims is counted less than in reality. http:// redcresearch.ie/wp-content/uploads/2012/08/RED-C-press-release-Religion-and -Atheism-25-7-12.pdf, accessed 20 May 2018.
3. The fieldwork for this chapter was conducted in 2013–14 as part of a wider project on the emerging cultures of "professionalism" in Accra, during which I encountered a number of Charismatic Christian producers of personal development, which this chapter focuses on.
4. See Rudnyckyj (2010) for a similar discourse of Islam as a vehicle for "marketplace reform" in Indonesia.
5. While the Charismatic Pentecostal personal development scene included a number of prominent female voices, the majority of the entrepreneurs I met were young men. They described themselves with labels such as "change makers" and "transformational leaders," fashioning themselves as responsible for changing the trajectory of the Ghanaian economy. Their partners, however, such as Richard's wife Lois, played key roles in the running of their enterprises and integrally participated in the scene. Yet, as Shipley remarks (2013), entrepreneurship remains a highly gendered concept in Ghana's contemporary public sphere and popular culture, and even more so when it comes to the "gendering of the speaking authority," personal development being mediated through various forms of public address. For instance, while Richard and Timothy understood their own strand of "spiritual entrepreneurship" as an inclusive mode of labour that incorporated women as integral participants, their closest business allies and masters of ceremonies of their events were almost exclusively men.

REFERENCES

Ahlman, J. S. 2017. *Living with Nkrumahism: Nation, State, and Pan-Africanism in Ghana*. Athens: Ohio University Press.

Asamoah-Gyadu, J. K. 2005. "Christ Is the Answer: What Is the Question?" A Ghana Airways Prayer Vigil and Its Implications for Religion, Evil and Public Space. *Journal of Religion in Africa* 35(1): 93–117.

Berardi, F. B. 2009. *Soul at Work: From Alienation to Autonomy*. Los Angeles: Semiotext(e).

Boltanski, L. and Chiapello, E. 2005a [1999]. *The New Spirit of Capitalism*. London: Verso.

Boltanski, L. and Chiapello, E. 2005b. The New Spirit of Capitalism. *International Journal of Politics, Culture and Society* 18: 161–88.

Comaroff, J. 2009. The Politics of Conviction: Faith on the Neo-Liberal Frontier. *Social Analysis* 53(1): 17–38.

Comaroff, J. & Comaroff, J. 2009. *Ethnicity, Inc*. Chicago: University of Chicago Press.

Comaroff, J. & Comaroff, J. 2016 [2012]. *Theory from the South: Or, How Euro-America Is Evolving Toward Africa*. New York: Routledge.

Davies, W. 2015. *The Happiness Industry*. London: Verso.

De Witte, M. 2003. Altar Media's Living Word: Televised Charismatic Christianity in Ghana. *Journal of Religion in Africa* 33(2): 172–202.

De Witte, M. 2008. Accra's Sounds and Sacred Spaces. *International Journal of Urban and Regional Research* 32(3): 690–709.

De Witte, M. 2011a. Fans and Followers: Marketing Charisma, Making Religious Celebrity in Ghana. *Australian Religion Studies Review* 24(3): 231–53.

De Witte, M. 2011b. Touched by the Spirit: Converting the Senses in a Ghanaian Charismatic Church. *Ethnos* 76(4): 489–509.

De Witte, M. 2012. Buy the Future, Now! Charismatic Chronotypes in Neo-Liberal Ghana. *Etnofoor* 24(1): 80–104.

Engelke, M. 2007. *A Problem of Presence: Beyond Scripture in an African Church*. Berkeley: University of California Press.

Ferguson, J. 2006. *Global Shadows: Africa in the Neoliberal World Order*. Durham: Duke University Press.

Foster, R. 2015. The Therapeutic Spirit of Neoliberalism. *Political Theory* 44(1): 82–105.

Foster, R. 2016. Therapeutic Culture, Authenticity and Neoliberalism. *History of the Human Sciences* 29(1): 99–116.

Guignon, C. 2004. *On Being Authentic*. New York: Routledge.

Harvey, D. 1990. *The Condition of Postmodernity*. Oxford: Blackwell.

Haynes, N. 2017. *Moving by the Spirit: Pentecostal Social Life on the Zambian Copperbelt*. Berkeley: University of California Press.

Illouz, E. 1997. *Consuming the Romantic Utopia: Love and the Cultural Contradictions of Capitalism*. Berkeley: University of California Press.

Illouz, E. 2008. *Saving the Modern Soul: Therapy, Emotions, and the Culture of Self-Help*. Berkeley: University of California Press.

Kirsch, T. 2001. Ways of Reading as Religious Power in Print Globalization. *American Ethnologist* 34(3): 509–20.

Lentz, C. 2014. "I take an oath to the state, not the government": Career Trajectories and Professional Ethics of Ghanaian Public Servants." In Bierschenk, T. & Olivier de Sardan, J.-P. (eds) *States at Work: Dynamics of African Bureaucracies*. Leiden: Brill.

Mahon, M. 2000. The Visible Evidence of Cultural Producers. *Annual Review of Anthropology* 29: 467–92.

Mann, L. 2014. Wasta! The Long-Term Implications of Education Expansion and Economic Liberalisation on Politics in Sudan. *Review of African Political Economy* 41: 561–78.

Meyer, B. 1998. The Power of Money: Politics, Occult Forces, and Pentecostalism in Ghana. *African Studies Review* 41(3): 15–37.

Meyer, B. 1999. *Translating the Devil: Religion and Modernity among the Ewe in Ghana*. Edinburgh: Edinburgh University Press.

Meyer, B. 2004. "Praise the Lord": Popular Cinema and Pentecostalite Style in Ghana's New Public Sphere. *American Ethnologist* 31(1): 92–110.

Meyer, B. 2007. Pentecostalism and Neo-liberal Capitalism: Faith, Prosperity and Vision in African Pentecostal-Charismatic Churches. *Journal for the Study of Religion* 20(2): 5–28.

Meyer, B. 2015. *Sensational Movies: Video, Vision and Christianity in Ghana.* Oakland: University of California Press.

Pedersen, M. 2011. *Not Quite Shamans: Spirit Worlds and Political Lives in Northern Mongolia.* Ithaca: Cornell University Press.

Piot, C. 2010. *Nostalgia for the Future: West Africa After the Cold War.* Chicago: University of Chicago Press.

Precarious Workers Brigade. 2017. *Training for Exploitation? Politicising Employability and Reclaiming Education.* London: Journal of Aesthetics and Protest Press.

Robbins, J. 2009. Pentecostal Networks and the Spirit of Globalization: On the Social Productivity of Ritual Forms. *Social Analysis* 53(1): 55–66.

Rudnyckyj, D. 2010. *Spiritual Economies: Islam, Globalization and Afterlife of Development.* Ithaca: Cornell University Press.

Salmenniemi, S. 2019. Therapeutic Politics: Critique and Contestation in the Post-Political Conjuncture. *Social Movement Studies*.

Shipley, J. 2009. Aesthetic of the Entrepreneur: Afro-Cosmopolitan Rap and Moral Circulation in Accra, Ghana. *Anthropological Quarterly* 82(3): 631–68.

Shipley, J. 2013. *Living the Hiplife: Celebrity and Entrepreneurship in Ghanaian Popular Music.* Durham: Duke University Press.

Skinner, K. 2009. "It Brought Some Kind of Neatness to Mankind": Mass Literacy, Community Development and Democracy in 1950s Asante. *Africa: Journal of the International African Institute* 79(4): 479–99.

Whitfield, L. 2011. Growth without Economic Transformation: Economic Impacts of Ghana's Political Settlement. Danish Institute for International Studies Working Paper 28.

8. Religion after work: Christianity, morality, and serious leisure

Ibrahim Abraham

INTRODUCTION

In the 'bourgeois age' in which we live (McCloskey 2006), leisure is an increasingly prominent aspect of our lives, not least because leisure creates jobs and wealth through the increasing commodification of our leisure time (Rojek 2010). The traditional moral view of leisure has been that there must be a 'natural' balance with work, and that the '"serious" side of life' focused on work and productivity must take precedence (Rojek 1989, p. 95). Leisure, in this traditional bourgeois morality, is properly understood as reward or recreation for work. As Marx explained the bourgeois view of leisure, 'pleasure-taking' must not override 'capital-accumulating', and to upset that balance would be to upset the moral order (ibid.). In certain contemporary contexts, however, this traditional hierarchical balance between work and leisure is being upset by changing social structures and technologies. Extended periods of unemployment or underemployment are becoming common, through lengthening periods of retirement, through the personal agency of those seeking to 'rebalance' their life and career, but also through lengthening periods of joblessness in low-growth economies and in industries undergoing automation, provoking policy debates about universal basic income (UBI), an unconditional welfare payment.

If work is becoming decentred, either through choice or through necessity, then the possibility arises for leisure to take its place as one's 'central life interest', the aspect of life in which one invests the most positive energy (Dublin 1992). This chapter seeks to explore the implications of such changes in the context of established religious and moral systems, in particular Protestant Christianity, which has seemed so connected to conventional bourgeois capitalist ideologies of work ever since Weber's (1930 [1992]) famous thesis on their 'elective affinity' in *The Protestant Ethic and the Spirit of Capitalism*. The particular focus of this chapter will be on the concept of 'serious leisure', developed by the Canadian sociologist Robert A. Stebbins to describe an approach to leisure in which, contra 'casual leisure', an individual makes a 'systematic' commitment to a leisure pursuit, gaining status and expertise, and experiencing various 'durable benefits' including self-expression and social belonging (Stebbins 1992, p. 7). In exploring serious leisure in the context of Protestant moralities of work and leisure, this chapter will draw upon data from ethnographic research in South Africa with abidingly evangelical serious leisure practitioners. In particular, the chapter focuses on youth-focused action sports projects (surfing and skateboarding) of the kind that have proliferated in the global development sector. An example of the individual capacity-building approach to poverty alleviation (Chandler 2016b, p. 76), the popularity of such projects increased after the United Nations Inter-Agency Task Force on Sport for Development and Peace (2003, p. 2) linked achievement of the Millennium Development Goals to the 'life skills learned through sport'.

I have found the serious leisure perspective to be a useful way of under-standing the importance of leisure activities in people's lives, and the perspective has helped me understand the anxieties conservative Christians experience trying to balance religious commitments with working lives and leisure pursuits. As this chapter will demonstrate, serious leisure emphasizes an 'auto-telic' approach to life; concentration and commitment to one's own actions and outcomes and deep awareness of one's own emotions. For Chandler (2016a), the autotelic self comes close to the self-governing neoliberal self, but the concept emerges organically elsewhere, notably in Mihaly Csikszentmihalyi's (1990) work on 'flow', foundational to the study of the emotional and physi-ological appeal of sport. Surfers 'live in a world of extremes', a youth pastor in Cape Town told me, 'if they apply themselves to something, they give it everything'. Surfers therefore tend to move between extremes, he argued, from loving Jesus to loving 'drugs and alcohol and the party lifestyle', such that there is an excluded middle of alienated obligation and begrudging neces-sity. Although there is a large body of literature on religion and leisure—with Watson and Parker (2014) offering an exemplary overview of literature on Christianity and sport, for example—studies written from within the serious leisure perspective ignore religion almost entirely. Aside from my own work (Abraham 2017, pp. 111–34), only one article employing the serious leisure perspective, on American dog sports enthusiasts, considers the impact of one's serious leisure pursuits on one's religious commitments (Gillespie et al. 2002).

In spite of the neglect of religion in the study of serious leisure, this chapter will show that not only can serious leisure demonstrate proximate moral values to traditional Protestant and secular bourgeois approaches to work, but that serious leisure is more capable of fulfilling the ideological or idealized values of work that Protestant and secular bourgeois morality preaches, such as authenticity. Although this chapter will draw on theoretical work from the global north, the empirical focus on South Africa will ground the chapter in a stagnant economy with an expanded unemployment rate (one that includes discouraged jobseekers) of 38 per cent in 2019 (Statistics South Africa 2019). If, as has been the case in Protestant thinking, work is essential for a conventionally moral life, then joblessness on this scale presents an ethical challenge beyond mere poverty. This chapter will therefore engage with ongoing debates around a UBI scheme in South Africa and in Finland, where a high profile UBI study took place. As a policy response to persistent unemployment, some formulations of UBI explicitly move away from the traditional emphasis on employment as the foundation of an individual's life. Rather, in Stebbins' (1998, p. 127) formulation of the UBI, recipients 'would literally be paid so they could play, "play" being synonymous with leisure'. If leisure, not work, becomes the foundation of an individual's life, then moral evaluations of leisure become all the more significant.

CHRISTIANITY AND THE MORALITY OF WORK AND LEISURE

In examining conventional moral approaches to work and leisure, this chapter makes use of the work of the economist and historian Deidre McCloskey (2006, 2010, 2016) to understand hegemonic moral approaches to work in modernity, and contrast those with moral approaches to leisure. This section will begin to demonstrate that work and leisure have more in common than one might assume, insofar as work has come to be thought of as something that provides subjective meaning, and certainly not as an aspect of life in which the self is merely repressed. While I do not share McCloskey's libertarian beliefs, her three-volume historical (and occasionally theological) exploration of bourgeois morality is a significant project, and although written in a witty manner, it is quite serious about identifying bourgeois morality as something other than an oxymoron. Her work emphasizes the importance of ideas, especially religious and otherwise moral ideas held by individual actors, in influencing social change in what she calls our 'bourgeois era'. There is certainly some strategic voluntarism in the project, and the work can perhaps best be read as a history of ideas, but it presents the modern salaried professional or entrepreneur as a rounded individual, someone influenced not just by a single 'p-value', in McCloskey's critique of quantitative social science and the idea of fundamentalist 'prudence', but by 's-values' as well: solidarity, sympathy, shame, and society (McCloskey 2010, pp. 407–15). She argues that the idea of a bourgeois subject driven purely by cynical utility or salvation anxiety does not come from empirical social science (McCloskey 2010, pp. 140–41, 2016, pp. 457–8), and that the bourgeoisie have led morally and spiritually richer and more agonistic and individualistic lives than has been acknowledged. Viewed from the perspective of Charles Taylor's (1989, p. 65) analysis of modern subjectivity, even if bourgeois prudence is a moral 'hypergood' that seems to supersede and judge earlier moral systems such as Christianity, moral 'struggle and tension' in private or public life is a more likely consequence than absolute moral transformation.

Drawing on literature and the history of bourgeois culture, McCloskey (2006, pp. 74–6) shows just how foundational the value of work is within bourgeois morality, and hence within the hegemonic moral system of the world the bourgeoisie has created. This 'work-admiring' middle-class morality is not merely directed at intellectual labour either, physical labour is also admirable in a moral system that privileges action and business above all else. In short, the morality of work (if not work itself) has been steadily moving away from the aristocratic virtue of idleness or, more specifically, from work as disengaged from the world or from one's self. There is a strong teleology in McCloskey's work in the form of a movement from almost total alienation in work, to something more egalitarian, and finally to something deeply personal, meaningful and socially engaging—even if individual experience does not match this ideal.

As with work, so it is with leisure. McCloskey's moral middle class have distanced themselves from the lives of disengaged casual leisure lived by those above them, but also those below them. Members of the species *homo ludens*, the 'carefree' and unjustifiably 'unworried' people of casual leisure, can be found among the idle upper class but also among the working class, as well as Bourdieu's (1979 [1984]) new middle class. McCloskey (2006, p. 76) cites 'weekends of proletarian soccer rioting in Amsterdam by yobs from Millwall' as an example of what Eva Swidler (2016, pp. 30–31) more generously labels 'proletarian forms of voluntary simplicity' and Chris Rojek (2005, p. 149) 'ceremonies of excess'. From the moral perspective of the middle class, the great sin of *homo ludens*, rich or poor, at work or at play, seems to be the lack of moral seriousness towards leisure as well as towards work.

In a more recent 'sermon' McCloskey (2013) analyses the morality of work from the perspective of both liberal economics and liberal Christian theology. She notes that in their professional capacity economists are less likely to moralize over idleness or pious withdrawal from the world than one might assume; 'leisure' is left to the exercise of one's utility-seeking choice. A somewhat similar critique of leisure studies is advanced by Rojek (2010, pp. 110–13). There is very little that an economist, or a leisure theorist, might say about Catherine of Sienna starving to death by consuming nothing but communion wafers, for example (McCloskey 2013, p. 68). But individuals' moral approaches and Christian theological approaches to work and leisure are quite different. McCloskey notes that St Paul's condemnation of idleness was directed 'against a particular type of *un*worldly excess, a laying down of tools in expectation of the Second Coming' (ibid.), and that the church continued to warn against '*excessive* withdrawal' and later from neglecting one's God-given gifts by refusing 'self-development'. There is something else here, though; the idea of work as a dignified or God-given activity that everyone should partake in is an alternative to the morality of the classical society of the biblical era, as well as medieval Christendom. McCloskey finds Jewish, Christian, and Muslim morality similar, and similarly remarkable, 'since in the Greek and Roman world work was so very undignified, and the collection of feudal rents by the genteel was precisely why they did not work at anything but war and courtesy' (ibid.).

Influenced by Weber and others, McCloskey (2006, p. 469) emphasizes the idea of work, commerce especially, as not just conceivably a 'calling'—and she tells us that she has 'God in mind here' because the idea of a calling has been thoroughly secularized (ibid.)—but also as self-actualizing and pleasurable. McCloskey seems to organically think about work the way others think about leisure, without making the critical jump to recognizing that meaning and self-expression are increasingly found in leisure activities rather than work itself. In fact, McCloskey writes about getting up on Monday morning to go to the office with the passion that others write about getting up on Saturday morning to go hit the surf. The durable benefits of serious leisure that Stebbins (1992, p. 7) lists would all be ones that McCloskey associates with work.

Illustrative of the sense of individual satisfaction, and almost ecstatic pleasure, that most would associate with leisure, McCloskey even makes productive use of Csikszentmihalyi's (1990) writings on 'flow' in describing work (McCloskey 2006, pp. 469–77). Csikszentmihalyi's mentor, Victor Turner (1974, p. 89), describes to 'flow' as 'to be as happy as a human can be'. McCloskey (2006, p. 470) cites Csikszentmihalyi's example of a railway engineer who had a preternatural ability to fix machinery; on the factory floor he was as much 'in the zone' as a surfer expertly riding through the tube of a giant wave. More typical of the use of flow in the social sciences, Bron Taylor (2007, pp. 941–2) invokes the concept to help explain surfing's 'religious aura' and the 'craving' of surfers to repeat the experience. He understands flow as a point of intense psychological concentration in which there is a unity of mind and body, and of the body with some deeper reality; the body obeys the mind and moves ideally through physical space, which creates something trance-like about the experience.

Victor Turner's collaborator, Edith Turner (2012, pp. 47–9), goes even further in her work on flow, making the concept's use in the world of work even more noteworthy. Turner offers a variety of cross-cultural musical and sporting examples of flow, from the music of Inuit shamans and Jean Sibelius, as well as a famous Manchester United victory. Her argument is that when we experience flow, we are tapping into a spiritual undercurrent that neither the social sciences nor institutional religion can comprehensively account for. As such, she presents an understanding of the phenomenon that resists full classification, in part because it exists apart from the 'system' of industrial modernity. Flow may come from God, Edith Turner infers, but 'not a god of judgment for sin or a god of authority or of any particular culture' (ibid., p. 47). As such, each 'shining moment' of flow may be considered 'a bit of the beatific vision [but] it cannot be claimed exclusively in the holy words of any one language or religion' (ibid., p. 49), nor, McCloskey would insist, in one social activity or system. Giving examples of bus drivers and garbage collectors, she insists that contemporary work can be as 'flowful' as leisure (McCloskey 2006, p. 476). If work offers individuals goals and control it can engage the autotelic self, and facilitate 'flow' just as surfing can; for McCloskey, what destroys this is alienation through over-regulation (by management or workers), or through cynicism (ibid., pp. 469–77).

Such bourgeois ideals of work as a source of self-fulfilment, and even joy, are rarely realized, even if the ideology of identity formation and meaning making through work remains strong. Sara James' (2017) study of the beliefs of Australian workers draws this out, emphasizing the importance of the value and rhetoric of authenticity in professional lives, even if this is rarely realized outside of television programmes, because of neoliberal structures of work including precarious and short-term contract labour. Charles Taylor's (1992, p. 14) theory of the 'age of authenticity' is foundational here, with the dominant ideology of 'expressive individualism' giving each individual the right 'to develop their own form of life, grounded on their own sense of what is really important ... to seek their own self-fulfillment'. In the contemporaneous study, *Habits of the Heart: Individualism and Commitment in American Life* (Bellah et al. 1985), professionals are seen to take pride in their careers, but lack any sense of professional calling. Precisely as Stebbins (1998, p. 122) recognizes in studies of contemporary attitudes to work, the appeal of work is 'external' to them, 'offering mainly a paycheck and social connections'. Stebbins (1998, p. 12) observed a shift towards 'reasoned wellness' among American professionals in the 1990s, the same group who seemed to embrace overwork in the 1980s. He argues that despite the desire of managers to 'wring extra hours of service from their employees' there has been a qualitative shift towards meaning making and identity formation beyond the workplace (ibid.).

If work is losing its centrality to the moral order, or at least losing its position as the 'central life interest' (Dublin 1992) of many people, then what about leisure? Looking specifically to Protestant views of leisure, especially sport, reveals something very similar to the normative bourgeois morality outlined above. It is not simply because Protestant morality both shaped and was shaped by secular bourgeois morality, but that Christian organizations were key agents in the instilling of 'the bourgeois attitude to leisure in the hearts, minds and bodies of the young' (Rojek 1989, p. 98). As with the case of the Protestant ethic in relation to work, the point is not that these values necessarily adhere in the same individual, but that they emerge within the same milieu and, at times, cross-fertilize. Earlier generations of Protestants made the distinction between frivolous leisure activities and productive leisure activities just as, for example, contemporary pedagogues or social workers might, but these Protestant values also help us understand why a life centred upon serious leisure rather than paid work may not be the moral scandal we might assume, why it need not signal a (re)turn to the 'carefree' amorality of some kind of welfare aristocracy. This is because just as McCloskey implies that ideals of work have shifted ever closer to the self, to be subjective forms of authentic expression, as Taylor would understand it, so too have certain forms of leisure and approaches to leisure undergone something akin to a moral reformation, to become *serious* leisure. In key ways, therefore, the practitioners of these forms of leisure approach them with the same moral outlook as the professional or entrepreneur approached his or her work according to the idealized bourgeois *work* ethic. In this way—and, I suspect, only in this way—can a life centred on serious leisure be considered a life well lived from within the conventional morality of work out of which it actually emerges.

In his historical study of sport and Protestantism, Overman (2011) argues that the Protestant ethic played an important role in not just further formalizing sport, but in moralizing it, such that sport became almost axiomatically a form of what would later be theorized as serious leisure. As Weber (1930 [1992], pp. 111–12) himself argued, Puritan objections to sport as ludic leisure were grounded in opposition to 'the spontaneous enjoyment of life' contra 'the ordered life of the saint', such that sport could be acceptable for the 'rational purpose' of increasing 'physical efficiency'. This is precisely the image of the one-dimensional bourgeois man that McCloskey wants to disabuse us of, and although sport and other forms of leisure have been used in the past as blunt moral instruments, distracting young people from sex and delinquency by simply physically exhausting them, Overman (2011) shows that the role of leisure in moral pedagogy has usually been more thoughtful. To the Victorians, a young person's leisure activities could be considered a reflection of their moral seriousness, and to certain Christians even a reflection of their family's salvation status (ibid., p. 244). Morgan's (2006, pp. 134–5) study of the morality of sport adds a twist to this, noting that it was the process of secularization, the stripping of religious authority from many fields of public life, that gave sport its added moral value in the United States. When religion was no longer the bedrock of social order, sport became a surrogate character and community-building resource. In the late twentieth century, American youth sport became so organized that it arguably ceased to be a part of a young person's leisure time at all, however, just one more part of the 'imposed regime of well-meaning adults' (Overman 2011, pp. 237–9). Repeating Stebbins' warning that seriousness can sometimes lead to joylessness, Siegenthaler and Gonzalez (1997, pp. 305–10) list overcompetitive coaches, schools, and parents as discouragements to young athletes.

Quite apart from the world of contemporary competitive youth sports, which seems to make even Puritan pedagogy seem permissive by comparison, critiques have also been made about the (mis)use of sport and leisure as a tool of moral regulation by governments, youth workers, and global non-governmental organizations (NGOs). To Rojek (2010, p. 134) this 'rational recreation' is a secularized form of an older Christian conservativism, and Richard Giulianotti (2004, pp. 356–7) labels 'sports evangelists' those who treat sport (not religion) as the opiate of the masses, especially in the developing world. As in historical studies of early Protestant moralizers of sport and leisure:

> Through the twentieth century, sports evangelists at home had sought to promote organized sporting activities to dissipate the lower orders' dangerous energies and to divert them from 'licentious' social practices (such as drinking, gambling, casual sex, and the following of youth subcultural styles). There is little convincing evidence to suggest that such evangelism has proved wholly successful among young people in the West over the years. However, it appears to be assumed, the young people in the old colonies may be more readily organized to receive and internalize the tendentious, self-controlling messages buried within sports. (Giulianotti 2004, pp. 356–7)

Whatever one makes of Giulianotti's critique, he is right that involvement in youth sport has been shown to have an ambivalent impact on the 'licentious' behaviour these so-called sports evangelists are seeking to dissipate (Coalter 2007, pp. 92–132). Like working life, leisure is a morally contested field, such that participation in sport or any other leisure activity cannot automatically promote positive moral choices in another field. As the Cape Town youth pastor observed, recognizing the autotelic values of the 'extreme' surfers, one might wholly commit to religion or hedonism. Leisure, in short, must be regulated by external moral values just as work has been in McCloskey's 'bourgeois era', not in a way that represses the modern self, but in a way that cultivates the self.

THE SERIOUS LEISURE PERSPECTIVE

Turning to the serious leisure perspective, we will see the way this concept undermines the 'polarized' view of work and leisure found in traditional bourgeois moral systems (Rojek 1989, p. 104), which we have seen in the previous section to be unsustainable, as serious leisure may be more planned and more systematized than even professional work. It may also be more vital to an individual's identity, and it may be more socially impactful—in spite of arguably being focused on cultivating the inner life of the individual—especially in the sports development projects discussed below. As such, serious leisure may well come closer to fulfilling the ideological claims about work found in more contemporary bourgeois moral systems, such as outlined in James' (2017) study of the ideology of authenticity, and in McCloskey's work on bourgeois virtue.

The basic definition of serious leisure is 'the systematic pursuit of an amateur, hobbyist, or volunteer activity that is sufficiently substantial and interesting for the participant to find a career there in the acquisition and expression of its special skills and knowledge' (Stebbins 1992, p. 3). 'Serious' leisure is contrasted along a continuum to 'casual' leisure which differs in its spontaneity and simplicity, such as watching television. Serious leisure is a 'career' in the sociological sense of a role with the possibility of advancement and increasing expertise, based on the investment of time and effort. Athletes and musicians improve their performance, for example, increasing their status along the way. In the South African sports development projects I observed, older participants were expected to take on a mentoring role, with organizers progressively handing over greater responsibilities. Serious leisure also differs from casual leisure insofar as it confers at least some of the eight 'durable benefits' which Stebbins has observed: 'self-actualization, self-enrichment, self-expression, recreation or renewal of self, feelings of accomplishment, enhancement of self-image, social interaction and belongingness, and lasting physical products of the activity' (ibid., p. 7). We can note that the first six items on this list are abidingly personal, but that the last two are more social. In public policy terms 'social belonging' is a matter of social cohesion and stability, and the creation of 'lasting physical products' might even be quantified; surfing tournaments, skate parks, and so on, all have demonstrable public benefits. Despite this, serious leisure is distinct from work, as it is not relied upon as a significant source of income, and in many cases serious leisure is a financial drain. In his study of amateur singers, Stebbins (1996, p. 63) found that 'self-enrichment' was the top motivation, with 'financial reward' listed last, quite probably an example of the autotelic self in operation.

Stebbins (1992, pp. 8–17) breaks serious leisure down into three particular forms; amateurism, hobby pursuits, and career volunteerism. Amateurism, firstly, refers to activities that are undertaken for the love of the activity, with an economic arrangement which differentiates amateurs from professionals. Amateurs exist on the 'margin of leisure', however, because they often pursue their activity with the seriousness of professionals (Stebbins 1979). This is especially observable in the lives of amateur surfers I have researched who constantly monitor weather conditions, rise extraordinarily early in the morning to catch the best waves, and deprioritize the secular and religious activities that interfere with surfing. The challenge of finding a balance between amateur surfing, work, and other life commitments was described to me as the ultimate 'quest of life' by one Christian surfer. Secondly, Stebbins (1992, pp. 8–17) cites hobby pursuits, activities in fields with no developed commercial sector, making the distinction with professionals less relevant. Underlining Rojek's (2010) lament that leisure time is being perpetually colonized by capital, some of the hobby pursuits Stebbins (1992, pp. 12–13) listed now have highly commercialized professional sectors, such as surfing and even video gaming. Thirdly, Stebbins refers to career volunteering, with the term 'career' in this case having the same sociological meaning as above of a role with the possibility of advancement. Career volunteering is differentiated from isolated charitable acts, as it implies the same sense of increasing expertise as for amateurs. Significantly, Stebbins (ibid., pp. 16–18) observes that volunteering is never wholly altruistic, as volunteers benefit from their involvement by increasing their social and cultural capital.

While McCloskey (2010, pp. 68–9) does not use the serious leisure perspective in her work, she nevertheless observes that contemporary life offers more opportunities for both serious and casual leisure than in the past. Casual leisure-as-pleasure, akin to 'a well-fed cat sitting in the sun', is celebrated in a certain parody of 'happiness studies' advocating downsizing and the simple life—a more sophisticated expression of this is the 'positive simplicity' practiced by many retirees (Stebbins 2013, pp. 5–6)—but contemporary life also offers us 'a uniquely enlarged scope to be fully realized human beings' (McCloskey 2010, p. 69). This builds upon the tradition of self-development and self-culture in Wilhelm von Humboldt's educational *Bildung* principle that so many universities are now struggling to defend against narrow vocational education. As McCloskey concludes, 'one can turn down *Bildung*, and watch reality TV all day. But billions are enabled to do more … if they wish' (ibid.).

The tradition of working-class sports teams and reading groups are one example of this, a feature of Richard Hoggart's (1957) study of working-class culture and leisure that sets this progressive respectability against the massification of casual leisure, even if this is seen now as a 'sentimental' view of working-class life (Rojek 2005, p. 150). We can also find a certain articulation of the *Bildung* principle recognizable in serious leisure practices—specifically serious leisure-based youth development projects—that emphasize the kind of individual resilience contra political change and group advancement that Reid (2016, p. 53) associates with neoliberalism; the creation of an individual subject 'that must permanently struggle to accommodate itself to the world: not a subject that can conceive of changing the world'. Such resilience is commonly referred to in sporting terminology as 'bouncebackability' and in sports development practices it is a value that can be adapted and applied by a young person navigating a hostile employment market, in an example of the development and deployment of the autotelic self. If they have been mentored to pick themselves up after a brutal wipeout on their surfboard, they may approach other tasks in life with the same emotional investment.

CHRISTIANITY, MORALITY, AND SERIOUS LEISURE IN PRACTICE

Looking at ways in which serious leisure has been utilized in sports-based youth development projects in the context of poverty and inequality in South Africa will demonstrate the ways in which serious leisure comes close to the traditional secular bourgeois or Protestant work ethic, as well as functioning as a potential surrogate for conventional work in the context of long-term joblessness. Given that youth unemployment in South Africa is around 55 per cent (Statistics South Africa 2019), and that approximately 50 per cent of South African children are living in 'income poverty', wherein they can only afford the very basics of life (Children's Institute 2018), the importance of the provision of serious leisure-based projects by NGOs and religious organizations is understandable. As Hartmann and Kwauk (2011, p. 287) outline the 'dominant' view of sports development, sport teaches the life skills and social skills 'individuals need to participate successfully in modern social life', and it does so organically through 'competition, respect for the rules, and dedication to a physical craft'. A Cape Town-based evangelical surfing coach explained this process, demonstrating the development of an autotelic self: 'surfing produces commitment, focus, and determination. It's the same in life; if a wave knocks you down you've got to get back on your board and stand up. You can relate surfing to a lot of life experiences.' Another South African evangelical youth sports facilitator, from the Cape Winelands, made a similar comment about skateboarding, 'You're never going to progress in your sport if you don't choose to get up and go practice for three hours, you know? There's a lot from the sport itself that can be carried over into life skills.'

When a young teenager in a surfing development project in Cape Town suffered a severe cut to their face from the fin of their surfboard, it was therefore a teachable moment on multiple levels. It reminded all the project participants of the importance of their safety and first aid training; accidents will happen but their frequency and severity can be reduced. But more importantly it reminded all the project participants that, after a period of healing, there is much to be gained from getting back in the water and back on your board. And, through the organic moral pedagogy of sports development, and its ability to inculcate the values of the autotelic self, one can observe that what is true in surfing is true in life; setbacks are inevitable but not always irreversible. So while Booth (2007, p. 318) reassures us that surfing is usually no more dangerous than fishing, and this particular youth sports facilitator told me her challenge is more often keeping injured youth out of the water long enough to heal than coaxing them back in the water once they have, the stage-managed sense of risk in action sports could be viewed as offering a parallel to the resilient neoliberal worldview that Reid (2016) describes, founded upon being secure in one's permanent and existential insecurity.

Managing risk in this manner is perhaps the most explicit example of the ways in which sports development projects instil the values of the autotelic self, as Csikszentmihalyi (1990, pp. 209–13) articulates them. In theory, an individual can metaphorically ride the waves of life's disappointment and unpredictability with the confidence of a surfer riding a monstrous wave, if their commitment is to the cultivation of the self through self-monitoring and individual ownership of the outcomes of their actions. Understood by Chandler (2016a, p. 45) as 'an individual capable of self-government in a world of contingency and radical uncertainty', the autotelic self can turn 'insecurity into self-actualization: into growth'. Illustratively, a vital feature of these surfing-based projects is the 'fish out of water' scenario of young, impover-ished, black South Africans engaging the same inner drive to enthusiastically commit to various activities—surfing, reading, computer skills—utterly unlike those undertaken by their peers, whose lives consist largely of spontaneous casual leisure. Prioritizing the development of the 'inner realm', rather than developing young people focused directly on transforming their external society (ibid.), does not mean that the protagonists of sports development projects are explicitly seeking to create neoliberal subjects. The youth workers, youth pastors, and volunteers who facilitate these schemes are doing so from within their own considered moral framework just as Weber's (1930 [1992]) Protestant bourgeoisie did. For example, when I have encountered the language of 'bouncebackability' from youth pastors involved in church-facilitated sports development projects, it is intended to be understood as a form of moral resil-ience, a way of 'not being controlled by your environment', as a Pretoria-based youth pastor explained to me, rather than resignation or conscious adaptation to a certain secular social logic.

The critique of implicit neoliberalism in leisure-based youth development projects runs into a further complication in the South African context, where it is not a case of a government abandoning or outsourcing existing social responsibilities, but rather a case of successive governments having little reach in much of the country, especially in the townships and impoverished rural areas that welcome religious and secular youth development projects. Further, as Rojek (2005, p. 179) observes, serious leisure projects can be 'a significant means of status acquisition and identity attainment and a strategy of resistance for individual and social integration and the generation of social capital'. This can happen within the welfare state, even in the global north in a welfare state fully committed to neoliberal policies. As Rojek (2010, pp. 134–6) notes in the British context, the inclusion of leisure activities in welfare systems began in the 1960s, with the state as the 'ringmaster of leisure and recreation', but transformed in the 1980s to a process to nominally empower individuals independent of the state, via an inward turn to cultivating individual moral capacities, and capacities to create and maintain social capital of the kind more or less associated with the autotelic neoliberal subject outlined above.

A more recent turn in the provision of leisure is the growing role of NGOs, including religious NGOs of the kind this chapter has focused on. While conceivably agents of neoliberalization—these are literally NGOs taking roles the state might assume—NGOs are often 'umbrellaed by governmental policy' which will not be uniform (Thorpe and Rinehart 2013, p. 119). In South Africa, serious leisure-based youth development NGOs often form productive relationships with youth affairs departments of local, provincial and national governments, as part of the piecemeal expansion of that country's welfare system. As if recognizing the limited possibilities of creating work for young people, there is a commitment to expand sporting and leisure opportunities in the country, as well as a growing recognition that this must go beyond support for the traditional masculine team sports in which South Africa has excelled—rugby, cricket, and to a lesser extent football—and embrace popular alternatives such as the individual action sports this chapter is concerned with.

In South Africa, therefore, one of the key tasks of sports development projects is to provide serious leisure activities to impoverished youth, in stark contrast to affluent youth who are typically overburdened with serious leisure activities, especially sport, organized by wealthy schools and parents. There is an irony here, for although sport is about achieving status through one's own efforts—which is also one of the virtues of work, for McCloskey (2006, p. 471)—one's ability to participate in sport often depends on ascribed status (Overman 2011, p. 264). This was a lesson affluent evangelicals needed to learn, illustrated by a history of the Australian-initiated Christian Surfers organization by its co-founder Brett Davis (2012, pp. 232–3): 'In South Africa, Christian Surfers explored how our mission—traditionally so focused on personal salvation—needed to develop a social justice edge. The black community traditionally did not enter the water, yet scores of black kids lived right at the beach and only felt they had drugs, sex, and alcohol to occupy them.'

The Christian Surfers organization has made a virtue of reasserting the 'rituals of bourgeois order' that surfing and other 'Californian sports' have sought to disrupt (Bourdieu 1979 [1984], p. 220), but this quote illustrates broader changes I have encountered from other evangelical serious leisure projects in South Africa, wherein the creation of serious leisure activities for impoverished youth becomes an end in itself, rather than purely a means to evangelize. Even so, in keeping with evangelical priorities such projects are never entirely secularized and instrumentalized, either to material outcomes like employment or even explicit moral outcomes. As one Cape Town-based youth pastor said of his surfing project; 'My hope is not that people would have good morals, my hope is that people would come to faith. That faith then outworks itself in people's lives. I hope my guys are living lives that reflect their beliefs.'

This creation of serious leisure activities is about the creation of something worth striving for, a foundational aspect of the serious leisure perspective, which Stebbins (2015) has more recently sought to position as a 'positive social science' insofar as it focuses on those things that make life worth living, rather than the common social scientific focus on inequality or injustice. To the Christian serious leisure participants and facilitators I have been researching, serious leisure will never be an entirely sufficient basis for one's identity or values, but in this latter, concise formulation of the serious leisure perspective, Stebbins (2015) suggests that the kind of outcomes associated with serious leisure, the durable benefits cited above, encompass relationships, spirituality, and various aspects of individual identity making. In short, any serious leisure activity will be substantive enough to fill up one's world, in the way that work or religion could. This is clearly why many evangelical serious leisure participants experience anxiety around their leisure pursuits, as the excessive tendencies of serious leisure can be a threat to religious commitments or identity. Serious leisure is not infrequently spoken of as a form of 'idolatry' one might overcommit to, just as one might overcommit to acquiring wealth or status (Abraham 2017, pp. 111–34).

LEISURE AND MORALITY AFTER WORK

Research on the 'positive' aspects of serious leisure, by Stebbins and others, typically emerges from the affluent global north; how to spend one's leisure time becomes a vital issue in societies that have achieved a 'basic tranquillity' (Elkington and Stebbins 2014, pp. 197–8), and in which Taylor's (1992) notion of expressive individualism has filtered down from the elite to the masses. Most obviously, then, serious leisure is an important topic in the context of societies with a reasonable work/leisure balance with a quest for these kinds of authentic individual lives, or in the context of extended periods of retirement. For example, McCloskey (2010, p. 361) cites the lifecycles of 'hundreds of millions of bourgeois and working-class Westerners, whose lives are spent in education up to their early-20s, and in retirement to a life of leisure twenty years longer than the life expectancy of their grandparents'.

The question of leisure is also a negative social phenomenon when it relates to joblessness through unemployment, rather than retirement. Far from contexts of social tranquillity, such ideas initially developed in the West in the economic downturn and early industrial globalization of the 1970s when unemployment and underemployment were on the rise. This so-called 'leisure society' thesis was undermined precisely by the neoliberal turn in the West, which not only normalized the idea of permanently contingent employment, but also privatized many leisure activities (Rojek 2010, pp. 21–2). The difference between chosen leisure and 'forced free time' is a significant one, as the definition of leisure as 'un-coerced activity' makes little sense if one has nothing else to be coerced into (Stebbins 1998, p. 122, 2015, p. 5). This leads to a quite different moral assessment of leisure, for focusing on the leisure lives of the working-age long-term unemployed runs up against 'the traditional capitalist principle that the entitlement to leisure must be earned through paid employment' (Rojek 2005, p. 150).

Within this context of inequality and unemployment, one can encounter a form of Christian morality labelled 'economic Arminianism' (McLeod 2007, p. 112) in which affluence or poverty, like salvation or damnation in normative evangelical theology, 'is a matter of individual free will' (ibid.). An alternative view, however, that is not focused on individual sinfulness but on structural changes, foresees a future of low employment in which there is very little that even the most righteous of the saints can do. Rather than the relatively short-lived leisure society thesis of the 1970s, predicated on economic crisis and stagnation in the West, this time technology is a vital agent of social upheaval, more likely to impact industrializing countries than the already post-industrial West. Martin Ford's (2015) *Rise of the Robots* has been influential in popularizing this view of the emerging economy; his argument is not about robots as such, but rather that contemporary technology has a 'general purpose' aspect to it that generates profit far beyond the capacities of a human workforce. Added to this is increasing concern about 'premature deindustrialization' in countries like South Africa, where local industrial employment growth is being outpaced by global technological developments, leaving workers in developing economies to hustle for jobs in the petty services sector (Rodrik 2016). Combining these two concerns, the financial journalist Ron Derby (2018) pessimistically observes that Netflix generates vastly higher income in South Africa with its global workforce of 5,400 than its local South African pay television rival Naspers can with its workforce of 25,000.

Unsurprisingly, Ford (2015), Derby (2018), and others concerned about permanent joblessness, and convinced of the relative moral blamelessness of the unemployed, advocate a UBI scheme, while McCloskey does so for her own 'bleeding heart' reasons (Solman 2014). In a foundational essay on the topic, 'Why surfers should be fed', Phillippe van Parijs (1991, p. 102) describes a UBI as 'an individual guaranteed minimum income without either a means test or a (willingness to) work condition'. Noting that it is 'the latter condition that has aroused most ethical controversy', he also observes that if the only likely candidates for the UBI were 'welfare hippies and Malibu surfers' there would be no debate on the topic (ibid.). Stebbins' (1998, p. 123) question about whether a society 'can afford to let a sizable segment of its population devote itself to non-paid amateur, hobbyist and career volunteer pursuits in lieu of working paid jobs', requires not just a financial evaluation, therefore, but a moral evaluation as well.

One view is that long-term unemployment, coupled with unconditional welfare payments, leads to an erosion of morals. I will take as representative the view of the Catholic neoliberal theologian Michael Novak (1996), often cited by McCloskey, who sees the welfare state as a key source of the decline of moral seriousness in society. Unconditional welfare payments, in this view, erode virtues such as personal responsibility and proper working habits among its recipients, as well as eroding values of kindness and decency manifested in voluntary charity. In Novak's view, the whole idea amounts to a contradiction of Christian anthropology, a basic understanding of human moral weakness (ibid.). However, in arguing for a UBI in South Africa, the economic historian Sampie Terreblanche (2002, p. 470) rejects such views as 'expedient excuses of the wealthy middle class' arguing that rather than being 'morally degraded' by welfare dependency, people become 'morally fractured by the heavy burden of poverty'.

Reviving the periodic UBI debate in South Africa 15 years later, financial journalist Peter Bruce (2017) is similarly critical of middle-class moralism, notably the suburban myth of impoverished women having children simply to receive the monthly 350 South African rand (26 United States dollars) child grant. 'You'd need 10 kids quickly just to earn the equivalent of the coming minimum wage,' he noted. Central to Terreblanche and Bruce's arguments are the recognition of the limited possibilities for significant jobs growth in South Africa. Between poor educational outcomes and low economic growth, the veteran journalist Allister Sparks (2012) warned about the emergence of a millions-strong 'redundant generation', unemployable for life. Masses of young people who have no meaningful role to play in the life of the nation are trapped in this precise scenario, in what Swartz (2009, p. 65) labels a 'morality of inevitability', a nihilistic moral framework that emerges from the quite reasonable belief that one is destined to live out one's life in meaningless poverty. Bruce's (2017) proposal is therefore a pragmatic one, based on a recognition of a likely sustained high level of unemployment, and the individual and collective impact that has. '[I]f you decided to pay every adult citizen (not in jail or in any way a ward of the state) 2000 [South African rand] [150 United States dollars] a month, the country changes. Poor people have real money in their pockets, most (not all) of which gets ploughed back into the economy.' But considering that it would be the relatively small South African middle class upon whom the burdens of such a scheme would fall, this does not answer the pragmatic moral questions that might be asked about whether such a scheme makes the poor better people, beyond simply being better off.

Stebbins (1998, p. 127) argues that '[m]ost of the supporters of guaranteed minimum income plans have in mind more fulfilling and deeply satisfying activities for the recipients than casual leisure', so the assumption must be that a UBI will have some moral force, and be more than a cynical abandonment of a large percentage of the population. As the UBI debate has emerged in the context of widespread joblessness, and the likelihood of permanent joblessness for a significant proportion of the South African population in this specific case, then the significance of serious leisure activities, including forms of creative self-expression and volunteering, emerge as a potential vital component of a new lifestyle, after work has ceased to become a central life interest and a central moral focus. For an example of this, it is worth looking at reporting on Finland's basic income experiment, run between 2017 and 2019, focused on a handful of research participants from among the 2,000 recipients of unemployment benefits randomly selected to receive a non-taxable unconditional payment of 560 euros per month in lieu of existing unemployment benefits. The most prominent research participant in the reporting of the experiment, conducting over 300 interviews, has been the artist and father of six Juha Järvinen, who praised the scheme for allowing him greater flexibility to participate in periodic short-term paid work which focuses his entrepreneurial ambitions, without the existing bureaucratic complexities of renegotiating family welfare payments and tax obligations (Yle 2017a, 2017b, 2018). Significantly, Järvinen's entrepreneurial ambitions are to monetize his serious leisure: film-making, woodworking (decorative window frames and shamanic drums), and organizing concerts and artistic retreats.

Although having some superficial resemblance to van Parijs' (1991) 'welfare hippie', Järvinen is a sympathetic spokesperson for the experiment, which he advocates be expanded even though it resulted in a slight reduction in his overall income. His previous business went bankrupt leaving him unable to access credit, a familiar scenario following the global financial crisis of 2008. Furthermore, although he was not engaged in formal paid work, Järvinen was actively focused on his serious leisure. Despite his unemployment and precarious financial position—he reports relying on church charities—Järvinen's serious leisure activities keep him from any sense of uselessness, which can accompany unemployment (Stebbins 1998, p. 122), and is foundational to the 'morality of inevitability' among impoverished South African youth (Swartz 2009). As he himself noted, 'One of the questions we are trying to work out [in the UBI experiment] is how many of us are going to end up lying on the sofa' (Yle 2018). Michael Novak might answer 'All of you!' but far from inculcating a morality of idle disengagement, by focusing on a research participant and welfare recipient with such a proactive serious leisure life, reporting on the basic income experiment could be seen to dispel some of the moral concerns about the scheme.

As someone deeply committed to serious leisure in spite of his adverse economic situation, Järvinen models the idea of the autotelic self, sketched above; whatever serious leisure activities he is pursuing, he is pursuing with a strong commitment, and with a sense of individual expression, in keeping with Taylor's (1992) idea of authenticity. His actions are not those of 'outside determining forces', but 'internally controlled' and mobilized in a variety of directions (Csikszentmihalyi 1990, p. 210). He explained that the burden of the conventional welfare system was being compelled to follow the directions of the employment office, when he was quite clear about his vocation in life (Vice News 2017). Järvinen does not present the image of an isolated egoist, however, but the image of someone whose serious leisure pursuits are embedded in overlapping creative social networks, and the image of someone whose serious leisure pursuits are formative and productive, in other words, self-disciplining in the autotelic manner discussed throughout this chapter.

CONCLUSION

It is here that we return to action sports, as representative of the kind of serious leisure activities being facilitated for young South Africans in the context of high levels of persistent poverty and unemployment. It is intentional—and entirely possible—that the life skills being instilled in young people through surfing and other action sports projects will increase their employment opportunities. But from the perspective of this chapter, that is as beside the point as the question of whether the serious leisure leads, in these evangelical-led projects, to the strengthening of the young people's faith. What is most clearly happening is the kind of discipline and commitment once associated with the Protestant work ethic, radically reoriented for life after work.

Accordingly, this chapter has analysed serious leisure as a source of individual fulfilment and public good, in light of concern around increasing joblessness, and in the context of conventional Protestant Christian and secular bourgeois morality. Drawing on the work of Deirdre McCloskey, it was argued that both conventional bourgeois and Christian attitudes towards work have viewed it as morally important to individuals, with bourgeois ideology emphasizing the possibility of finding fulfilment and pleasure in work contra the caricature of the joyless and repressed middle-class Protestant. It was nevertheless suggested that conventional morality has insisted upon a balance between work and leisure, and that leisure requires an element of moral seriousness just as work does. Even if the ideal of work as a source of personal fulfilment remains relatively hegemonic, there has nevertheless been a practical move towards leisure as the source of expressive individual fulfilment.

Offering an overview of Protestant approaches to the moral regulation of leisure, in particular sport, as well as contemporary secular sports development prospects, which similarly see leisure as a tool for moral pedagogy, the chapter noted the similarities between approaches to serious leisure and conventional approaches to work. Insofar as the sports development projects implicitly promote the creation of autotelic selves, capable of demonstrating self-control and commitment to a range of activities in a range of contexts, then moral approaches to leisure and work are fused. As McCloskey (2006, pp. 69–76) suggests, and sports development facilitators clearly state, a young person's approach to surfing can be carried over to the working world and other facts of life.

It is in this context of blurring moral lines between work and leisure that the chapter introduced Robert A. Stebbins' concept of serious leisure, a systematic approach to a leisure career, offering identifiably beneficial personal and social outcomes. Noting the specifically evangelical nature of the projects that were researched, it was recognized that within the facilitators' understanding of these projects, morality can only ever be a semi-articulation of one's material social context. While this chapter has acknowledged the critiques directed at serious leisure projects, accused, inter alia, of middle-class moralism, the religious grounding of these projects means they retain a certain utility independent of specific material outcomes, which is itself in keeping with the idea of the inwardly orientated autotelic self, capable of endless adaptation in a neoliberal age (Chandler 2016a; Reid 2016). In the context of high unemployment in South Africa, even absent explicit neoliberal policies, the overlapping religious and autotelic subjectivities could be considered adaptive virtues. Finally, with reference to ongoing debates around UBI schemes, it was argued with reference to reporting on the Finnish experiment that the presence of the autotelic self in serious leisure activities might be a source of moral comfort to those anxious about the ethical consequences of such schemes to address life after work.

REFERENCES

Abraham, Ibrahim (2017) *Evangelical Youth Culture: Alternative Music and Extreme Sports Subcultures*. London: Bloomsbury Academic.
Bellah, Robert N., Richard Madsen, William Sullivan, Ann Swidler and Steven Tipton (1985) *Habits of the Heart: Individualism and Commitment in American Life*. Berkeley, CA: University of California Press.
Booth, Douglas (2007) 'Surfing'. In Douglas Booth and Holly Thorpe (eds), *Berkshire Encyclopedia of Extreme Sports*, 317–23. Great Barrington, MA: Berkshire.
Bourdieu, Pierre (1979 [1984]) *Distinction: A Social Critique of the Judgment of Taste*. Cambridge, MA: Harvard University Press.
Bruce, Peter (2017) 'BIG Solution Would Change the Country'. *Business Day* (Johannesburg), 24 March.

Chandler, David (2016a) 'Resilience: The Societalization of Security'. In David Chandler and Julian Reid, *The Neoliberal Subject: Resilience, Adaptation and Vulnerability*, 27–49. Lanham, MD: Rowman and Littlefield.

Chandler, David (2016b) 'Development as Adaptation'. In David Chandler and Julian Reid, *The Neoliberal Subject: Resilience, Adaptation and Vulnerability*, 75–97. Lanham, MD: Rowman and Littlefield.

Children's Institute (2018) *South African Child Gauge 2018*. Cape Town: Children's Institute, University of Cape Town.

Coalter, Fred (2007) *A Wider Social Role for Sport: Who's Keeping the Score?* London: Routledge.

Csikszentmihalyi, Mihaly (1990) *Flow: The Psychology of Optimal Experience*. San Francisco, CA: Harper and Row.

Davis, Brett (2012) *Groundswell: The Christian Surfers Story*. Wollongong: Christian Surfers International.

Derby, Ron (2018) 'Instead of Swelling Social Grants, Why Not a Basic Income for All?' *Sunday Times* (Johannesburg), 2 September.

Dublin, Robert (1992) *Central Life Interests: Creative Individualism in a Complex World*. New Brunswick, NJ: Transaction Publishers.

Elkington, Sam and Robert A. Stebbins (2014) *The Serious Leisure Perspective: An Introduction*. London: Routledge.

Ford, Martin (2015) *Rise of the Robots: Technology and the Threat of a Jobless Future*. New York: Basic Books.

Gillespie, Dair L., Ann Leffler and Elinor Lerner (2002) 'If It Weren't for My Hobby, I'd Have a Life: Dog Sports, Serious Leisure, and Boundary Negotiations'. *Leisure Studies* 21(3–4): 285–304.

Giulianotti, Richard (2004) 'Human Rights, Globalization and Sentimental Education: The Case of Sport'. *Sport in Society* 7(4): 355–69.

Hartmann, Douglas and Christina Kwauk (2011) 'Sport and Development: An Overview, Critique, and Reconstruction'. *Journal of Sport and Social Issues* 35(3): 284–305.

Hoggart, Richard (1957) *The Uses of Literacy: Aspects of Working Class Life*. Harmondsworth: Penguin.

James, Sara (2017) *Making a Living, Making a Life: Work, Meaning and Self-Identity*. London: Routledge.

McCloskey, Deirdre (2006) *The Bourgeois Virtues: Ethics for an Age of Commerce*. Chicago, IL: University of Chicago Press.

McCloskey, Deirdre (2010) *Bourgeois Dignity: Why Economics Can't Explain the Modern World*. Chicago, IL: University of Chicago Press.

McCloskey, Deirdre (2013) 'Work in the World: An Economist's Sermon'. *Faith and Economics* 61, 62: 66–71.

McCloskey, Deirdre (2016) *Bourgeois Equality: How Ideas, Not Capital or Institutions, Enriched the World*. Chicago, IL: University of Chicago Press.

McLeod, Sean (2007) *Divine Hierarchies: Class in American Religion and Religious Studies*. Chapel Hill, NC: University of North Carolina Press.

Morgan, William J. (2006) *Why Sports Morally Matter*. New York: Routledge.

Novak, Michael (1996) *Business as a Calling: Work and the Examined Life*. New York: Free Press.

Overman, Steven J. (2011) *The Protestant Ethic and the Spirit of Sport: How Calvinism and Capitalism Shaped America's Games*. Macon, GA: Mercer University Press.

Reid, Julian (2016) 'Resilience: The Biopolitics of Security'. In David Chandler and Julian Reid (eds), *The Neoliberal Subject: Resilience, Adaptation and Vulnerability*, 51–71. Lanham, MD: Rowman and Littlefield.

Rodrik, Dani (2016) 'Premature Deindustrialization'. *Journal of Economy Growth* 21(1): 1–33.

Rojek, Chris (1989) 'Leisure and "The Ruins of the Bourgeois World"'. In Chris Rojek (ed.), *Leisure for Leisure: Critical Essays*, 92–112. London: Palgrave Macmillan.

Rojek, Chris (2005) *Leisure Theory: Principles and Practices*. Basingstoke: Palgrave Macmillan.

Rojek, Chris (2010) *The Labour of Leisure: The Culture of Free Time*. London: Sage.

Siegenthaler, K. L. and G. Laticia Gonzalez (1997) 'Serious Leisure and Youth Sport: A Critique'. *Journal of Sport and Social Issues* 21(3): 298–314.

Solman, Paul (2014) 'Why this "Gender Crossing" Economist Prefers "Motherly Libertarianism" to Government Paternalism', *PBS News Hour*, 24 April, www .pbs.org/newshour/nation/why-this-gender-crossing-economist-prefers-motherly -libertarianism-to-government-paternalism

Sparks, Allister (2012) 'How to Get around the Big Problem of Skills Training'. *Business Day* (Johannesburg), 25 April.

Statistics South Africa (2018) Quarterly Labour Force Survey Q1:2018. 14 May.

Stebbins, Robert A. (1979) *Amateurs: On the Margin between Work and Leisure*. Beverley Hills, CA: Sage.

Stebbins, Robert A. (1992) *Amateurs, Professionals, and Serious Leisure*. Montreal: McGill-Queen's University Press.

Stebbins, Robert A. (1996) *The Barbershop Singer: Inside the Social World of a Musical Hobby*. Toronto: University of Toronto Press.

Stebbins, Robert A. (1998) *After Work: The Search for an Optimal Leisure Lifestyle*. Calgary: Detselig.

Stebbins, Robert A. (2013) *Planning Your Time in Retirement: How to Cultivate a Leisure Lifestyle to Suit Your Needs and Interests*. Lanham, MD: Rowman and Littlefield.

Stebbins, Robert A. (2015) *Leisure and Positive Psychology*. Basingstoke: Palgrave Macmillan.

Swartz, Sharlene (2009) *The Moral Ecology of South Africa's Township Youth*. Basingstoke: Palgrave Macmillan.

Swidler Eva (2016) 'Radical Leisure'. *Monthly Review* 68(2): 26–34.

Taylor, Bron (2007) 'Surfing into Spirituality and a New, Aquatic Nature Religion', *Journal of the American Academy of Religion*, 75(4): 923–51.

Taylor, Charles (1989) *Sources of the Self: The Making of Modern Identity*. Cambridge, MA: Harvard University Press.

Taylor, Charles (1992) *The Ethics of Authenticity*. Cambridge, MA : Harvard University Press.

Terreblanche, Sampie (2002) *A History of Inequality in South Africa*. Pietermaritzburg: University of Natal Press.

Thorpe, Holly and Robert Rinehart (2013) 'Action Sport NGOs in a Neo-Liberal Context: The Cases of Skateistan and Surf Aid International'. *Journal of Sport and Social Issues* 37(2): 115–41.

Turner, Edith (2012) *Communitas: The Anthropology of Collective Joy*. New York: Palgrave Macmillan.

Turner, Victor (1974) 'Liminal to Liminoid in Play, Flow, and Ritual: An Essay in Comparative Symbology'. *Rice University Studies* 60(3): 53–92.

United Nations Inter-Agency Task Force on Sport for Development and Peace (2003) *Sport as a Tool for Development and Peace: Towards Achieving the United Nations Millennium Development Goals*. Geneva: United Nations Office on Sport for Development and Peace.

Van Parijs, Philippe (1991) 'Why Surfers Should Be Fed: The Liberal Case for an Unconditional Basic Income'. *Philosophy and Public Affairs* 20(2): 101–31.

Vice News (2017) 'Finland Is Giving Citizens $660 a Month for Free as an Experiment'. *Vice News*, 31 October. www.youtube.com/watch?v=vwjNrxVd-1E

Watson, Nick and Andrew Parker (2014) *Sport and the Christian Religion: A Systematic Review of Literature*. Newcastle-Upon-Tyne: Cambridge Scholars Press.

Weber, Max (1930 [1992]) *The Protestant Ethic and the Spirit of Capitalism*. London: Routledge.

Yle (2017a) 'Finland's Basic Income Experiment Begins: One Man Looks Forward to a New Start'. 9 January. https://yle.fi/uutiset/osasto/news/finlands_basic_income _experiment_begins_one_man_looks_forward_to_a_new_start/9394707

Yle (2017b) 'Six Months On: Feedback on Finland's Basic Income Trial'. 26 July. https://yle.fi/uutiset/osasto/news/six_months_on_feedback_on_finlands_basic _income_trial/9742149

Yle (2018) 'One Year Down, One to Go: A View on Finland's Basic Income Experiment'. 30 January. https://areena.yle.fi/1-4348029

9. The contemporary faith of innovationism

Katja Valaskivi

This chapter argues that the all-encompassing concept of innovation, which has spread into all spheres of life, can be understood as a contemporary faith or belief system that I call 'innovationism'.[1] The values of innovationism – competitiveness, progress, growth and success – direct and guide human action and societies around the world. Innovationism is analysed here as an implicit (Bailey 1990), globally circulating religion that permeates all levels of societies and ties organisations, nations, individuals and ultimately humankind as a whole, into its value system. At its core is the utopian belief that (technological) innovations will ultimately solve fundamental challenges faced by humankind, including the threat of death and extinction. This enables societies to continue to believe in an economic system based on growth despite the obvious limits of the planet. This faith, in the unlimited ingenuity and innovativeness of humankind, assumes that innovation will save us at the last minute before extinction. At the same time, innovationism paradoxically proposes that unless there are innovations (and growth), the result is waning and extinction. Ultimately, innovationism sees innovation as a path to human immortality, for example through the development of artificial intelligence and machine learning.

In this chapter, I will illuminate features of innovationism as an implicit religion. First, taking inspiration from religious studies, I will consider the dimensions (cf. Smart 1996) or aspects of innovationism. Second, I will analyse how these aspects tie into the core values of implicit religion to manage hopes and mediate a sense of threat in society. Third, I will explain, through different cases and examples, how innovationism works in practice. Two bodies of empirical data are drawn on in the chapter: interviews collected for the Challenges of Global Innovation Journalism (GINJO) research project in 2008–10, reported earlier in Valaskivi (2012), and media texts, interviews and ethnographic observations from the visit of Professor Steve Blank to Finland in 2008, reported earlier in Valaskivi and Sumiala (2013).

THE IDEA OF INNOVATIONISM

Finalising this chapter during my stay at the University of Pennsylvania's Annenberg School of Communication, I take the wrong transportation back home. The university provides a free bus service and, not having my bearings, I take the wrong one. The bus takes me to a shabby-looking industrial area with a new, fancy building in the middle. It starts to rain, and the irritated driver, at the end of his shift, tells me to wait for my Lyft ride inside the building. Stepping inside, I am greeted with a roll-up banner saying: 'Pennovation Center'. While waiting for my ride I learn on their website that:

> The Pennovation Center [is] a business incubator and laboratory that aligns and integrates researchers, innovators, and entrepreneurs for the commercialisation of research discoveries. Intended to marry entrepreneurs with an expert workforce and scientifically advanced facilities, key features of the Pennovation Center are the common creative spaces, including coworking areas, a cafe, and a venue for events and programs... By creating an atmosphere for collaboration, creativity, and productivity for innovators from all disciplines, the Pennovation Center... retain [sic] an industrial character to develop social space with a 'cool factor'.[2]

By sheer chance, I had arrived at the innovation incubator of my host organisation, the University of Pennsylvania.

This is an example of how innovationism appears in practice. Innovation is the purpose for action, as well as the desired end result: growth is the aim, innovations are perceived to lead to growth, thus innovations are the solution. Innovation is a contemporary buzzword, used in a great number of situations. A simple Google search[3] provides several illustrative examples: 'Innovation is vital for small businesses', 'The interplay between innovation, creativity and consciousness', 'How to build an innovation hub that's actually innovative', 'Japan Sets Aside 100 Billion Yen for Robotics and Innovation Research Programs', 'UW [University of Wisconsin] launching new innovation and entrepreneurship intern program', 'Innovation and the future of healthcare', 'UNESCO report: UK heritage sector "world-leading" on innovation and international development'.

As we can see, the concept of innovation circulates from economics to the media and is used in contexts ranging from national competitiveness strategies to university policies and even to the health and cultural sectors. It appears in business prospectuses and academic textbooks, strategy documents and funding applications, and local industry policy statements and guidelines for cultural enhancement. In each context, the concept gains new meanings, gradually becoming almost a blanket term, all-encompassing and inevitable in discussions about the future, organisational renewal, business models, science, society, education, development, the economy and so on. Innovation is seen predominantly as a good thing, something to be desired and enhanced. This pro-innovation bias (Rogers 1962; Kimberly 1981) has been recognised by innovation and organisational studies. The recently developed critical innovation studies makes the point that the pro-innovation bias leads to a collective blindness, innocence and lack of thought in studies of innovation (Godin and Vinck 2017a) as does, I suggest, wider usage of the term. However, this chapter goes further in arguing that innovationism can be understood as a faith that is not questioned; its doctrines are followed without question, relying on the presumed beneficial nature of the object of faith. Hence, I will look at innovationism as a worldview, faith or belief system that conforms to implicit religion. Implicit religion has been analysed and defined as something that does not explicitly belong to the category of religion, but which still provides existential meaning and purpose for human beings (Nesti 1990; Bailey 1990).

Despite the wide usage of the word 'innovation' and the hopes attached to it, most innovationism is quite practical and mundane – perhaps even banal (cf. Billig 1995; Beck 2004; Hjarvard 2008). Emphasis on innovation affects business organisations as well as public institutions, such as universities, as the example that opens this chapter illustrates. Most of the time innovationism – like another contemporary implicit religion, nationalism – is like the air we breathe (Anderson 1991). It thus becomes the invisible and self-evident condition of our lived experience.

UBIQUITY OF INNOVATION

In what follows, I will provide some examples of the ubiquity of the concept of innovation and its development. First, a search using Google Ngram illustrates how innovation has become a buzzword. Figure 9.1 demonstrates the prevalence of key words related to innovationism in science and technology policy, as well as in management and popular business literature.[4] The everyday experience of those who follow the media and/or social media and who take part in policy making and business culture suggests that the occurrence of 'innovation' is still growing, together with 'entrepreneurship' and 'start-up'. In contrast, 'technology transfer' and 'research and development' continue to decline. Similar observations have been made by Alasuutari (2015) who has studied the circulation of policy trends and related concepts (including 'innovation') in several countries.

The second example is the phenomenon called 'innovation journalism', a vague and nebulous term applied to journalism engaging with innovation that was developed in Sweden. The Swedish national agency for technology and innovation funding, Vinnova, launched a project on innovation journalism in 2003. This led to Vinnova initiating and partly funding a research centre at Stanford (Stanford Research Centre of Innovation Journalism), which aimed

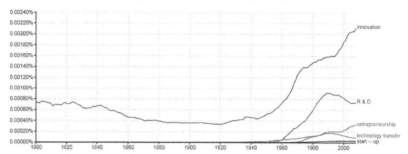

Source: Based on a search of Google Books for work published between 1800 and 2008; searched 30 May 2019

Figure 9.1   *Google Books Ngram viewer graph on 'start-up', 'technology transfer', 'entrepreneurship', 'research and development' and 'innovation'*

at joining the entrepreneurial spirit of the Silicon Valley to the field of journalism. The word circulated into other Nordic countries and was also used in Finland, mainly to direct some of the plentiful innovation-related research funding into the field of journalism research. There was a national association for innovation journalism founded by enthusiasts, and various research projects were initiated and funded. The concept of innovation journalism was always vague and referred to at least three things: 1) journalism on innovations and new technology; 2) innovations in journalistic practices and organisations; and 3) the usage of technological innovations in developing journalism and new business models for journalism.

The spread of innovation journalism inspired colleagues from the then Tampere Research Centre for Journalism, Turku Future Research Centre and University of Jyväskylä Media centre in Finland to apply for funding from the National Agency for Technology and Innovation for the GINJO project. This research set out to study how different actors in Finland, the United States (US) and Japan perceived innovation and the role of journalism in relation to it. Altogether around 40 interviews were conducted in Finland, the US and Japan. The interviewees were 'innovation system specialists', journalists and policy makers. The project ran from 2008 to 2010.

The GINJO project interviewed journalists and experts who at the time were called 'specialists of the innovation environment' in Finland, the US and Japan. In the research team I was assigned to study Japan, but I also had access to all the interviews produced in the other studied countries. The interviews consisted of discussions on innovation and journalism in relation to an ageing society and climate change. Some of the interviews for the GINJO project have been made use of in this chapter.

The fourth and final example demonstrates some of the intertwined practices through which innovationism has been advocated, circulated and promoted in public and political discourses, and how innovationism has changed the university sector in Finland. Around the time of the GINJO project, entrepreneurship associations were founded at universities by students, the leader in Finland being the Aalto Entrepreneurship Society (AaltoES) which began a systematic lobbying and media campaign to boost the start-up scene in Finland and find more investors for them (Valaskivi and Sumiala 2013). Innovationism-based politics in Finland over ten years (2009–19) led to a complete restructuring of the whole university system, prioritising technology-related areas likely to produce innovations, patents and start-ups. The initiators of the Aalto–university merging – the Helsinki University of Technology, the Helsinki University of Art and Design and the Helsinki School of Economy and Management – in 2011 first called their initiative the 'Top University' and then the 'Innovation University' (Ridell 2008). In the same year, prime minister Jyrki Katainen noted for the national broadcaster's radio news that there is nothing ideological about investing in start-ups and innovation. At the same time, all other fields of research, society and culture had to reformulate their discourses from the points of view of competitiveness and innovationism. The idea of 'social innovations' began to gain ground, and the social and health sectors were pushed towards privatisation in the name of competitiveness. The cultural sector began to emphasise its usefulness in increasing the health and welfare of citizens.

As the Ngram graph in Figure 9.1 demonstrates, there was a swift and loud policy discourse change from research and development policies to innovation policies at the end of the new millennium's first decade. Innovation began to be tied to entrepreneurialism, and the 'innovation environment' and its enhancement was on the lips of many governments and governmental bodies. The GINJO interviews, together with the public circulation of the concept of innovation, led me to think about how to understand these ubiquitous discourses on innovation as a belief system that provides the kind of answers that we consider part of the realm of religion, rather than that of science and technological development. It seemed apparent that the way innovation was used, both as an aim and a means, and as a way to manage hope and threat in society, the concept was more than a hegemonic ideology: it seemed like a faith, or implicit religion, that provided solutions to the problems of competitive society at all levels – individual, organisational, corporate and even humankind. Innovation appeared to be the answer to the existential questions human beings continue to have even if many have given up institutional religion and faith in a personal god. This thought experiment was published in an anthology of religious studies on post-secular society (Valaskivi 2012).

THE PRO-INNOVATION BIAS

Innovationism has grown in influence around the world in the last decades, despite the fact that the so called pro-innovation bias was recognised in the 1960s (Rogers 1962) and studied extensively in the 1970s (e.g. Downs and Mohr 1976). Early pro-innovation literature found that innovation was considered predominantly as a good thing, no matter the context. Because of this, it is usual to think that more innovation is better than less. Rogers (2003) considers this bias a particular problem in innovation dissemination research, which tends to focus only on rapidly spreading, successful innovations and ignore failures. Innovation research is also often funded by agencies and other actors particularly interested in enhancing innovations, which further strengthens the pro-innovation bias (Rogers 2003).

In the US, the idea of using innovations to boost growth and competitiveness had been spreading since the 1970s (Brint 2018), and had matured into full-fledged entrepreneurialism and start-up frenzy by the time the concept started to direct policies in the Nordic countries and Japan.

Innovation, together with entrepreneurship, continues to be at the centre of the contemporary understanding of progress as growth and an increase in competitiveness, while lack of innovation is connected with failure and extinction. Brint (2018) explains how 'academic innovationism' replaced 'academic professionalism' in the US university sector from the 1970s onwards. At the time of economic decline, solutions for growth and competitiveness were sought through stronger ties with entrepreneurialism, business and higher education institutions. These policy developments led to the marketisation of the university, but also to greater trends of inclusion and heterogeneity in universities. For Brint, then, innovationism is a systemic concept, an attempt to name the overarching change of the university sector in the US. At the same time, he comes to explain how the belief system of innovationism came about initially through practical, institutional and systemic changes. These were then copied, adopted and circulated into a whole belief system, which became both the aim and the means for development and policy decisions.

Through the discourse analysis of the organisation and management research literature, Segercrantz et al. (2017) conclude that innovation is usually spoken of as a good thing. They analyse the usage of 'innovation' from three perspectives: drivers, effects and practices. There are interesting parallels in Segercrantz et al.'s analysis with earlier work on innovationism (Valaskivi 2012). The latter identifies the core values of innovationism as success, progress, growth and competitiveness. Segercrantz et al. correspondingly observe that the drivers of innovation include the hope for the profit and growth or survival of the organisation that is applying innovation. They find that the effects of innovation are similar to the drivers: organisational competitiveness or survival, economic benefits and faster change and novelty. Although they do not call the phenomenon 'innovationism', Segercrantz et al. recognise that much of the discourse on innovations is based on faith. They conclude with three aspects of the discourse on the faith in innovation evident in management literature: 1) as a driver, the faith in the goodness of innovation drives innovation; 2) at the level of practices of innovation, the faith in the goodness of innovation creates a desire to invest in more efficient innovation practices; and 3) at the level of effects of innovation, faith in innovation leads to complete trust in the goodness of innovation – in other words, innovation is always seen as having desirable effects. These faiths form a circular system which sustains pro-innovation bias.

In what follows, I first briefly discuss the concept of implicit religion in relation to innovationism. I then move on to discuss the dimensions (Smart 1996) or aspects of innovationism observed in the GINJO project and reported in my earlier work (Valaskivi 2012). This section ends with Table 9.1 reflecting the aspects of innovationism as a way of engaging with hope for and threat to human action and existence.

IMPLICIT RELIGION AND INNOVATIONISM

Religious studies has, for decades, relied on the idea that with the secularisation of modern societies and its emphasis on the modernisation, industrialisation and rising levels of education in (Western) societies, the importance of religion as a public, societal phenomenon diminishes. Religion thus becomes primarily the concern of the individual and a private matter rather than a public, shared institution (Parsons 1960; Berger 1967; Luckman 1967; Bellah 1970). Casanova (1994) identifies three aspects of secularisation:

1. The differentiation of spheres of the social system, such as culture, politics, religion and economy.
2. The decline of religious belief and practice.
3. The marginalisation of religion into the private sphere.

Beyer (1994) uses the concept of subsystems to understand modern society and the role of religion within it. This functional perception of religion sees the differentiation and professionalisation of subsystems as a core feature of modern societies. In this kind of society, religion is no longer an all-encompassing authority, and subsystems operate relatively independently of religious norms, values and justifications.

However, the functionalist idea of subsystems often stands in the way of seeing aspects, dimensions or patterns of action that operate in religious ways in 'non-religious' subsystems. One of the concepts that attempts to grasp this phenomenon of religiousness beyond religion is 'implicit religion' (Bailey 1990; Nesti 1990). As Bailey (1990, 485) points out, 'Even in a differentiated society, the specialized functions (religion, politics, art, education, health etc.) are not exclusive to the role-bearing institutions'.

My aim here is to demonstrate that the collective reliance on innovations at all levels of human action can be seen as implicit religion with a global, circulating value system that has actual consequences on the ways in which public and private resources are allocated, nature is utilised and science is conducted in the world. In other words, given the pervasiveness of innovationism, it is imperative to understand the ways in which it communicates a belief system that manages power, funding flows and social relationships.

Innovationism works in the ways of religion, mostly outside of the realm of what we usually see as religion. This is how I construct innovationism as implicit religion. In religious studies, implicit religion has been conceptualised through individual experience, as the core beliefs of individuals beyond institutional religion. Bailey (1990) finds through an interview study that what people find most important, in the core of their existence, is an 'intensive concern with extensive effects', 'creating our own identities'. This drive for creating one's own identity

> was what people stood for, it gave coherence to much of their observable behavior; it made them comprehensible, in terms of meaning for themselves; it saw the ambiguity of their description as 'determined'; it enabled them to be driven by a chosen Cause or Causes, as well as causes, future hope as well as past inheritance; it recognized intentionality. (Bailey 1990, 495)

I argue here that implicit religion can also take the form of a societal belief system beyond individual perception of existence. It is, however, easy to see how innovationism ties in with the ideas of individualism, individual existence and individual core identity, and can act as a shared cause in societies. Implicit religion, thus, can also be something that is not considered to belong to the realm or subsystem of religion, but nevertheless provides core values and other aspects usually derived from religion, such as myths, rituals and social structures.

Innovationism is tied to the Western Enlightenment's emphasis on rationality and individual development contributing to the centrality of science as an orientation towards the world (cf. Turner 2011). Science and religion are often seen in binary opposition, with science as rational, public and secular and religion as emotional or mystic and private.

Recent texts on secularisation have begun to acknowledge that even in secularised societies there remains the human need to seek a deeper meaning and purpose in life. Charles Taylor (2007) acknowledges that in societies that have rid themselves of God there is nevertheless an aspiration for something better, and Habermas (2007) describes modern societies as having 'an awareness of what is missing'. Taylor borrows Luc Ferry's concept of the 'meaning of meaning' ('*sens du sens*') in explicating the notion that 'somewhere there is a fullness or richness which transcends the ordinary' (Taylor 2007, 676). In this sense, the issue is about the meaning of life. The question of (collective) meaning is intertwined with feelings of insecurity and a desire for security in (globalised) times. Secularisation does not remove the need for faith(s) that bring hope and help in managing the sense of threat caused by what Paul Tillich (1950) calls 'the ultimate frustrations'.

Tillich, the renowned 'theologian of hope', defines religion as being about the ultimate concerns of humankind. Thus, religion provides in the first place a meaningful set of ultimate values on which the morality of a society can be based. When these values are institutionalised, they can be spoken of as central values of a society. Second, religion provides an adequate explanation for the 'ultimate frustrations' which are inherent to the human condition, and are not manageable. Death is the typical case of (individual) ultimate frustration, while environmental concerns and climate change are current issues that threaten the whole of humankind (see also Bellah 1985). Ultimate values should be greater than ultimate concerns or frustrations; there should be hope beyond the ultimate concerns, in this (immanent) life or the next (transcendent) life. In this view, religion can provide an explanation for ultimate frustrations, so that an individual or a group can accept them without having their core values rendered meaningless (Bellah 1985). Tillich (1990, 182–93) emphasises the necessity of hope for human beings and for the collective: hope should exist as the driving force for a human being 'as long as he lives'.

Tillich's view on ultimate concerns has for some time been considered 'rather empty and too wide-ranging' (Smart 1996, 9) to facilitate an understanding of religion. Smart (1996) advocates for a comparative perspective, with the study of 'dimensions of worldviews'. According to Smart, there are seven dimensions that must be taken into account: 1) the mythic or narrative; 2) ethical; 3) material; 4) philosophical; 5) experiential or emotional; 6) organisational or social; and 7) ritual or practical. In this chapter, the seven dimensions of religion will be used to analyse the *aspects of innovationism*.

Like religious belief systems in general, innovationism is based on certain shared values. As noted above, these values are competitiveness, success, progress and growth. The circulation of these values not only contributes to the construction of an imagined (global) community (Anderson 1991) but is also the basis from which more practical dimensions are constructed. Thus, innovationism provides for contemporary developed societies both a set of ultimate values and a way of controlling ultimate frustrations – hope and transcendence beyond the existential threat of climate change and mass extinction.

In what follows, I will discuss the seven aspects of innovationism in relation to its core values and ability to manage hope and threat in society, using interview data from the GINJO project to illustrate.

ASPECTS AND VALUES OF INNOVATIONISM

First, *the mythic or narrative aspect of innovationism* refers to authoritative stories belonging to certain groups or traditions (Smart 1996). Myths are recited in the community, and are foundational to the worldview of the group in question. Myths are passed on through circulating narratives; through narration, myths enable the communication of the shared values of a community (Smart 1996).

By analysing the mythic dimension, it is possible to describe how the values of innovationism appear in the GINJO interviews. Here, values are understood as aims and aspirations toward which the actors strive. In the narratives which circulate in the GINJO project interviews, core values cut across individual, corporate, national and global levels.

The values of innovationism (success, growth, competitiveness and progress) appear in stories that recur within the interviews. The values appear on four levels within the narratives: the individual, the organisational, the national and the global (humankind). At the *individual level*, innovation becomes a means for *success* for the interviewees, in the US in particular. The myth of the American dream, the individual entrepreneur, is frequently repeated in the US interviews. In the technology sector, the story of Steve Jobs developing his breakthrough innovations in his mother's garage has gained mythical dimensions, and the lone introvert in his mother's garage is often mentioned in the interviews as a necessary beginning for innovations, but also as somebody who needs support in order to become a commercial success. The success of individual entrepreneurs can involve new start-up companies, which can generate *growth*. At the individual level, the narrative dimension has a connection with the second aspect, the *ethical* one (Smart 1996). The innovation system specialists emphasised how the behaviour of individuals should become suitable for creating innovations: mobility, flexibility, creativity, language proficiency and openness, plus a risk-taking mentality, are qualities required of the citizens of an innovative nation. In the discourses of the AaltoES, there is also an emphasis on embracing failure: the myth of the successful and innovative serial entrepreneur claims that one is supposed to fail nine times out of ten and be rewarded with 'outrageous wins' on the tenth try.

At the *corporate level*, innovation first and foremost provides a means for productivity and the possibility for *growth*. Innovations can also mark the beginnings of new corporations, which is one of the aspirations of competing nations: to produce more start-up companies. It is at the corporate level that the third aspect of innovationism, the *material*, is most visible: enterprises create new technology, new services and new markets through innovations. Innovations offer a way for corporations – and nations – to survive and flourish in the global market. This aligns with Segercrantz et al.'s (2017) observation of the self-preservation discourse in the innovation literature, wherein innovations are a means of survival for organisations. This is one way of sustaining organisational hope for the future.

The competitiveness of the nation-state is the third value identified in the interviews. The idea of global economic competition between nations, where growth is measured through gross domestic product and countries compete over growth and competitiveness (cf. Pilling 2018) is a myth that is rarely questioned. However, through innovativeness, the basic starting point of economic competition among nations is widened to include competition in general. National competitiveness is thus more than economic; it is about being useful for the global community, becoming visible and important – being meaningful – for others in the global setting, but also about being able to survive in the competition. This discourse is particularly prominent in relation to climate change: especially in Japan, interviewees talk about innovations as a way towards solving issues of climate change, but also emphasise the possibility of Japan being an example for other countries in changing the economic system towards a controlled degrowth when the population ages. In this way, there is a utopian aspect to innovationism.

At the *national level*, innovationism is a part of the political discourse on national competitiveness that was introduced during the 1980s throughout the industrialised world. In the narrative of innovationism, the globalising economy poses a threat to nation-states (Kantola and Seeck 2010). Thus, national actors express concerns about survival and success. At the same time, technology-driven ideas on innovation became influential in economics. It is important to note that although the discourse on competitiveness is global, the consequences and actions are taken at a national level. Thus, competitiveness measured by gross domestic product becomes an aim primarily at the national level, although it has value also at the corporate level. On the corporate and organisational level, the emphasis is on the acceleration of the innovation cycle and the amount of innovations, which is believed to lead to self-preservation, or success (Segercrantz et al. 2017).

Fourth and finally, at the *global level*, the narrative of innovationism appears through the emphasis on *progress*. This aspect could be considered *the philosophical aspect of innovationism*. Reliance on constant progress remains even when, occasionally, growth is questioned because of concerns of climate change or a looming ageing society. Innovations then become a means for the further enhancement of humankind, providing hope during times of global environmental threat. The values of progress and competitiveness are constantly intertwined in the GINJO project interviews when the national and the global circulate:

> in Asia relations between Japan, China, and Korea are complicated and difficult. We have been competing for hundreds of years. During the last twenty years Japan has been the underdog and has suffered severe mental [spiritual] damage. Should we progress [purely] with style or charm? With the arts? [Referring to the Cool Japan phenomenon and the global growth of sales in Japanese popular culture.] Our citizens are wondering about this as well. That is why we compete in science and want to compete for who is best in developing solutions for the [environmental] threats facing humanity. Our current prime minister has set a target to cut down carbon dioxide emissions by 25 per cent. This is a truly idealistic goal, and a significant one. It is something China and Korea cannot do. We no longer compete in food, fashion, or cars, but we want to be a presence and to be important in the world in other ways. We are looking for these ways now. (JP9)

This excerpt from an interview with a Japanese journalist also exemplifies the fear of failure in reaching what is aimed at. A nation that fails in competition is believed to be damaged and would need to seek out new areas in which to become competitive. The possibility of innovation brings determination and hope: 'We will be meaningful in the world of tomorrow.'

HOW INNOVATIONISM MANAGES HOPE AND THREAT

'The emphasis in religion is today on this world, not the world to come,' writes Frisk in her discussion of Woodhead's concept of the 'turn to life'. This refers to a focus on gaining desirable results in this world, in other words within the immanent frame. According to Woodhead, themes of punishment, hell, damnation and demonology have been losing their importance as societies have become more 'this-worldly' (Woodhead 2001; Frisk 2009–11). Innovationism can be seen as following this trend through its focus on human capabilities and abilities.

At every level, the management of threat and hope in innovationism can be analysed through the fifth, *emotional aspect of innovationism*. Innovationism creates a sense of threat by narrating ultimate frustrations and attempting to simultaneously manage these threats through positing innovations as solutions to the threats it narrates – thus developing hope for the future. At the organisational level, innovationism is used to alleviate the threat to existence through a self-preservation discourse, but also through a discourse of faith (Segercrantz et al. 2017). In the GINJO project interviews this appears as expressions of fear and uncertainty. The sense of threat is concentrated within issues of global warming and environmental change, phenomena that intensify an awareness of the limitedness of natural resources. To some extent, talk about the environment and demographics is invited by the framework of the interviews, in which innovations are discussed in the context of global warming and ageing. Nevertheless, the interviewees frequently list threats and challenges which correspond to multiple features of the risk society (Giddens 1990; Caplan 2000). The world is dangerous at every level: global, national, the level of (the media) industry and at the individual level. Exacerbated by global economic recession and the development of an ageing society in Japan in particular, ultimate frustrations are concentrated into the issue of sustaining the nation. However, at the core of global threats lies the question of competitiveness.

In *The Birth of Biopolitics*, Foucault (2008) points out that within neoliberalism, it is not the market mechanism that is new. What is new is the idea of constant competition and the aim of continuous growth. Taking up Foucault's identification of competition, I develop one of my central claims: through innovationism, competition is transformed into the source of the sense of threat. The operational environment of nation-states and corporations is one of constant competition for resources, for 'top' workers and for foreign investment. Similarly, individuals compete against each other: for jobs, for visibility, for fame. The necessity to innovate appears in expressions such as 'innovate or die', or 'innovate or perish' (cf. Cole 2019).

The outcome of possible failure was hardly ever explicated in the interviews, but can be read between the lines. Ultimate frustrations derivable from the interviews involve death, waning, chaos and extinction. On the corporate level, this means loss of competitiveness, and ultimately perhaps takeover or bankruptcy. These possibilities are rarely discussed in the GINJO interviews; there is rather just a present sense of indistinct threat.

Table 9.1 illustrates how innovationism manages hope and threat at different levels in relation to ultimate values and the most relevant corresponding aspects of innovationism for each level. At the core of innovationism is a belief in human ingenuity. According to the innovationist faith, humankind will eventually be able to solve the issues threatening our existence, including climate change and the mass extinction of species. Innovationism also carries the steadfast trust that humankind will be able to contain the development of artificial intelligence. Some even believe that technological innovation will eventually lead to individual transcendence, when human consciousness can be uploaded to a computer and live on beyond the death of the human body. In organisations – and nations – innovationism means prioritising values of competitiveness and competition, progress and continuous change. At a soci-

Table 9.1   *How innovationism is used to manage hope and threat at*
                 different levels

Level	Value (aim)	Hope	Outcome of failure	Threat	Dimension
Individual	Success	Memory	Unemployment	Death	Ethical
Corporate	Growth	Expansion	Takeover, bankruptcy	Merger or bankruptcy	Material
National	Competitiveness	Sustaining the nation	Falling of gross domestic product, falling credit rating	Waning, oblivion	Social and ritual
Global	Progress	Continuity	Climate change	Chaos, extinction	Philosophical

etal level, sectors and institutions can be seen as being a part of the innovation system, and both the ends and the means for the increase of innovations.

POWER AND SOCIAL ASPECTS OF INNOVATIONISM

Sustaining innovationism – like any belief system – is hard work. Any faith comes into existence through the relentless circulation of the values and perceptions of the belief system; this work is concrete and material, done by identifiable actors. I shall now move to the sixth aspect, the *organisational and social aspects of innovationism*, focusing on the actors and roles present in the production and circulation of innovationism. Next, I take a look at some of the actors involved in this circulation.

The most important actors in the circulation of innovationism are national elites. Among the GINJO project interviewees were innovation systems specialists and journalists, both of whom could be regarded as the elites of innovationism. Interviewees talked about 'the ordinary people' for whom they found two possible role positions in innovationism: they were either the audience, to be educated or informed about the benefits and urgent priority of innovations, or those who had the potential for creating innovations that the system was yet to tap into.

The actors of innovationism are tied between two contradictory logics at different levels of action. On the one hand, there is the conforming, global logic of innovation which emphasises the global setting, including the global, imagined centre of Silicon Valley. On the other hand, there is a strong emphasis on the nation-state, which plays the role of a mediator in the circulation of ideas. (Trans)national elites circulate innovationism to the national level;

while doing this, they apply a national framework and make use of the imagined community within the nation. The nation and the national political system is the frame within which resources are distributed, and elites with symbolic power themselves possess an interest in this distribution. The power struggle is tied to questions of national survival and a sense of threat and hope.

Silicon Valley appeared in the GINJO interviews as the 'centre' and the 'peak' of innovativeness. Smart (1996) describes the various ways in which height has symbolic value in most cultures and notes how height, size and centrality are often connected. Interviewees, in Japan and Finland, and the East Coast US, referred to Silicon Valley both as a source of innovative new solutions and as an ideal innovation environment: a place with a highly competitive atmosphere plus a creative buzz, both desired characteristics. In Silicon Valley, one sees a reversal of the norm: interviewees emphasised that there is no need to travel to see the world, since 'everybody comes here' (US1). This mentality can be understood through social practices belonging to the seventh and last aspect of innovationism: the *ritual* one. One ritual practice is *pilgrimage*. Groups and individuals travelling to Silicon Valley and Stanford University to learn innovativeness can be seen as pilgrims travelling to the centre of innovationism. In pilgrimage, travellers go to 'high sacral bumps in space, learn and gain from its merit, and convey it back to the periphery' (Smart 1996, 86–7). Within the experienced periphery, in Japan and in Finland and to some degree even in the East Coast of the US, there is a desire to become like the centre (Silicon Valley), or at least to overcome the spatial and mental distance between them.

The strength of the myth of the centre of society (Shils 1975; Couldry 2003) is underlined in interviews with the Japanese and Finnish elite experts, who are almost in despair over a national lack of innovativeness, mobility and openness, and express the desire to reach the level of innovation achieved in Silicon Valley. The sense of inadequacy cannot be assuaged by international comparisons that emphasise the innovativeness of Japan or Finland (see, e.g., Florida and Gulden 2005). Nevertheless, journalists, who act as mediators between the elites and ordinary citizens are not as certain of the circumstances: 'In Finland politicians appear to have taken on this [idea of developing innovations]. [They are] creating – I'm not sure if it is an illusion – but at least I have a perception of Finland being innovative' (FI17).

It is paramount that a country is perceived as innovative, because only in an innovative country will start-up companies be able to attract competitive funding from 'angel investors'. In order to develop the attractiveness of Finland in obtaining foreign investments, AaltoES began systematic development of events and support for start-ups in 2009, with the aim of 'becoming the Silicon Valley of Europe' (Valaskivi and Sumiala 2014, 85). The inspiration for this association came directly from the Silicon Valley, where founding members had visited. In 2011, the association invited Stanford University professor and private consultant Steve Blank to convince Finnish decision makers, politicians and the general public of the aim of making Finland the Silicon Valley of Europe. The event was carefully planned and publicised, and resembled more a revivalist service than a business event. A series of videos of all these events was available on the internet, and extensive attention was paid to stimulating media interest in Finland. Invited guests and speakers included ministers, high-level business leaders and rising start-up gurus (Valaskivi and Sumiala 2013). The audience was predominantly students from Aalto University. The three-day event organised around Steve Blank's visit was utilised as a kind of reformation of innovationism and a critique of earlier efforts to develop the Finnish innovation environment and organisations behind it.

AaltoES continues to support entrepreneurship and innovation-based start-ups including through an annual start-up investment event. In a few years, Slush has grown into a mega-event attracting thousands of participants from around the world. The development of AaltoES and the investment event demonstrates the ways in which innovationism organises resources and action. The example also demonstrates the role of media outlets in the circulation of a belief system. AaltoES paid special attention in both their own media production for different platforms and integrating journalist media outlets into their project. Without (mediated) circulation the belief system fails to spread and take on.

As explained above, the role of Silicon Valley is essential in innovationism – it is to innovationism what Rome is for the Catholic world. While GINJO interviewees emphasise national solutions for developing the innovation system, it is clear that innovationism is a global belief system. Although interviewees in other countries emphasise Silicon Valley as the model for national innovation systems, in Silicon Valley itself, interviewees emphasise the anarchic and unstructured nature of the innovation environment as being the source of its innovativeness (e.g. US1, US3). Nevertheless, in Finland and Japan, interviewees perceive the orientation first and foremost as a national one: innovations are a means to maintain (national) competitiveness and help solve problems on a (national and) global scale. In the US in general, but particularly in Silicon Valley, interviewees focus more on innovations as a means of individual as well as corporate success.

What distinguishes and differentiates elite actors of innovationism is their access to transnational sources of information and opportunities to take part in the circulation of information – in other words, the level of symbolic power that they possess (Bourdieu 1991; Hall 2003). Elite actors can exercise 'pastoral power' through the effects of words. Foucault (1982, 783–5; 792) emphasises that the power of the pastoral type has spread from religious institutions to enter the entire social body. Foucault (1982) refers to 'the power exercised by private ventures, welfare societies, benefactors, and … philanthropists'. This type of power is exercised by figures who take various roles within innovationism. As manifested in the interviews, pastoral figures include academics, consultants, some work for think tanks and others for multinational corporations. Politicians are rare, although some may have had a political career previously. At the present time they tend to be in a managerial position in relation to politics (Kantola and Seeck 2010; Valaskivi 2016). Their role can be understood as similar to a preacher or a theologian, who 'formulates the doctrines or teachings of a tradition or sub-tradition' (Smart 1996, 215–25).

In innovationism the role of the theologian is often played by consultants. Pastoral figures act as prophets who describe what a future with more and better innovations will be like. Alternatively, they issue predictions of a terrible future if national systems are not developed into a functioning innovation system, if new technology is not commercialised effectively, if social media is not made use of innovatively and so on. They speak at seminars or workshops and are called 'social media gurus'. Some carry the title of 'evangelist' and aim to achieve 'innovation development' or 'transfer'; and funding for innovative start-ups is provided by 'business angels'.

In the GINJO interviews, pastoral figures constituted the authorities of innovationism. They described the measures that need to be taken in order to enhance national innovativeness and develop the national innovation system. In the case of Finland, these figures included Pekka Himanen, who during the 1990s[5] was the youngest scholar ever to defend a dissertation in philosophy, and Jorma Ollila, the former chief executive officer (CEO) of Nokia. Younger-generation preachers are self-made entrepreneurs with fortunes made in ICT-related innovations. Pastoral power continues to be exercised by directors and employees of national funding bodies. Consultants and researchers working in think tanks and universities also fall into this category. The most influential pastoral figures, however, are CEOs, executives and founders of the global technology giants, Google, Facebook, Amazon, Apple, etc.

The visit of Steve Blank to Finland was a case of conscious utilisation of pastoral power in an attempt to shift political discussion, outflows of resources and emphasis of business funding towards innovation-based start-ups. The event was utilised by the organisers to critique the national institutions of innovation funding, as well as previous generations of business executives, although they were also committed to supporting the youth entrepreneurial movement. Innovationism, then, demonstrated itself in this event through the 'cool', rebellious young (men), those mythic innovators who will fail nine times, and hit it big the tenth. Steve Blank was an obvious pastoral figure, but he was also utilised by the Finnish hosts to creating a hype that would be noticed by the Finnish media.

The actors taking part in the circulation of innovationism are predominantly male. The overall picture is one of men dominating discussions concerning innovations, innovation policies and the measures that need to be taken. In practice, the women who are actually visible in this field are exceptions.[6] The innovation discourse exists as part of a continuum of science and technology policy discourses, and women have been side-lined for decades in national discourses relating to technological development (Vehviläinen 2002a, 2002b). Similar restrictions apply in discourses related to a number of areas of technology – ICT in particular (Stahl 1999). After the #metoo campaign, women attending the start-up event discussed above also came forward in the social media and the press saying that they had been harassed, and that the scene was very male-dominated. After this public dispute the organisers promised to change this and pay attention to the behaviour of attendees in the future. Nevertheless, specialists of start-up entrepreneurship and 'preachers' of innovationism are still mostly male, and the sexist and misogynist practices in the technology world and on the internet have only strengthened in recent years. Examples of this trend include Gamergate, the so-called 'incel-culture' and different forms of extreme-right platforms.

The symbolic, pastoral power that is represented and reproduced by elites through the circulation of innovationism is connected to economic and political power. Symbolic power in general differs from other forms of power in the sense that it affects 'not just what we do, but our ability to describe the social itself; it affects the perception of the inequalities in the social world, including the unequal distribution of those very symbolic resources themselves' (Couldry 2003, 39).

The elite interviewees saw society first and foremost as an environment for innovation – one whose purpose is to provide good circumstances for more innovative activities and competitiveness. The question is predominantly one of flows of public funding. Innovationism has meant that the flood of public money to the private sector has been plentiful and rapid. Among other things, it has meant that health-care institutions, schools and universities are seen as deserving of investment, insofar as they are basic elements of the innovation environment. In recent years there has been a growing tendency of privatisation of central institutions based on the idea that private organisations would automatically be more flexible, effective and innovative than the public sector.

One of the contradictions of innovationism lies in the relationship between the transnational and the national. The processes to which innovationism is attached – namely, the free flow of capital, economic growth and competition – are transnational, and could in fact lead to the dissolution and erosion of the nation-state. However, the particular actors and elites with symbolic power in the circulation of innovationism are always national, although they have access to the transnational mechanisms by which innovationism is circulated.

Pastoral figures from other countries – mostly from Silicon Valley, as in the case of Steve Blank – are used in a consecrating role and as a means to persuade national actors of a particular ideological setting and policy decisions. Consequently, national elites, while preaching innovationism within the nation, in fact use their symbolic power in a contradictory manner, to advance the globalising processes that are tightly bound up with their faith in innovation. The nation-state is a necessary vehicle for globalisation. And at the same time, global trends constitute the vehicle through which the elites attempt to sustain their power. This happens through twin endeavours – the summoning up of threatening images of globalisation and the preaching of innovationism.

HUMAN POTENTIAL UNLIMITED

This chapter has analysed the discourse on innovation as a religious belief system, or implicit religion which has four core values: competitiveness, success, progress and growth. These core values cut through four levels of action: individual, organisational, national and global (humankind). It has analysed these values in relation to the seven aspects of innovationism: mythic or narrative, ethical, material, philosophical, experiential or emotional, organisational or social, and ritual or practical. The chapter has argued that, as an implicit religion, innovationism acts in the ways of a religion although it does not belong to the realm or subsystem of religion. Innovationism, however, has its roots in the intertwined history of technology and Christianity, and can be seen as a form of religion of technology (Noble 1999). Our ability to recognise the existence of innovationism as a faith is hindered by the perception that innovation belongs to the realm of technology and science, and that this subsystem is completely separate from any kind of faith, belief or religion. However, this is a misunderstanding: believing in science becomes an ideology and a faith when it is assumed that science and innovation will solve all of the problems faced by humankind.

Innovationism, not unlike other religions, is a belief system with both immanent and transcendental implications: it justifies our contemporary way of life, while pointing a hopeful way to transcendence. Transcendence in this context means first and foremost the survival of humankind, but also the (still utopian and extreme) possibility for individual immortality through technology. This is the existential aspect of innovationism: providing hope in the time of grave threats, and also providing the kind of hope that does not require humans to give up their core values and beliefs: competitiveness, growth, progress and success. Innovationism aligns with capitalism and the oil economy, because it reassures us that we do not have to give up growth despite the global threat of climate change because innovations are seen as both the driver of growth and the remedy to destruction caused by it. Innovationism directs our attention astray: when it claims that without innovations individuals, companies, nations and humankind will wane and face extinction because innovations create growth, it actually contributes to the extinction. If innovationism instead generated innovations for degrowth, it could perhaps actually deliver what it promises.

Despite the transcendental and existential aspects of innovationism, its implications continue to be in this world – in other words, immanent. The last five years have shown how vulnerable society is in the midst of innovationism, which disrupts not only the climatic and natural environment of humans, but also the media environment in ways that challenge free, democratic societies. In Silicon Valley technology developers have for a couple of years been publishing mea culpa, regretting their naïve pro-innovation bias and faith in automatic benefits of technology (see Valaskivi 2018). They are resigning their positions in big media technology companies and founding initiatives to remedy what has been broken[7] and limit drastically the usage of mobile technology and social media of their own children. Simultaneously, the global university sector continues to establish 'cool' innovation initiatives and restructure along the lines of innovationism. Some changes might already be taking place in Silicon Valley and the technology industry, i.e. the centre of innovationism, but the periphery remains in a state of deep faith. There the pro-innovation bias continues to direct policy making, leading to constant, market-oriented restructuring in the public sector, and e.g. a growth of managerialism in universities, making universities first and foremost innovation factories. In Finland this has been particularly prevalent in recent years.

For myself, the latest practical implication of innovationism is my alma mater. In early 2019, what used to be the University of Tampere for over 50 years with a preceding history for over 90 years, was merged with the Tampere University of Technology forming Tampere University. The new joint university then acquired the Tampere Polytechnic. These three higher education institutions now form the 'Tampere higher education community'. The operation is innovationism come to flesh, with a focus on university–business cooperation, entertaining only 'top-notch' research, increasing the employability of the students through educating them in 'know-how', supposedly needed in work life, and questioning the importance of any disciplines without clear and direct potential of capitalisation or immediate field of application. The new slogan of the university is 'Human potential unlimited'. What is there to add?

NOTES

1. Parts of this chapter have been published in a different form as Valaskivi 2012.
2. www.pennovation.upenn.edu/pennovation-center (accessed 15 June 2019).

3. 6 August 2019 in Tampere, signed in to Google account with Chrome browser. As Google searches are sensitive to the user's browsing history, it is likely that searches by other users might provide different results.
4. Unfortunately, the search can go only up to 2008, so we cannot see how usage has developed since.
5. Pekka Himanen has since then fallen out of grace spectacularly, when in 2012 he prepared a report for the prime minister Jyrki Katainen's government about the future prospects of the society. Investigative journalism revealed that Himanen had been assigned without tender competition, which violated the Act on Public Procurement and Concession Contracts. After the public frenzy he has focused on his work abroad and remained silent in Finland. On Himanen's career and publications see pekkahimanen.net
6. It was difficult to find female interviewees in the GINJO project. Among the specialists, only one interviewees was female. The journalists specialising in science and innovations were predominantly male, while the journalists focusing on ageing were almost exclusively female in all three countries.
7. See e.g. https://humanetech.com/

REFERENCES

Alasuutari, P. (2015) *The Sychronization of National Policies: Ethnography of the Global Tribe of the Moderns*. London: Routledge.

Anderson, B. (1991) *Imagined Communities: Reflections on the Origin and Spread of Nationalism*. London: Verso Books.

Bailey, E. (1990) The Implicit Religion of Contemporary Society: Some Studies and Reflections. *Social Compass* 37(4): 483–97.

Beck, U. (2004) Cosmopolitical Realism: On the Distinction between Cosmopolitanism in Philosophy and the Social Sciences. *Global Networks*, 1 April.

Bellah, R. (1970) Civil Religion in America, in *Beyond Belief: Essays on Religion in a PostTraditional World*. New York: Harper and Row, pp. 168–89.

Bellah, R. (1985) *Tokugawa Religion: The Cultural Roots of Modern Japan*. New York: Free Press.

Berger, P. L. (1967) *The Sacred Canopy: Elements of a Sociological Theory of Religion*. Garden City: Doubleday.

Beyer, P. (1994) *Religion and Globalization*. London: Sage.

Billig, M. (1995) *Banal Nationalism*. London: Sage.

Bourdieu, P. (1991) *Language and Symbolic Power*. Cambridge: Cambridge University Press.

Brint, S. (2018), *Two Cheers for Higher Education: Why American Universities Are Stronger Than Ever – and How to Meet the Challenges They Face*. Oxford: Princeton University Press.

Caplan, P. (2000) Introduction: Risk Revisited, in P. Caplan (ed.), *Risk Revisited*. London: Pluto Press, pp. 1–9.

Casanova, J. (1994) *Public Religions in the Modern World*. Chicago: University of Chicago Press.

Cole, B. M. (2019) Innovate or Die: How a Lack of Innovation Can Cause Business Failure, *Forbes*, 10 January, at www.forbes.com/sites/biancamillercole/2019/01/10/innovate-or-die-how-a-lack-of-innovation-can-cause-business-failure/#17fe8d312fcb

192   *Spirituality, organization and neoliberalism*

Couldry, N. (2003) *Media Rituals: A Critical Approach*. London: Routledge.

Downs, G, W, Jr. and Mohr, L. B. (1976) Conceptual Issues in the Study of Innovation. *Administrative Science Quarterly*, 21(4), pp. 700–714.

Florida, R. and Gulden, T. (2005) The World Is Spiky. *Atlantic Monthly*, October.

Foucault, M. (1982) The Subject and Power. *Critical Inquiry*, 8(4), 777–95.

Foucault, M. (2008) *The Birth of Biopolitics: Lectures at the Collége de France 1978–1979*, ed. Michel Senellart. London: Palgrave Macmillan.

Frisk, F. (2009–11) Globalization: A Key Factor in Contemporary Religious Change. *Journal of Alternative Spiritualities and New Age Studies*, 5, i–xiv.

Giddens, A. (1990) *Consequences of Modernity*. Cambridge: Polity Press.

Godin, B. and Vinck, D. (2017) *Critical Studies of Innovation: Alternative Approaches to the Pro-Innovation Bias*. Cheltenham, UK and Northampton, MA, USA: Edward Elgar Publishing.

Habermas, J. (2007) An Awareness of What Is Missing, in J. Habermas et al. (eds), *An Awareness of What Is Missing: Faith and Reason in a Post-Secular Age*. Cambridge: Polity Press, pp. 15–23.

Hall, S. (2003) *Representation: Cultural Representations and Signifying Practices*. London: Sage.

Hjarvard, S. (2008) The Mediatization of Religion: A Theory of the Media as Agents of Religious Change. *Northern Lights: Film and Media Studies Yearbook*, 6(1), 9–26.

Kantola, A. and Seeck, H. (2010) Dissemination of Management into Politics: Michael Porter and the Political Uses of Management Consulting. *Management Learning*, 41(4), 1–23.

Kimberly, J. R. (1981) Managerial Innovation, in Paul C. Nystrom (ed.), *Handbook of Organizational Design*. London: Oxford: Oxford University Press, 84–104.

Luckmann, T. (1967) *The Invisible Religion: The Problem of Religion in Modern Society*. New York: Macmillan.

Nesti, A. (1990) Implicit Religion. *Social Compass*, 37(4), 419–509.

Noble, D. F. (1999) *The Religion of Technology: The Divinity of Man and the Spirit of Invention*. London: Penguin Books.

Parsons, T. (1960) Some Comments on the Pattern of Religious Organization in the United States, in *Structure and Process in Modern Societies*. New York: Free Press.

Pilling, D. (2018) *The Growth Delusion*. New York: Tim Duggan Books.

Ridell, S. (2008) Top University – Downhill for Humanities? Policing the Future of Higher Education in the Finnish Mainstream Media', *European Educational Research Journal*, 7(3), 289–307.

Rogers, E. M (1962) *Diffusion of Innovations*. New York: Free Press.

Rogers, E. M. (2003) *Diffusion of Innovations*, 5th edition. New York: Free Press.

Segercrantz, B., Sveiby, K.-E. and Berglund, K. (2017) A Discourse Analysis of Innovation in Academic Management Literature, in B. Godin and D. Vinck (eds), *Critical Studies of Innovation: Alternative Approaches to the Pro-Innovation Bias*. Cheltenham, UK and Northampton, MA, USA: Edward Elgar Publishing.

Shils, E. (1975) *Center and Periphery: Essays on Macrosociology*, Cambridge, MA: Harvard University Press.

Smart, N. (1996) *Dimensions of the Sacred: An Anatomy of the World's Beliefs*. Berkeley: University of California Press.

Stahl, W. A. (1999) *God and the Chip: Religion and the Culture of Technology*. Waterloo, ON: Wilfred Laurier University Press.

Taylor, C. (2007) *Secular Age*. London: Belknap Press of Harvard University.

Tillich, P. (1950) *Systematic Theology I*. Chicago: University of Chicago Press.

Tillich, P. (1990) The Right to Hope, in R. H. Stone (ed.), *Theology of Peace.* Louisville: Westminster/John Knox, 182–93.

Turner, B. (2011) *Religion and Modern Society: Citizenship, Secularization and the State.* Cambridge: Cambridge University Press.

Valaskivi, K. (2012) Dimensions of Innovationism, in P. Nynäs et al. (eds), *Post-Secular Society.* London: Transaction.

Valaskivi, K. (2016) *Cool Nations: Media and the Social Imaginary of the Branded Country.* London: Routledge.

Valaskivi, K. (2018) Strategic Analysis February 2018: Beyond Fake News: Content Confusion and Understanding the Dynamics of the Contemporary Media Environment. 28 February. www.hybridcoe.fi/publication-tags/strategic-analysis/page/2/

Valaskivi, K. and Sumiala, J. (2013) Yhteisöt liikkeessä: innovaatiouskon kiertoa jäljittämässä [Mobile Communities: Tracing the Circulation of Innovationism], in L. Mikko (ed.), *Liikkuva maailma: liike, raja, tieto [Mobile World: Movement, Border, Knowledge].* Tampere: Vastapaino, 77–94.

Valaskivi, K. and Sumiala, J. (2014) Circulating Social Imaginaries: Theoretical and Methodological Reflections. *European Journal of Cultural Studies,* 17(3), 229–43.

Vehviläinen, M. (2002a) Gendered Agency in Information Society: On Located Politics of Technology, in M. Consalvo and S. Paasonen (eds), *Women and Everyday Uses of the Internet: Agency and Identity.* Oxford: Peter Lang Publishing, 275–91.

Vehviläinen, M. (2002b) Teknologinen Nationalism [Technological Nationalism], in T. Gordon, K. Komulainen and K. Lempiäinen (eds), *Suomineitonen hei! Kansallisuuden sukupuoli* [Greetings, Maiden of Finland! Gender and Nationality]. Vastapaino: Tampere, 211–29.

Woodhead, L. (2001) The Turn to Life in Contemporary Religion and Spirituality, in U. King and T. Beattie (eds), *Spirituality and Society in the New Millennium.* Portland: Sussex Academic Press, 110–23.

Index

Café Gratitude 15, 17–20, 22–3
capitalism
    changing spirits of *xix–xxv*
    disenchanted *xxiii*
    global
        entrepreneurial spirit of *xxix*
        precarization of life under
            29–30
        Third World's population
            involvement in *xxx*
    and innovationism *xxix*, 189–90
    logic
        of accumulation 132
        as irreducible fabric of human
            society 16
        as supernatural 4, 6
    neoliberal *xii–xiii*, *xx*, 6, 13–14,
        23–4, 31, 109
    principle of entitlement to leisure
        163
    and Protestant Christianity 149
    really-existing 4
    relegitimization 129
    requirement for enhanced
        productivity *xxii*
    self-help offering tools to master 30
    and self-transformation 41
    service-intensive 130–31
    spirituality *xx*
    see also new spirit of capitalism
capitalist spiritualities *xx*
Carrette, J. *xx–xxi*, *xxx*, 87
Chandler, D. *xiv–xvi*, *xvii*, *xviii*, *xxviii*,
    109, 150, 160, 167
character building *xxvi*, 126, 128, 132–4,
    138, 141, 144–5
Charismatic Pentecostalism
    ascertaining impact 143–4
    bettering self for God 134–7
    and citizenship 144
    collective reading 143
    commodification of 129
    entrepreneurs 128
    in Ghana 146
    rising popularity of 126
    as type of new spirit of capitalism
        129
    young male involvement 146
Chiapello, E. *xiii–xiv*, *xxvi*, *xxviii*, *xxx*,
    28, 41, 48–50, 60–61, 129, 131

Christian personal development 128–9,
    134, 136, 142, 144–5
Christianity
    ability to blend with indigenous
        forms of worship 146
    innovationism having roots in 189
    and morality of work and leisure
        151–6
    and neoliberalism in Ghana 134–7,
        144–5
    serious leisure and morality in
        practice 159–62
citizenship
    politics of, in Ghana 129, 132–4,
        144
    productive *xxvi–xxvii*, 126, 128, 129,
        132–4, 138, 144
    republican model of 28, 33
Clearing ritual 20–22
coaching
    conceptualizing self as business or
        commodity 30
    credo of assuming personal
        responsibility 33, 36
    Dov's story 34–5
    as form of personal development
        work 27
    Gila's story 38–40
    in Israel *xviii–xix*, 29, 30–31, 40–42
    language of *xviii–xix*, 29, 41
    reasons for embracing *xviii–xix*,
        40–42
    Tamar's story 35–7
    as therapeutic discourse 28
collective structures 35–8, 41
colonialism *xxiv*, 111, 132
    see also post-colonialism
commodification
    of authenticity 128
    of Charismatic Pentecostal
        Christianity 129
    of leisure time 149
    as manifest in and through labouring
        body *xxiv*
    of re-sacralised work 87–105
    of religion *xxii*
    of spirituality *xxiii*
community
    building 69, 80, 83, 155, 179
    communicating shared values of 180

blurring moral lines between
167
and morality after 162–6
morality of, and Christianity
151–6
as 'love in action' 87, 89–90, 91,
93–4, 101–2, 103, 104
neoliberal structures of 154
and processes of attunement and
sharing 91–4
Protestant and secular bourgeois
approaches to 150, 166
re-sacralisation of 89–104
and sense of usefulness 99–101
serious leisure perspective 156–9
and yoga 77–9, 80–81, 83
workplace spirituality
and American business 1–3, 23–4
as form of neoliberal governance 6,
8, 23
as neoliberal project 5–6
neoliberal spirituality in American
business education 9–14
as neoliberal subject formation 3–9
overview *xvii–xviii*
representing 'technology of the self'
2, 6, 7–8, 13, 23

Yankellevich, A. *xviii*
yoga
Cartesian trap of emphasizing either
mind or body *xxi*
and family 75–7, 80, 82, 83
and health 73–4, 80, 82
as spiritual practice
highlighting altruistic giving
and self-care 79

postfeminist and neoliberal
69–72
responsibility for health 74
secularized form of *xi*
study discussion 79–83
teaching
context of study 67–8
embodied and economic
precarity of *xxiii*
as form of body work 68
as insurance policy for difficult
financial periods 78–9,
80
life history methodology 72
underpinning belief systems *xx*
and work 77–9, 80–81, 83
Young Pioneers 132–3
youth
angry young men 108–10
as disconnected from land 166
folk tales embedding knowledge 111
gardening as unusual choice for 114
involvement in Charismatic
Pentacostalism 146
mobilisation around food gardens
108, 117–21, 122
'morality of inevitability' among
impoverished 165
sports developments projects 150,
156, 158–62
training programmes 132
urban unemployed, in Africa 107,
109–10

Zionism 28, 31–2, 33, 35–6, 37–40